Environments for Student Growth and Development: Libraries and Student Affairs in Collaboration

Edited by Lisa Janicke Hinchliffe
and Melissa Autumn Wong

D1564576

Association of College and Research Libraries
A division of the American Library Association
Chicago, 2012

Table of Contents

Acknowledgements

We gratefully acknowledge the work of James Elmborg and Sheril Hook and their approach in *Centers for Learning: Writing Centers and Libraries in Collaboration*. Thank you for giving us a model to follow.

We are also thankful for the students we have taught in our Information Professionals in Higher Education course and the librarians who have taken our ACRL Libraries and Student Affairs: Collaborating to Support Holistic Student Development e-learning course. You, along with the authors of the chapters in this book, have challenged us to deepen our understanding of collaboration and the role of librarians and libraries in academic institutions.

~ Lisa and Melissa

I must begin with gratitude for my co-editor, Melissa Wong. We have come a long way from when we first met as library science graduate students and coworkers at the information desk of the University Library at the University of Illinois at Urbana–Champaign. Our work together, on this project and many others, is a constant source of joy and satisfaction. Our friendship is even more a treasure.

I also thank my loving husband, Joe, who continues to encourage and support me as I pursue my passion for academic libraries and student learning. I am fortunate to have the love of such a devoted husband.

~ Lisa

I have had the pleasure of working with many fine student affairs colleagues in my career and am grateful for their willingness to teach me about their work. I owe an especially deep debt of gratitude to Susan Garman and Shane Armstrong, student affairs professionals *par excellence*. They have served as my guides to the world of student affairs and taught me much about students and their development, outreach, programming, and collaboration. Along the way, they became personal friends and sources of professional and personal inspiration.

I am also grateful for the support and encouragement of my former dean, Robert Matthes, who listened to my ideas about what an academic library could do and let me run with them, and for my colleagues in the Marymount College Library, particularly Alice Cornelio and Nikki Gomez, who embraced the model of a student-centered library and opportunities for collaboration with enthusiasm. Thank you for making work an energizing and inspiring place to go each morning.

My appreciation goes to Cheryl Tarsala for the support she offered in our weekly phone calls. Thanks for helping me keep my balance and being firm when needed.

This book would not have happened without my co-editor, Lisa Janicke Hinchliffe, since she first suggested we edit a book together. Thank you for being my collaborator in the course, the book, and everything in between; work is always more fun when it is with you. Thanks most of all for your personal friendship and encouragement; I am so glad we became friends all those years ago at the Info Desk.

Most of all, to my husband, Bob, and our children, Erica and Craig, for your love, patience, and support while I worked on this book and during all my professional endeavors, more thanks than you can "shake a stickit." You make my world wonderful every day.

~ Melissa

Introduction
The Power of Library and Student Affairs Collaborations

Lisa Janicke Hinchliffe and
Melissa Autumn Wong

This book about collaboration grew out of collaboration. And, like many collaborations, our multiyear relationship is so continuously generative that it is hard to know where this specific project began. Nonetheless, it has its roots in years of professional practice and a strong orientation towards improving outcomes through working with others.

In our own practice, we had found that working with student affairs professionals was a powerful avenue for outreach and partnership. These collaborations did not replace our work with faculty and integration into the formal curricula at our institutions but rather served as complementary to that work. Inspired by our colleagues in student affairs and, in particular, by their emphasis on integrative and holistic student learning and development, we began to see how librarians are uniquely situated to bridge the academic affairs/student affairs gap that unfortunately exists at all too many institutions.

Over the past few years, awareness of the importance of outside-of-class learning has continued to increase in higher education. The National Survey for Student Engagement has been particularly important in bringing attention to the fact that learning is impacted by more than what happens inside the walls of a classroom, be they literal walls or the virtual walls of online learning. Within libraries, the emergence of learning commons and other collaborative ventures demonstrates the power of integrative approaches to student learning and development.

Partnerships between libraries and academic departments or academic services are often treated in the literature. Partnerships between libraries and student affairs units are discussed less often. This book fills a gap by exploring how librarians and student affairs professionals can expand their reach through collaborative programming and other joint efforts. As the chapter authors reveal, there are opportunities to create stronger campus environments for student growth and development inherent in library and student affairs collaborations.

The book has two parts. The first part is an introduction to student affairs. We invited Dallas Long to author the chapters The Foundations of Student Affairs: A Guide to the Profession and Theories and Models of Student Development as we have found that librarians often have little knowledge about student affairs and the philosophies that underlie their work. This lack of knowledge is unfortunate since academic librarians and student affairs share many common values and approaches as well as similar challenges in engaging students outside the classroom.

The second part of the book is devoted to case studies of successful collaborations. Not all of the projects discussed were successful; however, the collaborative relationships remain strong. There is inspiration to be gained from successful projects but especially from collaborations that persevere in the face of challenging circumstances. Each chapter is co-authored by at least one student affairs professional and one librarian. The result is powerful stories of relationships that are grounded in a shared vision of improved student learning and growth. We hope that the chapters in this book will demonstrate the potential for shared vision that can be used to further the value inherent in such collaborative approaches.

1

The Foundations of Student Affairs: A Guide to the Profession

Dallas Long

Student affairs is a large, complex area of campus operations and is comprised of many departments with professionals from a wide variety of educational backgrounds. Long provides a short history of the student affairs profession, followed by an overview of the departments in a typical student affairs division and the responsibilities and goals of the professionals in those departments. Long also describes the values that guide the work of student affairs professionals and the contemporary challenges they face.

The classroom is not the sole province of student learning. Learning is interwoven throughout the students' college experience—from the day they move into their first dormitory as freshmen until the day they hold a diploma in hand. They are shaped by their experiences—the lessons in conflict management from sharing living spaces with other students, the leadership skills acquired in leading a student organization, the critical thinking honed by challenging academic work, and an emerging sense of identity as they make meaning out of their experiences. Student learning takes place in a classroom, but the college or university itself is the classroom. There is no doubt that college is a transformative experience for students. Student learning is, therefore, also about student development.

There are many experts on student development at every college, university, and community college in the nation. They work in a variety of scenes—as academic advisors who help students select majors and build their class schedules; as residential life staff who supervise the students living in residence halls; as admissions officers who help students decide if the college is the right fit; as career counselors who assist students with finding the right internships and the right careers that fit their talents and aspirations. All of these professionals are as focused on student learning as the English professor who strives to improve students' writing skills. These professionals develop students' cognitive and interpersonal skills, foster leadership, ethics, and cultural understanding. They also stress the importance of wellness, help establish the students' identities, and spark their exploration of careers and of service to society. Student learning encompasses a breadth of people who educate predominantly outside of the classroom. They belong to the domain of education called *student affairs*. The field has a long history in higher education and, over the years, has been called *student personnel, student services, student development,* and other names. *Student affairs* is the most common phrase today.

The purpose of this chapter is to serve as a primer on the profession of student affairs. Who are the people and what are the functions that comprise student affairs organizations at colleges and universities? How did student affairs evolve as a profession within the academy? What are the core values that guide their work? What are the emerging trends and issues that are transforming student affairs today? This chapter answers each question with an overview of the history, values, essential competencies, functions, and new directions for the field of student affairs. It will provide a foundation for librarians who want to collaborate with student affairs professionals and will help librarians identify values, issues, and trends that they share with their student affairs colleagues.

A BRIEF HISTORY OF STUDENT AFFAIRS

Student affairs as a distinct profession within higher education—with graduate programs, professional associations, journals, and scholarship—is a relatively new phenomenon. However, the roots of the student affairs profession reach all the way back to the colonial era and the earliest years of American higher education. The doctrine of *in loco parentis* (literally "in place of the parent") empowered colleges and universities to manage students closely, as students were viewed in those times as emotionally immature and requiring strict adult supervision.[1] Colonial colleges were often poorly staffed, with faculty serving as live-in teachers who supervised the students in the dormitories and dining halls as well as in the classrooms. The faculty developed rules and regulations that governed students' behavior, conduct, and dress, and they enforced college rules and expectations even when students were not on the college premises.[2]

By the mid-1800s, academic life at American colleges and universities had changed radically. The faculty at this time were significantly influenced by European—predominantly German—universities. European universities viewed the faculty's exclusive responsibility to be the training of the intellect. Subsequently, American faculty began to earn doctorates in large numbers, developed expertise in specific disciplines, and maintained active research agendas. They began training graduate students who shared the faculty's interests and who participated in the faculty's research pursuits better than undergraduate students. As the faculty became subject experts, they had little time for or interest in tending to matters of undergraduate student discipline and mentorship. At the same time, students gradually rebelled under the strict discipline and were not satisfied with merely classical programs of study. Instead, students developed an interest in extracurricular activities to educate the whole student: intellect, spirit, and body. Literary societies, fraternal organizations, campus publications, sports teams, and debate and student clubs emerged as informal but integral aspects of college and university life.[3]

By the turn of the twentieth century, faculty involvement in student discipline had significantly diminished. Elizabeth Nuss states, "The paternalism associated with colonial colleges … had given way to almost complete indifference."[4] Students participated in their own governance, creating student governments, drafting honor codes, and adjudicating allegations of rule violations. In the 1920s, the first administrators were hired. Their principal area of work was student personnel matters. The presidents of Harvard and many land grant universities appointed the first "deans of men" (later "deans of students") to investigate student conduct and enforce university rules.

Many of the traditional functions of the student affairs profession emerged in the early part of the 1900s. Student health services developed as physicians joined the faculty, either as professors of medicine or as attending physicians. College staff were hired to monitor the students' academic records and to advise students on vocational guidance and job placement. John Seiler Brubacher and Willis Rudy observed that "in the years following World War I, the student personnel movement gained national recognition and professional stature. It was becoming self-conscious, confident, and widely influential."[5] The national professional associations were founded around this time. Deans of men, deans of women, and other staff who were focused on student personnel issues had previously worked in relative isolation, but now they corresponded and met to share ideas and concerns related to their work.

The core values of the student affairs profession gained widespread recognition and acceptance in higher education with the publication of the *Student Personnel Point of View*, a landmark report issued in 1937 by the American Council on Education. The report emphasized the education of the whole student—intellect, spirit, and personality—and insisted that attention must be paid to the individual needs of each student. The report was revised in 1949 and proposed a comprehensive suite of student services that represented thirty-three functional areas. The guidelines proposed in the *Student Personnel Point of View* provided the philosophical and organizational foundations for the student affairs profession as it stands today.[6]

The relationship between students and colleges and universities changed significantly during the 1960s. The legal concept of *in loco parentis* was greatly eroded by the courts. The US Supreme Court's decision in *Dixon v. Alabama State Board of Education* in 1961 defined a person over the age of 18 years as a legal adult. Subsequent court rulings granted students a right to due process and viewed the relationship between students and colleges and universities as largely contractual in nature—if students paid their tuition and met the college or university's published academic requirements, they were entitled to a diploma. Consequently, student discipline diminished as the student affairs professional's most crucial role; instead, the critical purpose turned to educating the students on making appropriate choices and decisions.

Simultaneously, student activism proliferated on campuses. Crises erupted at many universities such as Kent State University that resulted in student deaths, injuries, and property damage. As pressures in the campus environments increased, student affairs professionals were tasked with greater roles in conflict resolution, communication, and social justice.[7]

In the 1960s and 1970s, the student affairs profession established a theoretical base as the framework for its knowledge and practice. Many theories that explained student development emerged in the fields of education, psychology, and sociology. Student affairs professionals and the professional associations embraced the advances in student development theories, and graduate programs were founded that included student development theo-

ries as the cornerstone of the curriculum. The marriage of professional practice and theory received profound attention in the student affairs field with
the release of the American College Personnel Association (ACPA)'s 1972
report *Student Development in Tomorrow's Higher Education: A Return to the
Academy*. The report argued that student affairs professionals could not have
a significant impact on students' intellectual, psychosocial, or emotional
growth without first understanding the motivations, abilities, and environments which drive, create, and define students.[8] Consequently, the report
called for student affairs professionals to collaborate with faculty, participate
actively in the learning process, and create curricular experiences that spur
student development inside the classroom as well as outside.[9]

The student affairs profession matured in the 1980s and 1990s, with
much professional practice grounded in student development theory. Many
of the theories, however, were developed with a "traditional" undergraduate
student in mind—between the ages of eighteen and twenty-two years, usually white, and most frequently male. The intervening decades challenged
student affairs professionals on a new definition of a student.

During this twenty-year period, the diversity of students increased
in every respect.[10] The number of African American, Hispanic, and Native
American students enrolled in higher education grew at all types of colleges and universities. Women students increased to more than 60 percent
of college students nationwide. Gay, lesbian, bisexual, and transgender students were significantly more visible on college campuses. Online education
brought a new face of students—older, with full-time work or family obligations, and remaining geographically distant from the campus.

Community building, advising, and career development were not the
only areas in which student affairs professionals were challenged to adapt to
an online learning environment. Student affairs professionals and scholars
noted that each diverse group of students brought new needs and interests,
and many student development theories were revised with new research specific to the growth of each group. A strong understanding of diversity and its
implications for student affairs practice became an essential competency for
student affairs professionals.

The globalization of higher education in the 1990s and 2000s has certainly affected the student affairs profession. The American model of student
affairs practice and the organization of student affairs functions spurred great
interest at colleges and universities in Europe, Latin America, and Asia. The

Fulbright Scholar program facilitated the placement of American student affairs professionals at colleges and universities abroad, and the Association of College and University Housing Officers and the Association of College Unions added *International* to their names to highlight the inclusion of colleagues at colleges and universities outside North America.[11]

Student affairs professionals in North America also began to integrate international perspectives into their work as well. As the number of American students who participate in study abroad programs has grown over the past twenty years, student affairs professionals have addressed the needs of their students abroad and have studied how students' experiences abroad have shaped their subsequent identity and learning.[12] The heightened security in the years following the attacks on September 11, 2001, has also brought attention to international students studying at American colleges and universities. Student affairs professionals have delicately addressed the increased government scrutiny international students face but also recognized the need to educate themselves and their communities on the values and cultures the students bring to the campuses.[13]

Nuss observes that student affairs was established as a profession to support the academic mission of colleges and universities and to foster the development of the student intellectually, psychosocially, and emotionally.[14] The education of the whole student is likely to remain the core focus of student affairs in the future, but student affairs professionals will be challenged to think about educating the student differently. How do student affairs professionals create a meaningful sense of community for students in a virtual classroom? What should intellectual, psychosocial, and emotional development look like for adult students? Does identity development progress differently for minority students than for white students? These are only a few of the questions that pose significant challenges for the future of theory and practice in student affairs.

THE VALUES OF STUDENT AFFAIRS

"Values are the essences of philosophy that guide our actions in important ways," writes Robert Young, a leading voice in student affairs scholarship.[15] This section outlines the fundamental values and best practices, identified by Young and others, that bridge the diversity of student affairs and direct the way that student affairs professionals manage their services, programs, and policies. Young identified the following values as those most fundamentally held by student affairs professionals throughout the history of the profession.[16] These values provide the greatest context for student affairs practice.

Educating the Whole Student

Student affairs is committed to the ideas that student learning does not occur exclusively within the classroom and that college affects students profoundly in many different dimensions. Essentially, student affairs professionals accept that college is a critical period of life during which students discover a meaningful identity and develop core values for how they will perceive and experience their adult lives. This holistic view of education focuses on the growth of the intellectual and emotional capacities of students, as well as their development of a stable sense of identity, interpersonal skills, moral and spiritual values, ethics, career goals and vocational skills, and physical wellness. Subsequently, student affairs professionals deliberately create programs, services, and experiences that will advance the students' growth in one or more dimensions of their lives.

Care for Students

Student affairs professionals respect students as individuals who matter and who have dignity. They recognize that each student is unique in his or her own personal experiences, circumstances, and needs. Accordingly, each student deserves attention, respect, and fair treatment. Every interaction with a student should serve the student's best interests.

The underlying value is care. Student affairs professionals must ultimately care about the well-being of the students they serve. On a higher level, the value of care is demonstrated through student affairs professionals' advocacy for special groups of students. Student affairs professionals educate university administration and others on the needs of special populations of students in order to change policies or procedures that remedy disadvantages or unfair circumstances. Additionally, care is a fundamental value that student affairs professionals strive to instill in students. This generally takes the form of service learning, as students learn to understand the situations of others and want to advocate on their behalf.

Service to Students and to the University

The underlying fundamental mission of student affairs, however, is to serve; the profession exists to ensure that students are safe, cared for, well treated, and (more or less) satisfied with their higher education. Young suggests that the value of service inherent to the profession extends not only to students but to faculty as well; to "provide teachers of subject matters with information about their students—when, where and how they find significant experiences inside and outside the classroom."[17] Service to students may seem an obvious value of the profession, given its name *student* affairs. Nonetheless student affairs represents such a wide and diverse range of functions that many student affairs professionals may be in direct contact with students infrequently. Many student affairs professionals—those concerned with assessment, for example—may serve primarily administrative functions, but their overall work is still centered around services for students.

Community

Dennis Roberts, a leading expert in community development, characterized community as "the binding together of individuals toward a common cause or experience."[18] Building a sense of community between students has many educational benefits, including the potential to create opportunities to develop leadership skills; instill a sense of belonging for students who might otherwise be marginalized; instill empathy and responsibility for violations of the community's standards; and advance interpersonal skills through communication and conflict resolution. Other benefits of community are not strictly educationally meaningful but contribute to a safe and healthy environment. Incidents of vandalism, property theft, and assaults decrease when students perceive a relationship with each other and with their surroundings.[19] Students are also more likely to persist to graduation if others value their involvement.[20]

Equality and Social Justice

Equality is at the center of many campus issues. As a value of the student affairs profession, equality originated in student discipline cases and demonstrated the college or university's commitment to fair proceedings and due process. However, equality for student affairs professionals today is more concerned with fair access to resources and treatment. Admissions, financial aid, student discipline, and health services are frequent areas of higher education in which students are concerned about a lack of fairness in the distribution of opportunities and services. Student affairs professionals tread a difficult territory—they are often charged with developing policies and procedures that ensure equal access and treatment, while also needing to explain the rationale to students who perceive policies and procedures as unjust.

Social justice as a value of the student affairs profession expands on this concept of equality. Scott Rickard defines social justice as "fairness and equity in the distribution of opportunity, in the treatment of individuals, in the assurance of personal and economic security, and in the protection of civil and human rights."[21] He identifies ways in which student affairs professionals promote social justice in higher education—by ensuring that the campus is committed to remedying policies or procedures which historically disadvantaged groups of people, that the campus serves as a model of fairness and inclusion for all people, and that staff and students are encouraged to recognize and be prepared to remedy inequality within the campus and the surrounding community.

ESSENTIAL COMPETENCIES FOR STUDENT AFFAIRS PROFESSIONALS

Core values create the underlying culture of the profession, but how do student affairs professionals design and implement programs that will reflect these values on the front lines? Core values such as caring, counseling, and faith focus on improving the individual and require that the student affairs professional possess finely honed interpersonal skills. Student affairs professionals must listen carefully, observe nonverbal cues, and be insightful into the students' backgrounds and concerns. Other core values such as community development, social justice, and career exploration are contextual in nature—demanding student affairs professionals perceive the complex layering of the campus environment and how the interaction between individuals supports or inhibits student development and success.

Consequently, student affairs professionals must be skilled in a multitude of interpersonal and contextual skills. Eight core competencies, identified by the Council for the Advancement of Standards in Higher Education, are expected of new student affairs professionals.[22] Many graduate programs in student affairs have adopted curriculum and practicum experiences that help graduate students develop the core competencies they will need to succeed as new student affairs professionals.

Effectively Working with Diverse Populations

Students are increasingly more diverse in race, ethnicity, gender, sexual orientation, socioeconomic status, and religion. Each special population has encountered unique barriers and obstacles in higher education, including disparity in admissions, financial aid, housing, and campus climate. Student affairs professionals are actively engaged in making their campuses more welcoming and accessible to the increasing diversity of students. However, student affairs professionals recognize that advocacy is difficult without truly understanding the perspectives of the students.

Student affairs professionals must develop a sophisticated range of multicultural competencies: appreciation for diversity and a thorough, deep knowledge of the cultural values of the students at their colleges and universities. They must be able to perceive the organizational barriers that exist at the campus, demonstrate their genuine concern for minority students' success, and work with college and university administrators to develop strategies for creating a welcoming, inclusive environment. Self-awareness is also important for student affairs professionals; an individual who is not aware of his or her own identity and cultural values cannot perceive how others are shaped by their own identities and cultural values.[23]

Community Building and Development

Building a sense of community between students is complex but has many advantages for a college or university. Such benefits include creating a welcoming space for difficult discussions and student learning outside the classroom, bringing the campus together in a time of crisis, reducing unwanted incidents such as vandalism, and creating an enduring loyalty to the college or university after the students have graduated. Student affairs professionals shape the process of community development, but first they must decide what the "community" is that they are shaping—students residing on a floor of a residence hall, the entire population of first-year students, adult learners in an online environment, or all the students, faculty, and staff on the campus. Student affairs professionals must also decide what a healthy community looks like. Is it one that follows rules and experiences few disciplinary measures, or is it one that encourages and respects diverse viewpoints and perspectives? What does a healthy community look like that encourages both?

Community building is therefore a very intentional process for student affairs professionals. Many models of community development emphasize the students' building of the community through their involvement with each other and with the planning of activities that bring members of the community into direct contact. Student affairs professionals, therefore, must identify students who are potential leaders in the community; help students with envisioning programs that appeal to the larger student body; plan, manage, and market programs; and hold students responsible for their contributions. These "involved" students begin to see themselves as responsible for the programs they create, and the participants in the programs begin to see that they can initiate change themselves. Ultimately, a community emerges. If student affairs professionals negotiate the community's development carefully, they can ensure that the community reflects the values and learning outcomes that are desired. As Roberts said, "people support what they create."[24]

Conflict Resolution

Most students lack the interpersonal skills to effectively resolve conflict. Student affairs professionals help students address and resolve immediate conflicts, but they also teach life skills. While disputes between students (especially roommates) are the most common type of conflict, students experience conflicts in many areas of campus life. Conflicts may occur between students and faculty over academic performance, between student organizations and the university over speech, access to resources, or institutional culture, or between students and family regarding expectations for programs of study and career decisions.[25] Each of these types of conflict is mediated carefully by student affairs professionals.

They use different perspectives for managing conflict depending on the nature of the conflict and the parties involved. A *student development perspective* emphasizes the opportunity for growth and understanding as the desired outcome of the conflict, such as helping a student recognize a roommate's perspective. An *organizational development perspective* links the outcome of the conflict to the college or university's mission, such as negotiating for greater institutional support for an unpopular student organization on the basis of promoting diversity of opinion. A *community development perspective* emphasizes a resolution that best serves the interest of the community—whether that community is the students living in a residence hall, a student organization, or the campus as a whole. The community development perspective might be applied when resolving a conflict that affects a community—for example, a student whose loud parties disrupt the sleep of neighboring students. Open dialog, sharing of information, patience, and the exercise of fairness and good judgment are essential for effective conflict resolution skills.[26]

Counseling/Helping

Most student affairs professionals are not trained or licensed counselors, but the overwhelming number of them must develop helping skills because of their direct contact with students. Helping skills are not necessarily intended to address a student's emotional well-being, but to provide the student with coping skills and with the context for making decisions that solve his or her own dilemmas. Counseling and helping skills increase a student affairs professional's capacity to create positive relationships and environments for students. Lawrence Brammer and Ginger MacDonald identified three characteristics that are necessary for an effective counselor or helper: *genuineness*, or truly wanting to help; *unconditional positive regard*, or respect for students who hold contrary or unpopular values; and *empathy*.[27]

Robert R. Carkhuff developed a model that provides the basis for student affairs professionals to assume a helping role.[28] In the *attending* phase of Carkhuff's model, the student affairs professional is alert to individual students and reflects the appearance and behavior of someone who is prepared to listen. A good example is a residence hall director who notices that a new student doesn't often leave her room in the residence hall. Checking in with the student reveals a problem—she isn't happy at the college.

In *responding*, the student affairs professional frames the student's concern through acknowledging his or her feelings, asking probing questions, and connecting the student's responses (e.g., "You are unhappy at the college because you are lonely."). In *personalizing*, the student affairs professional brings the student's problem back to the student's own control (e.g., "You are unhappy living at the college because you are lonely because you have not participated in any social activities and not talked to many new people."). In *initiating*, the student affairs professional prepares the student for solving the dilemma by setting a reasonable goal (e.g., the student decides, "I will attend the movie night on Friday evening and talk to three people. Then I will have met new people, and then I will not be as lonely.").

Advising

Advisors help students identify choices and make responsible decisions—an inescapable facet of so many dimensions of student affairs, from residential life and financial aid to career services and health services. Many interpersonal characteristics essential to good helping skills are also vital interpersonal characteristics for good advising—genuineness, positive regard, and empathy. However, the advising process, unlike helping skills, requires the advisor to have a thorough and comprehensive knowledge of the college or university's resources and options for an appropriate resolution. Many available options can affect a student's success very differently, such as the selection of a major that suits a student's abilities, interest, and career goals. The advisor must perceive how each possible option can affect the student. Just as students may not be certain of their information needs when they interact with a reference librarian, students are not always able to fully articulate a problem to an advisor either.

Academic advisors must have sharp interviewing skills to diagnose why something isn't working for a student and why one option might be a better alternative than another. Love and Estanek identified the advising process that student affairs professionals engaged in advising should follow: *identifying the problem* (e.g., "I don't like my chemistry class."); *gathering information about the problem* (e.g., "I don't like my chemistry class because the homework is too difficult, and I'm not interested in it"); *proposing solutions* (e.g., "Let's do a career inventory test to see if there are careers that interest you that don't require a degree in chemistry."); *implementation* (e.g., "Let's enroll you in Horticulture this next semester to see if that is a better fit for you."); and *evaluation* (e.g., "You earned a high A in the Horticulture class. Do you think horticulture is a good fit for you as a new major?").[29]

Students' advising needs not only evolve as they progress through college, but advisors report that students are also increasingly underprepared for the rigor of college courses.[30] Many students now require at least some remedial education. As a consequence, advising is an increasingly complex skill for student affairs professionals and requires a sophisticated understanding of institutional resources, plans of study, student development theory, and continuous assessment of student learning.

Leadership

Because student affairs is a profession that tolerates, by necessity, a high degree of flexibility and ambiguity, many student affairs professionals and scholars have stressed the importance of leadership as a core competency. No student's situation is exactly like another, and student affairs professionals are frequently faced with times where a resolution is required quickly and immediately, without the benefit of seeking input from colleagues or supervisors. Not only does student affairs work often require quick decision making, but student affairs organizations must also adapt readily to serve students differently. Emerging technologies, trends in student culture, and changing student demographics demand different responses from past practices.

The college or university's organizational culture is generally slow to adapt to change, but student affairs organizations operate within a much tighter time frame in which policy decisions, technology, and organizational structures must evolve. Komives, Lucas, and McMahon assert leadership in student affairs is really about positive change that creates a flexible organizational culture.[31]

Love and Estanek suggest that leadership in student affairs reflects the value of the profession in educating the whole student and in students building a sense of community and being accountable for the success of the organization. To have meaningful experiences that stimulate development, student affairs organizations need to be more inclusive and collaborative in decision making than other areas of colleges and universities.[32] Love claims that leadership in student affairs "incorporate[s] holism, has an emphasis on relationships, thrives on uncertainty and ambiguity, is based on trust, and thrives on bottom-up efforts. Any member of an organization … can challenge a process, inspire a shared vision, enable others to act, model the way, and encourage the heart."[33]

Citizenship

Florence A. Hamrick describes citizenship as "actively attending to the well-being, continuity, and improvement of society through individual action."[34] Examples of good citizenship can range from implementing green initiatives to reduce energy consumption, organizing service opportunities in underserved communities, to challenging discriminatory laws and practices. The practice of good citizenship is not limited to the municipality or community in which a person lives—it extends to their participation with their department, campus, and college or university, such as celebrating a colleague's notable accomplishment.

However, scholars of citizenship education stress that good citizenship must be taught and is therefore both a skill and a learning outcome.[35] For student affairs professionals, citizenship is a two-fold competency: a skill to be practiced as a citizen of the department and of the campus in which they work, and also as a value to be instilled to students. Collegiality, teamwork, and staff recognition are certainly ways in which student affairs professionals practice citizenship in their roles as colleagues and employees. Creating experiences for students which teach citizenship skills are arguably more intricate. In practical terms, student affairs professionals must respect dissenting opinions, allow others to express their ideas, and help each other and students work towards a mutually acceptable resolution within a civil and respectful context.

Assessment

Assessment in student affairs is increasingly important for justifying costs, services, and programs; guiding policy and staffing decisions; and improving the quality of student services, programs, and learning outcomes.[36] Generally, assessment in student affairs is not intended to assess an individual student's learning or experience, but to collect data that provides answers on larger questions—such as why a particular group of students has lower rates of persistence or graduation than other students or why students choose to move out of residence halls after their first year of college. At some colleges and universities, only student affairs professionals with specialized training and expertise conduct assessment, but assessment skills are increasingly expected among many student affairs professionals regardless of their principal area of work.[37]

The assessment studies undertaken by student affairs professionals could and should be of great interest to librarians. Student affairs professionals are founts of qualitative and quantitative data about student populations and services. For example, librarians who are weighing whether or not to reduce computer labs and public workstations in libraries are probably interested in whether students have access to computers elsewhere. Their colleagues in housing and residential life may have already surveyed the student population to determine how many students bring laptops and desktops to campus as they decide how much network infrastructure is required in the residence halls.

FUNCTIONAL AREAS OF STUDENT AFFAIRS PRACTICE

Student affairs organizations at many colleges and universities compose a diverse set of functional areas that provide student services and academic support. Many student affairs organizations are organized very differently depending on the unique needs of the campus. Therefore the functional areas of student affairs organizations are very different between two-year and four-year colleges and universities, small liberal arts colleges, comprehensive universities, and research universities. A chief student affairs administrator is generally responsible for the operations of student affairs organizations, but student affairs and academic affairs are unified as a single reporting unit at some colleges and universities. Other colleges and universities have recently aligned some student affairs functional areas, such as admissions and financial aid offices, with academic affairs.[38]

Student affairs scholars generally regard the following functional areas as the core functions of student affairs organizations. These functional areas are among the oldest domains of student affairs and are organized under a chief student affairs administrator more consistently than other functional areas.[39] Each of the functional areas has its own professional associations, conferences, journals, and other publications that provide support, continuing education, and investigations of emerging trends.

Academic Advising

Wesley R. Habley declared, "Academic advising is the only structured activity on the campus in which all students have the opportunity for one-on-one interaction with a concerned representative of the institution."[40] Academic advisors help students develop a plan of study that successfully leads to the student's goals. The process involves learning the student's desired outcomes; guiding the student through declaring a major and course selection; career counseling; and connecting the student with opportunities for internships, independent study, and experiential learning. Faculty might act as academic advisors to students with declared majors in their respective academic programs at many small colleges and universities, but frequently academic advisors are student affairs professionals dedicated to advising cohorts of students throughout their college experience.

Academic advising is linked to a number of important outcomes, including students' satisfaction with their academic programs, achievement for underprepared and underperforming students, and—arguably most important—student persistence.[41] Consequently, academic advising is increasingly following a developmental advising model. The academic advisor is a mentor for the student, appreciating the student's preferred learning styles, identifying the student's life goals, and promoting campus and community resources. As Richard Light claims, "Good advising may be the single most underestimated characteristic of a successful college experience."[42]

Admissions/Enrollment Management

Admissions is a complex function. Admissions officers develop comprehensive plans for identifying and recruiting the right mix of students for the college or university. They provide information to prospective students on the breadth of academic programs and opportunities available at the campus. They also help the student and the family decide if the college or university is the right match for the student's academic talent, aspirations, and background. Consequently, admissions officers are uniquely trained to listen carefully to students' interests and to quickly develop a keen insight into the student's background. Admissions officers are not simply seeking the brightest or most academically gifted prospective students, but they are also complementing the college or university's diverse student body by seeking students with creative and athletic promise.

At some campuses, admissions functions are organized into an enrollment management function. In an enrollment management function, the admissions, financial aid, marketing, and student records professionals work together closely to craft a comprehensive recruitment and retention plan. It is increasingly common that the enrollment management functional area reports to a college or university provost or chief academic officer rather than a student affairs organization.[43]

Campus Ministries

Many student affairs professionals believe that spiritual development is an integral part of educating the whole student. According to Jennifer Capeheart-Meningall, "Spirituality is one of the ways people construct knowledge and meaning."[44] Spirituality and religious beliefs affect the development of students' identities, but also provide opportunities for self-reflection and reasoning. Alexander W. Astin noted that students who are involved in religious or spiritual programs at their colleges or universities are likely to report greater satisfaction with campus life, a stronger sense of community, better physical and psychological well-being, and stronger academic performance than students who are not involved.[45]

This functional area of student affairs organizations is commonly referred to as campus ministries. Colleges and universities affiliated with a specific faith often employ chaplains and other spiritual advisors who coordinate spiritual programs and activities across the campus. Chaplains might also play a role in academic affairs at faith-affiliated colleges and universities which integrate spiritual teachings into the curriculum. They may lead religious services, especially if the college or university maintains houses of worship. Public colleges and universities will often coordinate spiritual programs and activities with houses of worship located in their communities. Off-campus spiritual advisors tend to the needs of the students who belong to their faiths, but public colleges and universities will often make space and resources available for faith-affiliated student organizations.

Campus Safety and Police Services

Campus safety and police are the principal law enforcement and public safety officers for colleges and universities. The culture and climate of campus safety and police services are subtly different from municipal police agencies. Whereas the focus of municipal police agencies is often law enforcement, the focus of campus safety and campus police services is frequently crime prevention because of the educational mission of higher education.[46]

There are multiple organizational models for campus safety and police services, depending on what the college or university administration values about safety and its security initiatives. At many colleges and universities, campus safety and police services report directly to the president or chancellor to facilitate more efficient, rapid communication regarding incidents on campus. A reporting line to business affairs is also a common organizational model and often reflects the campus's desire to coordinate campus safety with facilities, human resources, and public relations operations.

When campus safety and police services report to a student affairs organization, however, the emphasis of their work is often on crime prevention and educating students on personal security and campus safety. These initiatives often include coordinating volunteer safety escorts and student patrol officers to monitor campus during off hours, educating students on traffic and pedestrian safety, and participating in outreach to students residing in campus housing.[47]

Career Services

Advising students on career exploration and planning is the principal responsibility of student affairs professionals employed in career services. They help students locate information on internships, prospective employers, and current job openings. Frequently, career services provides students with resume-writing skills and resume critiques, interviewing skills, and strategies for negotiating salaries and benefits. Most importantly, however, student affairs professionals working in career services are skillful counselors who help students identify their career interests, recognize their personal strengths and loves, and hone their job search to professional areas that best match their preferences. Increasingly, career services professionals are reaching out to first-year students to instill career planning early in the academic experience.[48] Many also work with alumni who are exploring new careers or experiencing a career interruption.

Commuter Services

Commuter services is often responsible for addressing the needs of students who reside in off-campus housing. The most common functions of commuter services include helping students locate affordable housing and information regarding landlords and leases. It helps students negotiate tenant and landlord relationships and educate students how to be good neighbors and roommates. However, commuter services professionals also advocate for off-campus students in regards to access to and information about recreational facilities, events and programs, dining options, and representation in student organizations. At some college and universities, commuter services is also responsible for parking services and adjudicating parking fines and other disputes.

Community Service and Service Learning

Community service and service learning programs promote volunteer activity among students and are often designed to foster civic responsibility. Many student affairs professionals who work in this area collect information regarding volunteer opportunities in the community, conduct outreach with community agencies, and coordinate campus service learning days. They also advise individual students, student organizations, and Greek houses on service opportunities within the community. Many student affairs professionals working in community service and service learning programs also act as consultants for university administration on matters of civic engagement and responsibility. Educating administrators on the concerns of community residents and businesses that are neighbors to campuses has become especially prevalent as universities engage in capital expansion projects.[49]

Dean of Students Office

The student affairs professionals who compose the Dean of Students office help students find solutions to dilemmas that threaten to disrupt their academic studies. This includes resolving conflicts between students and faculty, providing guidance on select legal issues, and working with students to find a voice in the campus on student-related concerns. The Dean of Students office is also typically charged with upholding standards of behavior and integrity among the students, such as mediating allegations of plagiarism. Often it serves as the college or university's touchstone for student-related issues. The Dean of Students office coordinates the work of many of the other student affairs programs and services.

Disability Support Services

The goal of disability support services is generally to help students with disabilities participate fully in campus life and derive the greatest benefit possible from their educational experience. As such, they assess students' unique needs and plan ways in which students succeed despite physical or academic impediments. This might include facilitating transcription services for hearing-impaired students or negotiating with publishers for the rights to convert a print source to an audio source so that a textbook may be narrated for the student. The student affairs professionals employed in this area assume many roles—educating college or university administration on the physical access of the campus and its resources, ensuring legal compliance to laws and rules regarding accommodation, helping faculty identify ways to accommodate the needs of particular students, and advising students on their rights under the Americans with Disabilities Act.

Greek Affairs

Student affairs professionals who manage Greek affairs serve as liaisons between the college or university and the fraternity and sorority chapters that are chartered in the area. They monitor the Greek houses for standards of safety and responsibility, and they help the houses determine their autonomy and accountability. Student affairs professionals working in Greek affairs are generally responsible for enforcing the rigors of scholarship, service, and leadership that enable the houses to remain on the campus. They might also provide training to house officers on the management skills necessary for running their houses successfully and help mediate incidents that violate the houses' rules of conduct and personal responsibility.

Health Services and Counseling Services

Health and counseling services for students are commonly organized under student affairs organizations. Physicians and mental health counselors tend to the physical and psychological well-being of students, but educational programming is also a significant mission of many student health services centers. Student affairs professionals are employed as health educators, who participate in student outreach and create awareness of health-related issues, prevention, and resources. They help students identify strategies for healthy living, regulating stress, and anger management. Health services and counseling professionals collaborate closely with other functional areas, such as housing and academic advisors, to coordinate referrals.

Housing/Residential Life

The principal responsibility of housing and residential life is to provide safe living experiences for students who reside in campus housing. At many colleges and universities, housing and residential life is a single functional area, but other colleges and universities manage the functional areas separately. Housing may be charged with managing room assignments, dining operations, and the facilities of the residence halls. Residential life may be charged with educational and social programming, conflict resolution between students, and the supervision of students and the resident assistants. Residence halls are recognized as one of the primary settings for student learning and growth, and many housing and residential life programs have created living-learning communities where students who share common interests or aspirations live together and participate in classes and educational programs in the residence halls.[50]

Many of the student affairs professionals employed in housing and residential life live in the residence halls to ensure student safety and rapid responses to emergencies. "Living in" is a good way for student affairs professionals to develop intimate knowledge of the campus and insight into student experiences and backgrounds. Consequently, housing and residential life are areas where many entry-level student affairs professionals begin their careers.[51]

Judicial Affairs

The student affairs professionals who coordinate the activities of judicial affairs offices are principally charged with enforcing the student code of conduct and campus rules. Generally, they investigate claims of behavioral misconduct referred to their office by faculty, campus safety and police officers, housing and residential life professionals, and municipal police agencies. Judicial affairs professionals listen to students' perspectives on infractions and attempt to work with the students to develop a sense of personal accountability.

Student discipline provides a unique moment for student affairs professionals to gauge the level of moral reasoning employed by students and to make a developmental impact on students' moral reasoning. The role of judicial affairs professionals has traditionally offered an opportunity to foster the personal growth of students as part of the educational process.[52] The problem of student discipline has long posed a dilemma for student affairs professionals, however. The student's right to due process and the potentially serious consequences of discipline demand a judicial process with tightly followed rules and policies. Nonetheless, the responses to student discipline provide a valuable opportunity to foster a student's moral development and ethical decision making.

Judicial affairs professionals formulate educational responses to student discipline rather than mere punitive measures. The judicial affairs officer can challenge the student's current level of development and facilitate development to a more sophisticated level of moral reasoning. Judicial affairs officers are frequently trained in conflict resolution, higher education law, and due process; such student affairs professionals are commonly attorneys.[53]

Leadership Programs

Leadership programs are focused on developing leadership skills in students, primarily through a combination of programs and experiences. Programs can be connected with an academic program and take the form of credit-bearing courses or can be a series of extracurricular programs that lead to a certificate. Leadership programs that are embedded in an academic program are generally focused on developing leadership traits specific to a field of study. The student affairs professionals will frequently collaborate with faculty to teach credit-bearing courses in which students learn skills such as strategic planning within a business context or collaborating with community agencies to design parent-outreach programs within a school district.

Leadership programs take a different shape when the programs are extracurricular. The student affairs professionals facilitate problem-solving exercises and workshops that foster teamwork, strategic planning, vision, and other vital skills. Additionally, student affairs professionals help the students connect leadership skills to daily living situations and bring students together with local industry leaders.

Multicultural Student Services

Offices of multicultural student services are focused on supporting and integrating students who are traditionally underrepresented in higher education with the majority culture of the campus. The student affairs professionals who work in this area foster a campus climate that is welcoming and inclusive for all students, coordinate celebrations of cultural heritage and expression, connect students with academic and community resources, and help underrepresented students navigate the complexity of majority culture campuses.

Improving student retention is one of the underlying goals for multicultural student services, particularly at campuses that are working towards increasing the racial and ethnic diversity of the student community.[54] Services and programs that support African American, Latino/a, Asian and Pacific Islander, and Native American students are commonly integrated into a functional area that serves the particular needs of each community, but larger colleges and universities might have decentralized services where each group of underrepresented students is served by its own office and programs. Women students and gay, lesbian, bisexual, and transgender students are sometimes included in multicultural student services functional areas, but may be served by other student affairs programs specifically tailored to their particular needs.[55]

Orientation/New Student Programs

Student affairs professionals are often responsible for coordinating orientation programs for first-year and transfer students and for managing programs which help students transition successfully to higher education. Their primary purpose is to orient the students to the college or university's history, traditions, and expectations, while preparing the students to be responsible campus citizens. They educate the students on campus and community resources and provide information regarding housing, financial aid, course registration, and dining options. They facilitate discussions on sexual harassment, underage drinking, violence, and other topics related to expectations of conduct and community living. Student affairs professionals working in this area may arrange campus tours for prospective students and provide information to parents.

New student programs have recently begun to expand beyond campus tours and orientation sessions that last one or a few days. Such programs are evolving to include first-year experience programs that integrate student affairs and academic programs, learning outcomes, and faculty participation in an orientation that spans the students' first year of college.[56] Programs are increasingly designed to focus on at-risk or underperforming students, developing a cohort that brings the students together throughout their college experience and providing workshops that strengthen students' research, writing, and study skills.[57]

Recreation and Fitness

Recreation and fitness programs are increasingly important areas of student affairs organizations. Their primary purpose is educating students on wellness, which can include coordinating a variety of physical activities and maintaining facilities but is increasingly expanding to educate entire campus communities on proper nutrition, lifestyle choices, and awareness of healthy living. Recent studies indicate as many as 90 percent of undergraduate students use recreation and fitness facilities.[58] Many campuses are experiencing a construction and expansion "boom" in recreation and fitness facilities and programs. Such facilities are perceived as being increasingly critical to student satisfaction and prospective students' decisions to enroll.[59]

Student Activities

Student activities represents a broad range of programs and services for students. It provides a way for students to become engaged in campus life outside of the classroom. Student activities encompasses cultural programs such as heritage celebrations, entertainment and recreational activities such as film festivals and dances, and sponsored outings such as day trips to museums or nature preserves. Students involved in activities are more likely to persist to graduation than students who are not involved, and involved students also make greater gains in intellectual and psychosocial skills and are more satisfied with their college experiences than uninvolved students.[60] As a result, many of the programs are designed to expose students to new perspectives and to encourage participation in campus governance, community service, and student organizations.[61] Many of the programs and services coordinated by student activities may, in fact, be coordinated by other student affairs functional areas, such as student unions or multicultural student services, at larger colleges and universities with a decentralized student affairs organization.

Student Unions/Student Centers

Student unions or student centers are generally organizations that serve as the "hub" of student activity and programming on campuses. They are gathering places for students to study, lounge, and connect with convenient services, such as coffee houses, food courts, bookstores, and computer labs. Campuses with centralized student affairs organizations will often bring career services, student activities, multicultural student services, and other areas together in the student union. At campuses with decentralized student affairs organizations, the functional areas are frequently located at other areas of the campus. The student union will consequently serve as the primary entertainment venue for recreational activities. Student affairs professionals with experience in programming and event planning frequently manage student unions.

EDUCATION AND PREPARATION IN STUDENT AFFAIRS

Many student affairs professionals hold master's degrees, and many colleges and universities require a master's degree for an entry-level student affairs position. Graduate programs that traditionally place students into student affairs positions are variously called higher education administration, college student personnel administration, educational leadership, college student affairs, and college student development. Many of these programs are offered through colleges or schools of education.

Each program emphasizes different core skills. Some programs focus on administration, others focus on counseling (and might even require licensure for graduation), and others on teaching and communication skills. Some programs provide a stronger theoretical foundation for student affairs practice, and still others will emphasize practical experiences. Most graduate programs will provide opportunities for graduate students to participate in an assistantship or practicum, either at their home campus or with a partner campus, as a way of providing students with professional experiences. As in librarianship, many students enrolled in student affairs graduate programs will find their first position after graduation based on the context and strength of their assistantship and practicum experiences.

Doctoral degrees are rarely required for entry-level positions in student affairs. However, doctoral degrees are increasingly expected among student affairs professionals who hold dean and associate dean positions or serve as directors of housing and residential life, academic advising, student unions, career services, admissions, and financial aid. Like the master's degree, a doctoral degree in a specific discipline is not always required, but higher education administration is the most frequent doctoral degree held by student affairs professionals.[62]

However, not every student affairs professional earns a master's degree in an academic discipline that provides a theoretical or practical foundation for working in student affairs. A bachelor's degree and relevant work experience are sufficient at some colleges and universities, while others employ student affairs professionals who earned master's degrees outside of the traditional areas of study. A business student might gain relevant professional experience by developing a business plan with a department of housing and residential life that maximizes the number of occupied beds in the residence halls. A nursing student could acquire significant knowledge of the needs of people with disabilities during an internship with a department of disability support services. Student affairs professionals with law degrees are not uncommon in judicial affairs, and masters of business administration are reasonably common for positions in business affairs and management.[63]

How do people "find" student affairs as a profession? Just as in librarianship, many people are introduced to the profession through their experiences in student employment. James Conneely speaks for many student affairs professionals, "Some found the profession by accident, but many enjoyed their experiences as a student leader or student worker. The truth is, very few children talk about being a student affairs professional when they grow up! Many people find the profession through work as an undergraduate or graduate staff person."[64] Housing and residential life employ large numbers of students as resident assistants and in other capacities; student unions hire students to participate in programming events and manage service desks; counseling and health services manage peer counselors; and recreation and fitness facilities have significant numbers of student staff to operate the physical facilities.

PROFESSIONAL ASSOCIATIONS AND CORE PUBLICATIONS

There are many professional associations and organizations that cater to the many dimensions of the student affairs profession—too many to be addressed in this chapter! Each of the functional areas mentioned earlier in this chapter has its own associations and organizations that are specifically tailored to its unique issues, trends, research, and professional development needs. However, a few associations merit an overview here because of their broad scope of interests, appeal to student affairs professionals across the breadth of functional areas, and traditional collaboration with faculty and staff outside of student affairs.

The American College Personnel Association (ACPA) and NASPA— Student Affairs Administrators in Higher Education (formerly the National Association of Student Personnel Administrators)—are the oldest professional associations for student affairs professionals. Their annual conferences bring together student affairs professionals from many functional areas at many diverse colleges and universities. ACPA represents more than 8,500 members at more than 1,500 private and public colleges and universities in the United States and globally. NASPA is the older and larger of the associations. Founded in 1919, it represents more than eleven thousand members at more than 1,400 colleges and universities.

The missions and scope of ACPA and NASPA are very similar, with many members belonging to both associations simultaneously. ACPA is favored by mid-career student affairs professionals based on the association's emphasis on leadership development, supervisory skills, and other continuing education programs. NASPA has attracted greater numbers of new student affairs professionals in recent years through its partnerships with the Association of College and University Housing Officers–International (ACUHO-I) to provide job placement exchanges and networking opportunities.

ACUHO-I is specifically focused on the residential living experiences of students. It has more than nine hundred college and university housing organizations and more than two hundred corporations as members. Together, its members provide housing for approximately 1.8 million students. The annual conferences emphasize current research on student learning outside the classroom and innovation in housing services, facilities, and architecture.

There are also a number of key journals that are worth exploring which delve deeper into emerging research, policy analyses, and literature reviews of student affairs. The *Journal of Student Affairs Research and Practice, Journal of College Student Development, New Directions for Student Services, Career Development Quarterly, Journal of College and University Student Housing, Journal of College and University Law, Higher Education Review, Research in Higher Education,* and the *Journal of Higher Education* are leading, peer-reviewed scholarly journals which publish emerging research. *NACADA Journal, About Campus, Campus Law Enforcement Journal, Journal of College Admissions, Journal of Student Financial Aid, Journal of Career Planning and Employment, Talking Stick, Journal of Technology in Student Affairs, Diverse: Issues in Higher Education,* and *Black Issues in Higher Education* are not peer-reviewed journals but share perspectives from practitioners across student affairs and higher education.

EMERGING ISSUES IN STUDENT AFFAIRS

Student affairs is evolving rapidly to meet the needs and expectations of today's college students. The millennial generation has brought greater diversity to college campuses. Greater numbers of students are also attending college with complex personal and health issues that profoundly challenge the capacities for student health services and notions of campus and personal safety. Legal issues present ambiguous expectations for student affairs professionals in regards to student privacy and confidentiality and blur the boundaries for ensuring the welfare of students. Parents are also playing a significantly stronger and more visible role in students' lives. Technology is radically shaping the way the students interact with each other and with the university, as well as transforming how student affairs professionals communicate with each other in times of crisis. The issues that pose the greatest challenges to student affairs professionals are different for each college and university, but there are many emerging issues that are common to most campuses today. The following emerging issues have generated significant discussion in recent years in the student affairs profession.

Diversity

A racially and ethnically diverse campus provides educationally meaningful experiences for students. There is a growing body of research that proposes that critical-thinking skills, teamwork, tolerance, cultural appreciation and knowledge, and inclusion are strengthened when students are exposed to students with perspectives and backgrounds different from their own.[65] Diversity scholars contend that students make the strongest gains on diversity-related educational outcomes through interactions that students of diverse backgrounds have with each other on a daily, informal basis.[66] These interactions take place in residence halls, social activities, workplaces, and student organizations. The first-year housing arrangement might be the very first time that a white student from rural Minnesota has met an African American student from urban Chicago. The subsequent tension can result in serious consequences including isolation and victimization—but also incredible benefits if negotiated carefully.

Student affairs professionals are ideally suited to help students learn about diversity and negotiate the complex interactions that can result in conflict. Tolerance, openness, acceptance, and respect for others are core values of the profession, and student affairs professionals are front and center in students' daily interactions outside of the classroom. Their knowledge and insight about student experiences, backgrounds, and frustrations have often resulted in better institutional policies, programs, and services.[67] Consequently, the student affairs profession has addressed diversity at national conferences since the 1960s and continues to aggressively emphasize diversity skills and multicultural competencies in graduate programs and in continuing education opportunities for student affairs professionals.[68]

Student affairs professionals seek collaborations with faculty and with administrators to resolve tensions that stem from diversity, remedy grievances, and advocate for stronger academic and social support for students who are underrepresented at the campus. Arthur Sandeen and Margaret J. Barr call such a leadership role "the most critical of all for student affairs professionals to assume" and emphasize the importance of the steps that student affairs professionals should take in making diversity a cornerstone of their professional lives.[69]

Student Safety and Security

Are students responsible for their own personal safety on campus, or should the college or university play a role? The message provided to colleges and universities by society and by the courts has grown ambiguous over the decades. For much of American higher education's history, the courts have charged colleges and universities with safeguarding students. Historically, the legal concept of *in loco parentis* means literally "in place of the parent." Colleges and universities carefully monitored student behavior, enforced codes of conduct, and had significant latitude in deciding where and when students could socialize, spend their leisure time, and return to campus. Much of the monitoring and enforcement fell to student affairs professionals. However, *in loco parentis* eroded with changes in society and legal opinion during and after the 1960s. Responsibility for student conduct and for personal safety and security rested largely with the individual student. Today, student affairs professionals report that they are actively studying ways to teach students greater responsibility for personal security.

They are also creating mechanisms to make the campus safer. The shooting rampage at Virginia Tech University in 2007 left thirty-two students and faculty dead. Attitudes on student safety and security changed almost overnight. Many colleges and universities have moved towards implementing emergency alert notification systems and adopting crisis response plans. The scale of such crisis planning is immense—many crisis plans involve students directly for the first time. Student affairs professionals are training students in how to protect themselves in the event of an active shooter on campus, and they encourage students to monitor their surroundings closely and report suspicious activity immediately.[70] Cameras and other monitoring devices are strategically placed on campuses in increasing numbers as well.[71]

Mental Health Issues

The number of students entering higher education with previously diagnosed mental health issues has increased dramatically since the 1990s.[72] Previously, such students may not have attended college or may have attended a local college while living with family. Improvements in medications and counseling services have enabled many students with mental health issues to pursue educational opportunities unencumbered. However, not all students adjust to campus life easily. Some students stop taking necessary medication when they are not under the supervision of their parents or family physician, while other students' mental health issues are aggravated by new stresses. Still others exhibit signs of unusual behavior or disorganized thinking for the first time during college.

Student affairs professionals are challenged to quickly recognize signs of mental health issues. Is inappropriate, immature, or impulsive behavior masking an underlying psychological issue? Does the student demonstrate signs of depression, withdrawal, or anger? Does the student have the potential to harm himself or others? Whatever the behaviors, student affairs professionals are trained to intervene and decide if the student should be held accountable for his or her behavior through contracts for good community living, campus judicial processes, or mandated referrals to counseling services.

Parent Involvement

While librarians may not hear *helicopter parent* very often, student affairs professionals are intimately familiar with the phrase! Helicopter parents "hover" over their college student children, often intervening in situations or making decisions on behalf of their child that should be left to the student to resolve. Student affairs professionals have reported that parents' involvement in their children's college education has increased dramatically since the 1990s.[73]

Many student affairs professionals blame the cell phone. With so many families connected by family calling plans, it's easy for a student to quickly call home after the latest disagreement with a roommate or frustration with a class assignment. The millennial generation of students seem particularly attached to their families.

Many colleges and universities have responded to parents' involvement in their children's higher education and established an office of parent concerns. These offices employ student affairs professionals to listen to parents' concerns—which range from receiving information on tuition and fees to explaining grading policies. Student affairs professionals also ensure that parents have a voice in campus decisions. Alumni affairs, fundraising offices, and other areas of campus have reported excellent benefits by involving parents more closely in campus life.

Campus Environments

Academic programs and student services are not enough to create a learning community. Students must *believe* in something that brings people together for a shared experience and identity. Traditions, demography, and institutional mission are all vital elements of creating a campus culture. However, the environment does not prove easy terrain for all students, nor are all environments healthy for student learning.

Small campuses might be stifling to some students, and very large campuses can make students lonely or homesick if they are unable to make connections with others easily. Some colleges and universities rely heavily on codes of conduct to regulate student behavior, whereas others follow an honor code that encourages individual styles of learning and expression. Racially and ethnically diverse colleges and universities stimulate tolerance between different student groups when mutual respect is observed; sadly, other diverse campuses experience racial tension or convey unintended messages that chill the campus environment for certain student groups. Campus traditions and symbols impact student culture—the Aggie Bonfire at Texas A&M University grew from a simple bonfire that celebrated a college rivalry seventy years ago to an elaborate ritual with five thousand participants constructing a forty-foot pyramid the year that the elaborate structure collapsed and killed twelve students.

Increasingly, student affairs professionals use the college or university's culture as a lens for analyzing and understanding how students' experiences influence their behavior and their learning. Are the faculty touting a high standard of achievement yet providing little feedback to students in regard to written work and research? The result will probably be student frustration, complaints about lack of access to instructors, and lower retention rates. Student affairs professionals, however, are among the first who notice the effect on the students and hear their confusion. Frequently, university leaders call upon student affairs professionals to interpret student culture, facilitate discussions with vocal student groups, and remedy situations that have reached crisis proportions. Student affairs professionals understand how the campus influences student learning and student development and helps the campus adapt its culture to promote a successful learning environment. As Sandeen and Barr say, "Campus culture as a learning environment is a bit like religion… . We have to believe in it to make it work."[74]

Alcohol Issues

Alcohol use and abuse have increased significantly on college campuses. Fifty percent of today's college students have consumed alcohol prior to entering college.[75] The National Advisory Council on Alcohol Abuse and Alcoholism announced four hundred thousand self-reported incidents of sexual assault involving alcohol occurred on college campuses in 2002, and 1,400 college students died from alcohol poisoning or accidents involving alcohol. Student injuries, vandalism and destruction of property, sexually transmitted diseases, and academic problems are reported to be significantly higher on college campuses where high percentages of students consume alcohol.[76]

Certainly student affairs professionals are concerned with how to educate students on alcohol issues while maintaining standards for campus and community safety. However, this is no easy task. The consumption of alcohol is illegal for most traditional-aged college students, and many campuses ban the possession of alcohol even for students over the age of twenty-one. Alcohol use has largely moved to areas of campus life where student affairs professionals have little direct control—off-campus apartments, fraternity and sorority houses, and bars and nightclubs with lax enforcement. Binge drinking has subsequently become more widely practiced in recent years.[77]

Role of Technology

If librarians are at the forefront of the emerging technologies that are shaping how educators connect with students, student affairs colleagues are at the front lines along with librarians. Growth in technology has exploded in student affairs and is rapidly changing how student affairs professionals communicate with each other and with students, respond to campus crises, facilitate student learning, and transform facilities and services. Students expect technology threaded through their living and learning experiences, and student affairs has risen to the challenges in a number of ways. Academic advisors offer virtual advising appointments via webcams and instant messaging. Tours of campuses and demonstrations of fitness machines are available on YouTube. Residence halls provide wireless networks and notification by text messaging when laundry facilities have finished students' laundry. Students are encouraged to join Facebook groups created by student affairs professionals to advertise upcoming programs and resources.

Parents' expectations, too, are evolving, as they want information and updates more consistently from student affairs professionals. Many student affairs organizations have responded by creating sections of their websites specifically aimed at parents, with important dates (such as room assignments), programs of interest to parents, and ways for parents to become involved in campus affairs. Some colleges and universities even strategically place webcams that broadcast in real time to give viewers a window into campus life without having to set foot on the physical campus.[78]

Social networking has certainly had an impact on student behavior. Student affairs professionals working in residential life and judicial affairs have counseled students whose alcohol consumption and misconduct are chronicled on Facebook and YouTube. Residential life staff report mediating roommate conflicts that occurred wholly via instant messaging—sometimes with the students sitting in the same dorm room with no verbal communication at all.[79] Career counselors advise students on removing questionably tasteful Facebook photos and carefully considering the implications of their online presence while seeking internships and entering the workforce. Multicultural student services staff document racially hostile anonymous postings on campus websites, online student newspapers, and online bulletin boards that create a chilling effect for minority students.[80]

Many colleges and universities with distance learning programs are integrating student affairs programs online, especially academic advising, financial aid, and career services.[81] An emerging discussion among student affairs professionals is how to build a sense of community among students who principally interact with each other online. This is particularly of interest to student affairs professionals who are employed at campuses with strong distance learning programs. However, student affairs professionals at residential colleges and universities are rethinking ways to connect with the students who live in their residence halls—they report that it's increasingly difficult to interest students in programs and facilitate discussions when virtual worlds, social networking, and video-on-demand services compete for the students' attention and time.[82]

Rapid crisis response is especially critical as emergencies unfold. Voice over Internet Protocol (VoIP) technologies, public broadcast systems, and emergency notification text-messaging systems are often managed by student affairs professionals. Mobile devices and pagers are becoming standard tools of the trade for student affairs professionals who must respond to crises at any hour of the day or night. Winston, Creamer, and Miller wrote at the start of the last decade, "The key word for student affairs in the twenty-first century is *connectivity*."[83] Given the urgency on many campuses for better coordination and faster communication, connectivity is certain to play an ever-increasing role in the coming years.

CONCLUSION

The role of student affairs in higher education is complex. Historically, the student affairs profession emerged from the need to attend to issues of student conduct and the administrative functions of the college or university. Today, student affairs professionals work in a variety of functional areas throughout colleges and universities, ranging from admissions to academic advising to housing and residential life. The role of student affairs professionals has also changed from one focused on administration to one focused on education. As institutions have shifted away from acting *in loco parentis*, the purpose of student affairs changed from a disciplinary role to an educational role. Student affairs professionals perceive that considerable learning and growth take place for students outside the classroom.

The core purpose of student affairs today is to understand how students develop intellectually, psychosocially, and emotionally and to create meaningful experiences that stimulate student development. Core values such as caring, helping, equality, and social justice inform much of the environments that student affairs professionals strive to create as the best conditions for student learning and success. In helping students develop stable identities, values, conflict resolution skills, communication skills, ethical standards, and tolerance, student affairs professionals help students prepare for career, leadership, and civic roles throughout their lifetimes.

A rich body of scholarship grounds student affairs practice in theory and research based in social science, education, law, and other disciplines. Professional associations and scholarly and trade literature connect student affairs professionals with each other and establish standards for professionalism and essential competencies. Emerging issues in higher education, such as the increasing diversity of students, the rise in mental health issues and alcohol consumption, the evolving role of technology on college campuses, parental involvement, and increased attention to safety and security are radically shaping the future of student affairs. Educating the whole student, however, remains the foundation of the profession, and collaboration with faculty and others will become increasingly paramount as student affairs professionals seek to understand and foster student learning in new and innovative directions.

Notes

1. John R. Thelin, *A History of American Higher Education* (Baltimore, MD: Johns Hopkins University Press, 2004), 28.

2. Ibid., 33.

3. John Seiler Brubacher and Willis Rudy, *Higher Education in Transition: A History of American Colleges and Universities, 1636–1976* (New York: Harper Row, 1976), 332.

4. Elizabeth M. Nuss, "The Development of Student Affairs," in *Student Services: A Handbook for the Profession*, 4th ed., edited by Susan R. Komives (San Francisco: Jossey-Bass, 2003), 5.

5. Brubacher and Rudy, *Higher Education in Transition*, 336.

6. Nuss, "The Development of Student Affairs," 76.

7. Tony Chambers and Christine E. Phelps, "Student Activism as a Form of Leadership and Student Development," *NASPA Journal* 31, no. 1 (1993): 21.

8. Robert D. Brown, *Student Development in Tomorrow's Higher Education: A Return of the Academy* (Washington, DC: American Personnel and Guidance Association, 1972), 48.

9. Ibid., 67.

10. Nuss, "The Development of Student Affairs," 78.

11. Patrick G. Love and Kimberly Yousey, "Gaps in the Conversation: Missing Issues in the Discourse of the Student Affairs Field," *Journal of College Student Development* 42, no. 5 (2001): 432.

12. Patrick G. Love and Sandra M. Estanek, *Rethinking Student Affairs Practice* (San Francisco: Jossey-Bass, 2004), 175.

13. Ibid., 177.

14. Nuss, "The Development of Student Affairs," 86.

15. Robert B. Young, "Identifying and Implementing the Essential Values of the Profession," *New Directions for Student Services*, no. 61 (1993): 6.

16. Ibid., 19.

17. Robert B. Young, "Philosophies and Values Guiding the Student Affairs Profession," in *Student Services: A Handbook for the Profession*, 4th ed., edited by Susan R. Komives (San Francisco: Jossey-Bass, 2003), 102.

18. Dennis C. Roberts, "Community: The Value of Social Synergy," *New Directions for Student Services*, no. 61 (1993): 36.

19. Gary J. Margolis and Noel C. March, "Campus Community Policing: It All Started with Us ... ," *Campus Law Enforcement Journal* 38, no. 3 (2008): 22.

20. Craig Vivian, "Advising the At-Risk College Student," *The Educational Forum* 69, no. 4 (2005): 336.

21. Scott T. Rickard, "Truth, Freedom, Justice: Academic Tradition and the Essential Values," *New Directions for Student Services*, no. 61 (1993): 21.

22. Laura A. Dean, *CAS Professional Standards for Higher Education*, 6th ed. (Washington, DC: Council for the Advancement of Standards, 2006), 33.

23. Derald Wing Sue, *Counseling the Culturally Diverse: Theory and Practice*, 4th ed. (New York: Wiley, 2003), 21.

24. Dennis C. Roberts, "Community Building and Programming," in *Student Services: A Handbook for the Profession*, 4th ed., edited by Susan R. Komives (San Francisco: Jossey-Bass, 2003), 545.

25. Margaret J. Barr, *The Handbook of Student Affairs Administration* (San Francisco: Jossey-Bass, 1993), 315.

26. Ibid., 325.

27. Lawrence M. Brammer and Ginger MacDonald, *The Helping Relationship: Process And Skills*, 7th ed. (Boston: Allyn and Bacon, 1999), 34.

28. Robert R. Carkhuff, *Helping and Human Relations: A Primer for Lay and Professional Helpers* (New York: Holt, Rinehart and Winston, 1969), 18.

29. Love and Estanek, *Rethinking Student Affairs Practice*, 189.

30. Abdusalam A. Addus, David Chen, and Anwar S. Khan, "Academic Performance and Advisement of University Students: A Case Study," *College Student Journal* 41 (2007): 316.

31. Susan R. Komives, Nance Lucas, and Timothy R. McMahon, *Exploring Leadership: For College Students Who Want to Make a Difference* (San Francisco: Jossey-Bass, 1998), 15.

32. Love and Estanek, *Rethinking Student Affairs Practice*, 39.

33. Ibid., 42.

34. Florence A. Hamrick, Nancy J. Evans, and John H. Schuh, *Foundations of Student Affairs: How Philosophy, Theory, and Research Strengthen Educational Outcomes* (San Francisco: Jossey-Bass, 2002), 183.

35. Alexander W. Astin, "The Role of Service in Higher Education," *About Campus* 1, no. 1 (1996): 15; Chambers and Phelps, "Student Activism as a Form of Leadership," 21.

36. John H. Schuh and M. Lee Upcraft, *Assessment Practice in Student Affairs: An Applications Manual* (San Francisco: Jossey-Bass, 2001), 5.

37. Ibid., 18.

38. Gwendolyn Jordan Dungy, "Organization and Functions of Student Affairs," in *Student Services: A Handbook for the Profession*, 4th ed., edited by Susan R. Komives (San Francisco: Jossey-Bass, 2003), 340.

39. Ibid., 341.

40. Wesley R. Habley, *Key Concepts in Academic Advising* (Manhattan, KS: National Academic Advising, 1994), 10.

41. Addus, Chen, and Khan, "Academic Performance and Advisement," 320; Vivian, "Advising the At-Risk College Student," 336.

42. Richard J. Light, *Making the Most of College: Students Speak Their Minds* (Cambridge, MA: Harvard University Press, 2001), 8.

43. Dungy, "Organization and Functions," 342.

44. Jennifer Capeheart-Meningall, "Role of Spirituality and Spiritual Development

in Student Life Outside the Classroom," *New Directions for Teaching and Learning*, no. 104 (2005): 32.

45. Alexander W. Astin, *The Spiritual Life of College Students: A National Study of College Students' Search for Meaning and Purpose* (Los Angeles: Higher Education Research Institute, University of California Los Angeles, 2004), 4.

46. Margolis and March, "Campus Community Policing," 22.

47. Ibid., 25.

48. Addus, Chen, and Khan, "Academic Performance and Advisement," 320.

49. Komives, Lucas, and McMahon, *Exploring Leadership*, 82.

50. James F. Conneely, *Planning a Career in College and University Student Housing* (Columbus, OH: ACUHO-I, 2002), 17.

51. Ibid., 24.

52. Elizabeth M. Baldizian, "Development, Due Process, and Reduction: Student Discipline in the 1990s," *New Directions for Student Services*, no. 82 (1998): 29.

53. Ibid., 30.

54. Patricia Gurin et al., "Diversity and Higher Education: Theory and Impact on Educational Outcomes," *Harvard Educational Review* 72, no. 3 (2002): 330.

55. Ibid., 335.

56. Erin Bentrim-Tapio and Kim Sousa-Peoples, "Student Learning Outcomes Assessment for Orientation Programs: A SOARing Transformation," *Journal of College Orientation and Transition* 15, no. 2 (2008): 28.

57. Vanessa K. Johnson et al., "Managing the Transition to College: The Role of Family Cohesion and Adolescents' Emotional Coping Strategies," *Journal of College Orientation and Transition* 15, no. 2 (2008): 23.

58. James R. Kilcherman, "The Impact of College Recreation Center Renovation on Overall Participant Utilization and Frequency," (master's thesis, Wright State University, 2009), 38, http://etd.ohiolink.edu/send-pdf.cgi/Kilchenman%20James%20R.pdf?wright1246041960.

59. Ibid., 53.

60. Hamrick, Evans, and Schuh, *Foundations of Student Affairs*, 199.

61. David Jacobson and Ethan Shimer, "Student Activities and Greek Affairs: Goals, Expectations, and Learning Outcomes," June 17, 2009, accessed July 14, 2010, http://www.slideshare.net/djacobson/student-activities-and-greek-affairs.

62. Conneely, *Planning a Career*, 2.

63. Ibid., 12.

64. Ibid., 17.

65. Gurin et al., "Diversity and Higher Education," 337; Anthony Lising Antonio

et al., "Effects of Racial Diversity on Complex Thinking in College Students," *Psychological Science* 15, no. 8 (2004): 507; Jeffrey F. Milem, Mitchell J. Chang, and Anthony Lising Antonio, *Making Diversity Work on Campus: A Research-Based Perspective* (Washington, DC: Association of American Colleges and Universities, 2005), 17; Sue, *Counseling the Culturally Diverse*, 68.

66. Gurin et al., "Diversity and Higher Education," 333.

67. Arthur Sandeen and Margaret J. Barr, *Critical Issues for Student Affairs: Challenges and Opportunities* (San Francisco: Jossey-Bass, 2006), 57.

68. Lamont A. Flowers and Mary F. Howard-Hamilton, "A Qualitative Study of Graduate Students' Perceptions of Diversity Issues in Student Affairs Preparation Programs," *Journal of College Student Development* 43, no. 1 (2002): 99.

69. Sandeen and Barr, *Critical Issues for Student Affairs*, 66.

70. Margolis and March, "Campus Community Policing," 23.

71. Ibid., 22.

72. Sandeen and Barr, *Critical Issues for Student Affairs*, 110.

73. Johnson et al., "Managing the Transition to College," 25.

74. Sandeen and Barr, *Critical Issues for Student Affairs*, 62

75. Barr, *The Handbook of Student Affairs Administration*, 43.

76. Jennifer L. Crissman Ishler, "Today's First-Year Students," in *Challenging and Supporting the First-Year Student: A Handbook for Improving the First Year of College*, edited by M. Lee Upcraft (San Francisco: Jossey-Bass, 2005), 26.

77. Ibid., 29.

78. Sandeen and Barr, *Critical Issues for Student Affairs*, 88.

79. Roger B. Winston, Don G. Creamer, and Theodore K. Miller, *The Professional Student Affairs Administrator: Educator, Leader and Manager* (New York: Taylor & Francis, 2001), 67.

80. Ana M. Martinez Aleman and Katherine Lynk Wartman, *Online Social Networking on Campus: Understanding What Matters in Student Culture* (New York: Routledge, 2008), 45.

81. Winston, Creamer, and Miller, *The Professional Student Affairs Administrator*, 45.

82. Aleman and Wartman, *Online Social Networking*, 68.

83. Winston, Creamer, and Miller, *The Professional Student Affairs Administrator*, 82.

2

Theories and Models of Student Development

Dallas Long

Long's chapter provides an overview of the theoretical models of student development that are most often used by student affairs professionals in their work. These theories guide student affairs professionals in developing programs and services, setting strategic goals, and interacting with students. Understanding these theories provides librarians with insight into the aims and values of the student affairs profession, a shared vocabulary for discussing student support efforts with colleagues, and frameworks for creating programs that encourage holistic student development.

Why do some students succeed in college while others do not? Why do some students identify very strongly with their cultural or racial background, while other students of the same background do not? Why do first-year students respond very differently to a conflict with a roommate than fourth-year students? As Ivey suggested about student growth and development during the college years, "there is too much going on that meets the eye ... and development is too complex for us to be aware of it all."[1]

Student affairs, as a profession, is highly practical but also well grounded in theory. As in librarianship, theories serve as a foundation for the knowledge, expertise, and practice of student affairs. Theories and models advance most—if not all—of the daily work of student affairs professionals, from academic advising, to career exploration, to leadership development, to student discipline. This chapter provides an introduction to the family of theories and models that student affairs professionals most commonly use to create meaningful educational experiences and programs.

Many of the theories and models which inform the work of student affairs professionals derive from the disciplines of education, psychology, sociology, anthropology, gender studies, ethnic studies, law, business administration, and communication. However, student affairs ultimately exists as a profession to support student learning and student success. Therefore, student development theories, which describe how students grow and change throughout their college experience, are the cornerstones for the theoretical framework of student affairs.

FAMILIES OF THEORIES

Student development theories fall into four broad families of theories. *Psychosocial theories* focus on the self-reflective and interpersonal dimensions of students' lives. These theories describe how students' perspectives of their own identity and of society evolve through the conflicts and crises they experience. *Cognitive-structural theories* explain how students think, reason, organize, and make meaning of their experiences. These theories are often sequential in nature, with cognitive development unfolding by stages as students build upon past experiences. *Person-environment interactive theories* focus on how the student's behavior and growth are directly affected by the educational environment. This family of theories is used extensively in academic advising and career services. *Humanistic-existential theories* describe how students make decisions that affect themselves and others. Counselors and other student affairs professionals engaged in helping skills heavily use this family of theories.

The most influential student development theories are briefly and very simplistically described in this chapter. They provide significant context for student affairs research and practice and underpin many of the educational experiences and programs that student affairs professionals create.

PSYCHOSOCIAL THEORIES OF STUDENT DEVELOPMENT

Psychosocial theories of student development explain how people grow and develop over their life span. This family of theories examines development as sequential in nature, generally accomplished through tasks, stages, or challenges that must be mastered or overcome before advancement to the subsequent phase of development. These tasks are frequently age-related, and most theorists working in the area of student development have focused on the developmental stages most closely related to the traditional age of college students—ages eighteen to twenty-two years. Conflict, independence, interdependence, and autonomy are the underlying values of many psychosocial theories. Student affairs professionals engage psychosocial theories frequently in situations that require students to resolve conflict with others or to develop independence and autonomy; these theories are also used to frame discussions of identity, gender, race and ethnicity, and sexual orientation.

Identity Development

Chickering's "seven vectors" theory of identity development is arguably one of the most widely known and widely applied theories of student development. He referred to identity as students' concepts of themselves as autonomous, independent people with carefully articulated opinions, beliefs, talents, skills, and ethics. He suggested that the development of students' identities is the foremost issue during students' college years and that students move through seven distinct vectors.[2] Each vector can be considered a developmental stage or phase of the students' lives.

Developing competence is the first vector of identity development. During this vector, students acquire a wide range of new cognitive, psychosocial, and technical skills as they encounter new academic challenges, living environments, diversity, and technology. Students develop new competencies and, subsequently, confidence as they master new skills. In the vector of *managing emotions*, students develop the ability to recognize the appropriateness of certain emotions and reactions in different contexts. They are able to control and express their emotions accordingly.

In the third vector, *moving through autonomy*, students achieve autonomy by learning to solve problems on their own. They recognize that their goals must be accomplished largely through their own actions and decisions rather than through reliance on parents, peers, and others. During the fourth vector, *developing mature interpersonal relationships*, students develop an appreciation for others based on the qualities they possess. This leads students to develop both a tolerance of differences and the capacity for intimacy.

In the vector of *establishing identity*, students construct a secure and comfortable sense of identity in regards to physical appearance, gender, race, and sexual orientation. They are aware that their identity is composed of multiple dimensions and how their identity is integrated with the broader society, culture, and history. In *developing purpose*, students develop a set of clear career goals, personal aspirations, and commitments to family, friends, and self. In the final vector, *developing integrity*, students progress from "black and white" thinking on complex moral and ethical issues to acknowledging the perspectives of others as valid. Students' behavior aligns with the values and goals they have established previously.

According to Chickering, students progress through the first four vectors during their first and second years of college and through the last three vectors during their third and fourth years of college.[3] Students move through the vectors at different rates and may move back and forth between vectors as they re-examine issues and experiences. Other researchers and theorists have examined the applicability of Chickering's theory of identity development to specific groups, such as women, African Americans, nontraditional-aged students, and gay, lesbian, and bisexual students. Other theories of identity have subsequently been formulated in regards to each special population of students.

Phinney's Theory of Racial and Ethnic Identity Development

There are many models and theories of racial and ethnic identity development. Cross developed one of the first theories of racial identity development, focusing on African American students. Garrett and Walking Stick Garrett examined racial identity development in regards to Native American students. Torres examined Hispanic students; Sue and Ibrahim respectively proposed theories for Asian American and Indian American students. Spickard addressed multiracial identities, and Helms proposed a theory of white identity development. All the racial and ethnic identity models focus on the psychosocial process of discovering and defining a sense of self through the lens of culture.[4]

Phinney developed a theory describing an identity process applicable to all minority racial or ethnic groups.[5] Her model features three stages: diffusion-foreclosure, moratorium, and identity achievement. She proposes that students who belong to minority racial or ethnic groups experience fundamental conflicts that occur as a result of their membership in a minority group. Students experience threats to their identities as they experience stereotyping and prejudicial treatment. Students must critically examine their racial or ethnic identity to successfully resolve the threats.

Students at the *diffusion-foreclosure* stage have not examined their ethnic identity. They may lack interest in what their membership in a minority racial or ethnic group means to them; such students are diffused. Students at this stage experience a fundamental conflict with their identity as they experience stereotyping and prejudicial treatment. Students may accept the majority culture's negative views of their race or ethnicity; such students risk a fore-closed identity, which might lead to internalized racism and self-loathing. If students reject the majority culture's negative views of their racial or ethnic group, they begin to question what it means to be a member of their racial or ethnic group.

Phinney's second stage of ethnic identity development is a search for ethnic identity, which she calls *moratorium*. During moratorium, students will explore their ethnic background and seek to understand what being a member of the minority race or ethnic personally means to the student. The exploration may be spurred by harsh personal encounters, such as racism, or a gradual awareness that not all racial and ethnic backgrounds are treated equitably.

Phinney's third stage of ethnic identity development is *identity achievement*. As the students accept their membership in a minority racial or ethnic group, they become comfortable with their identity. They demonstrate a knowledge of their racial or ethnic group's customs, history, and contributions to society. They are proud of their racial or ethnic identity. Students at the third stage also attain an openness to other cultures and tolerance for differences.

Theories of racial and ethnic identity development are employed by student affairs professionals in a variety of settings. Student affairs professionals use such theories to frame discussions and dialog about diversity and social justice. Counselors help minority students connect with mentors who share their racial or ethnic identities. Student affairs professionals working in minority student services create educational experiences that teach students about their respective cultures, and many student affairs organizations create cultural houses and other programs that offer welcoming, safe environments for minority students who might otherwise feel isolated or unsupported.[6]

Super's Theory of Career Development

There are a number of theories of career exploration and development, but Super's theory of career development is the most widely adopted by career counselors today.[7] Super proposed that career preferences and competencies change with time and experience. He developed the concept of vocational maturity, in which people pass through five developmental stages during their lifetime.

In the growth stage, people build a general understanding of the world of work and the need to work. In the exploratory stage, people try out a variety of occupational choices through classes, work experiences, and hobbies. This stage corresponds most closely to the experience of college students as they collect information about careers, build an understanding of the skill sets and qualifications for specific careers, and develop career interests. In the establishment stage, people acquire the entry-level skills for their chosen occupation and focus on expanding their knowledge and expertise. The maintenance and decline stages are focused on career advancement and ultimately retirement.

Super identified six factors associated with the exploratory stage that help students select appropriate career choices and advance to the establishment stage. He argued that decision-making skills; long-term planning skills; knowledge and use of information resources; general information about the culture, rules, and etiquette of the work world; and detailed information about occupations were essential for students in the exploratory stage to master.[8] Consequently, many student affairs professionals engaged in career services and counseling are focused on helping students build interview skills and knowledge of workplace etiquette and on arranging internships and other professional experiences that introduce students to the daily environments of their career choices.

Although Super framed his theory as a life-span model, with each stage corresponding to a chronological period in life, he acknowledged that people cycle through multiple careers as workers adapt to workplace trends and lifestyle choices. Consequently, people of varying ages might occupy similar stages in their career development—or move through all the stages more than once through their working lives.[9]

COGNITIVE-STRUCTURAL THEORIES OF STUDENT DEVELOPMENT

The cognitive-structural family of theories explain how students interpret and make meaning out of their experiences. Teaching, learning, reflection, change, and empathy are values that underlie many cognitive-structural theories. Student affairs professionals engage cognitive-structural theories frequently in situations that require students to reflect, learn, and adapt their perspectives and behaviors to their environment.

Perry's Theory of Cognitive Development

Perry's theory of cognitive development describes how students perceive and organize knowledge. Perry's theory identified nine sequential positions which are grouped into four major periods of students' cognitive development.[10] While in the *dualistic* period, students exhibit rigid, inflexible attitudes towards knowing. Students resist learning new information or interpretations that challenge their established beliefs. Students accept most information as indisputable facts with little or no inclination for critical inquiry. Teachers, parents, and the media are the absolute experts and not questioned. The dualistic period is most commonly associated with primary school–age children.

In the *multiplicity* period, students recognize that knowledge has shades of gray and that the information imparted by teachers and parents is imperfect. Nonetheless, students perceive knowledge as still absolute—but ultimately unknowable because not all facts are known about certain issues or questions. Kurfiss described the viewpoints typical of such students: "Values? Ideology? Why have any? Just go with the flow. All we have is opinion, and one opinion is just as good as another."[11] This period of cognitive development is most commonly associated with secondary school–age children, but sometimes with students in the early years of college.

In the *relativistic* period, students recognize the strategies of information seeking and analysis: designing experiments, comparing interpretations, and analyzing evidence. In the *commitment to relativism* period, the students commit to a value system or ideology through which they construct their worldview or paradigm for perceiving knowledge. This period of cognitive development is most often associated with students in the later years of college.

Student affairs professionals apply Perry's theory of cognitive development for facilitating student learning outside of the classroom through programs, service learning, and other opportunities designed to challenge their beliefs. Subsequent researchers have adapted Perry's work to improve strategies for college teaching, first-year experience programs, and student discipline.

Kohlberg's Theory of Moral Development

Kohlberg's theory of moral development explains how students' ability to reason affects their behavior and conduct. He describes six stages of moral development through which students develop a sense of personal responsibility for their own actions and ultimately for the actions of a morally just society.[12] Each stage requires a moral conflict before progression to the subsequent stage can occur. The six stages are categorized into three distinct levels: pre-conventional morality, conventional morality and post-conventional morality.

Pre-conventional morality consists of the first and second stages of moral development and is characterized primarily by a wish to avoid punishment or injury and a limited interest in others only when one's own interest is fulfilled. Children exhibit pre-conventional reasoning most commonly. Kohlberg believed that adolescents and adults demonstrated pre-conventional reasoning, too, but rarely.[13]

Conventional morality is composed of the third and fourth stages of moral development. During the third stage, people shift from egocentricity to a desire to conform to a specific social role, such as a "good little boy." People's motivations are significant, and they view rules as existing primarily to support social roles. During the fourth stage, people recognize the need for law and order to maintain a healthy, functioning society. The concepts of right and wrong are dualistic and idealized, and shades of gray are often unrecognized. Many older adolescents and traditional-age college students operate at a conventional level of moral reasoning, according to Kohlberg.[14]

Post-conventional reasoning is composed of the fifth and sixth stages and is characterized by the recognition that situations are often ambiguous and law and order are not unfailingly just. People develop a sense of ethics and consider moral dilemmas in light of those ethics. People develop integrity through their consistent application of those ethics.

Kohlberg argued that people must experience moral dilemmas and reflect upon their own responses in order to progress through his proposed stages of moral development. Kohlberg stated, "We get into discussions and debates with others, and we find our views questioned and challenged and we are therefore motivated to come up with new, more comprehensive positions. New stages reflect these broader viewpoints."[15] Kohlberg's theory of moral development has profoundly affected the way student affairs professionals approach student discipline and conduct. Like that of Chickering and Perry, Kohlberg's work has inspired new theories by subsequent researchers. Theories in development of college students' ethics, faith, and spirituality have arisen from Kohlberg's work.

Parks's Theory of Faith Development

Parks's theory of faith development is arguably the most dominant theory of spiritual or faith development in student affairs. Parks describes faith development as "the process of discovering and creating connections between among experiences and events."[16] She explains that faith is the process of spiritual development that is concerned with meaning making, and spirituality is the activity of faith. Spirituality is the recognition and acceptance that unknowable higher powers exist and influence the direction of one's experiences.[17]

Parks's theory adapts Perry's theory of cognitive development and proposes that faith development emerges in sequential stages, moving from a dualistic perspective where students accept the belief system of their communities without question to an integrated belief system that acknowledges multiple explanations. Parks focuses her theory on young adulthood as a critical point of life where faith develops. Young adulthood is marked by *probing commitment*, in which students recognize that it is necessary to choose their own path in the world. Students may commit tentatively to multiple ways of knowing or making sense out of their experiences through the lenses of different belief systems.

Parks claims that forms of community are vital to fostering students' faith development. Students' belief systems are "fragile and vulnerable" during their stage of probing commitment but are "healthy and full of promise" when supported by forms of community.[18] Parks argues that the form of community needed by students during this time is a mentoring community. She defines a mentoring community as "a compatible social group of belonging in which young adults feel recognized for who they really are, and as who they are becoming. It offers … good company for both the emerging strength and the distinctive vulnerability of the young adult."[19] She argues, too, that the culture of the community must be flexible and nonjudgmental in its shared values—the stronger the culture, the less the student is able to tentatively probe a commitment.

Student affairs professionals work to integrate the recognition of spiritual development into student affairs programs and activities. Campus ministries are frequently viewed as the avenue where spiritual development is best supported and explored, especially at state-supported colleges and universities. However, the close connection between students' spiritual development and their cognitive and psychosocial development leads many student affairs professionals to create educational experiences and environments that promote students' self-reflection on their value systems. Love explains, "Students' involvement in social, volunteer, leadership and community service activity may be a manifestation of their spiritual development and quest for meaning."[20]

HUMANISTIC-EXISTENTIAL THEORIES OF STUDENT DEVELOPMENT

The humanistic-existential family of theories is focused more on the students' relationship to others and to society. These theories emphasize more the conditions for healthy growth and development and less the development itself. Balance, harmony, and purpose are significant values that underlie humanistic-existential theories. Student affairs professionals engage humanistic-existential theories frequently in situations that require helping, counseling, or advising students.

Hettler's Model of Wellness

Student affairs professionals recognize that dimensions of student development do not exist independently of each other. Identity development is intrinsically linked with psychosocial and intellectual development—it is difficult for a student to reflect on his or her cultural identity without also reflecting on the social dynamics of race relations or the social constructs of race and ethnicity. Hettler proposed that students cannot develop psychosocially and intellectually without wellness. Hettler defined wellness as a state of complete physical, mental, and social well-being. He developed a holistic model of wellness that integrates six dimensions of a student's life: physical, intellectual, social/emotional, spiritual, environmental, and occupational. Each dimension requires a deliberate personal commitment and time to reach an optimum level necessary for balance. A student must achieve between each of the six dimensions to fully experience learning and development that is positive, healthy, and complex.[21]

In the *physical* dimension, students must be well nourished and well rested and maintain a regular regimen of physically activity. The *intellectual* dimension involves students' continuous active learning and the effort to acquire new knowledge and skills. In the *social* dimension, healthy friendships, relationships, and social interactions help students make meaningful connections and find a sense of belonging. Exploring students' values systems and philosophies is the focus of the *spiritual* dimension. The *environmental* dimension explores the students' connections and interdependence with their physical and natural surroundings. The *occupational* dimension involves finding a fulfilling career or vocation as well as developing lifelong learning as an occupational value.

Student affairs professionals recognize that students will struggle in their academic work, personal and social lives, and career development without a critical understanding of the dimensions of wellness. Consequently, they promote wellness deliberately in a variety of ways in campus activities, which range from residence hall programs that stimulate physical activity, to service-learning programs that focus on sustainable living, to recreational programs that teach students to reduce and manage stress.

PERSON-ENVIRONMENT INTERACTIVE THEORIES

Although the theories described previously are widely accepted in student affairs, no theory adequately describes the complexity of the college experience. Many student affairs scholars remark that theories of student development are more truly theories of personal development. Given the right learning conditions—be it in college, the military, or the working world—most young people will experience conflicts that challenge their perspectives and subsequently spur their progress through the developmental stages of Chickering's, Perry's, and Kohlberg's theories.

What unique role does the experience of being a college student college play in development? College impact models examine the process of student development. They are focused on context—how does the environment of the college or university affect the student's development? How do the background and individual characteristics of the student foster or impede development?

Astin's Theory of Student Involvement

Astin proposed that students are more academically and socially proficient the more they are involved in the academic and social aspects of college life. He defined involved students as those who participate actively in student organizations, spend considerable time on campus, interact often with faculty outside of the classroom, and devote considerable time to studying.[22] He focused on the motivation and behavior of students and recognized the integral role of students' time and the quality of available programs and resources.

He stressed that involvement has a quantitative feature, the amount of time devoted by students, and a qualitative feature, the seriousness with which students approach their involvement. If students invest significant amounts of time and approach academic work and campus life with seriousness, their overall learning will increase because they are emotionally and physically invested in the outcomes.

Astin believed that students are more likely to be involved if they have access to high-quality programs and services that stimulate and challenge their learning. If extracurricular activities and classroom assignments are not directly relatable to students' goals and lives, and if faculty, student affairs professionals, and resources are not accessible to students at their convenience, students will not be directly involved in campus life. Astin encourages faculty and student affairs professionals to make academic work and other activities relatable to students' lives, connect directly to an outcome that students value, and be flexible to accommodate the external demands on students' time, such as jobs, family, and friends.[23]

Tinto's Theory of Student Departure

Tinto developed a theory to explain student retention. He argued that students depart higher education without earning a degree because of the nature and quality of their interactions with the college or university. He claimed that students enter higher education with unique and individual characteristics ranging from socioeconomic circumstances, family support, clarity of purpose for higher education, and cultural and social values.[24] Colleges and universities, too, are composed of unique individual characteristics. The characteristics of students and the colleges or universities they attend may not match and therefore may bring the students into conflict with the college or university. Students may depart, or drop out, if the sources of conflicts are not resolved.

Tinto proposed that the sources of student departure are primarily in three specific areas—academic problems, failure to integrate socially and intellectually with the culture of the college or university, or a low level of commitment to the college or university.[25] He argued that colleges and universities must integrate students deliberately in all three areas to decrease the chances of departure. Colleges and universities should create intentional opportunities for extracurricular activities, informal student interactions, and faculty/student interactions.

Tinto cautioned that students and colleges and universities define failure differently.[26] Often colleges and universities interpret the students' lack of attaining a degree at that particular college or university to be a failure. Students leave colleges or university for a variety of reasons, however, such as career advancement, family obligations, or health reasons. Students may transfer to other colleges or universities or return to higher education to attain degrees at a later time. Thus the student may not interpret departure as a failure at all.

Student affairs professionals help students make the academic and social transitions at their colleges and universities through early contact with students and community building. They monitor students' academic performance and make referrals to counselors, academic advisors, and tutors. Student affairs professionals help create supportive social and educational environments in which students are valued and full members of their communities.

Pascarella's Model for Assessing Student Change

Pascarella proposed a model for the assessment of student development, or change, in which he considered the direct and indirect effects of a college or university's structural characteristics as well as its campus culture. He suggested that students' growth and development are affected by five sets of variables: students' precollege traits, the college or university's structural or organizational characteristics, the campus culture or environment, socializing agents on the campus, and the quality of effort put forth by the students.[27]

Students' pre-college traits include students' socioeconomic backgrounds, preparation for college-level work, and demographic traits. A student body composed predominantly of wealthy students who attended college preparatory schools will present significantly different opportunities and challenges to colleges and universities than students coming from predominantly working-class backgrounds and less academically proficient secondary schools. The size, selectivity, geographic location, secular or faith affiliation, and residential character of colleges and universities define their structural or organizational characteristics. Together the variables shape the third variable: the campus culture or environment.

Pascarella defines the fourth variable as the frequency, content, and quality of the students' interactions with the socializing agents on the campus, namely the faculty, administrators, and student affairs professionals.[28] The fifth variable, the quality of effort expended by students, will be directly affected by the fourth variable, as well as by their own individual character-istics and the cultural norms and expectations of the college or university. Students who are less involved because of work or family obligations, have little access to faculty and student affairs professionals, and attend a college or university whose culture tolerates mediocre academic performance will not develop as vigorously as they would under different circumstances.[29]

CONCLUSION

Theories of student development are helpful for student affairs professionals in several different ways. Theories explain and describe student behavior and create meaning for students' unique perspectives and experiences. Student affairs professionals intentionally design educational experiences and pro-grams using theories of student development. For instance, first-year stu-dents are concerned with skills acquisition and developing competency, as suggested by Perry. Therefore, writing workshops, study skills programs, and other programs that emphasize developing competencies in academic skills are more likely to be successful when marketed heavily to first-year students. As Evans wrote, "Theory suggests questions to ask, avenues to explore, and hypotheses to test. It provides shortcuts to exploring students' concerns and analyzing how they are addressing them."[30]

Notes

1. Allen E. Ivey, *Developmental Therapy: Theory into Practice.* (San Francisco: Jossey-Bass, 1986), 312.

2. Arthur W. Chickering, *Education and Identity* (San Francisco: Jossey-Bass, 1969), 38.

3. Ibid., 51.

4. Alicia Fedelina Chavez and Florence Guido-DiBrito, "Racial and Ethnic Identity and Development," *New Directions for Adult and Continuing Education,* no. 84 (1999): 47.

5. Jean S. Phinney, "Ethnic Identity in Adolescents and Adults: Review of Research." *Psychological Bulletin* 108, no. 3 (1990): 502.

6. Jean S. Phinney, "Ethnic Identity and Acculturation," in *Acculturation: Advances in Theory, Measurement, and Applied Research.* edited by Kevin M. Chun (Washington, DC: American Psychological Association, 2003), 76.

7. Linda Brooks and Duane Brown, *Career Choice and Development: Applying*

Contemporary Theories to Practice (San Francisco: Jossey-Bass, 2002) 42.

8. Ibid., 56.

9. Ibid., 72.

10. William G. Perry, *Forms of Intellectual and Ethical Development in the College Years* (New York: Holt, Rinehart and Winston, 1970), 23.

11. Joanne Kurfiss, *Intellectual, Psychosocial and Moral Development in College: Four Major Theories* (Washington, DC: Council for Independent Colleges, 1983) 19.

12. Lawrence Kohlberg, *Moral Development and Behavior: Theory, Research and Social Issues* (New York: Holt, Rinehart and Winston, 1976), 34.

13. Ibid., 35.

14. Ibid., 38.

15. Ibid., 45.

16. Sharon Daloz Parks, *Big Questions, Worthy Dreams: Mentoring Young Adults in Their Search for Meaning, Purpose, and Faith* (San Francisco: Jossey-Bass, 2000), 18.

17. Patrick G. Love, "Spirituality and Student Development: Theoretical Connections." *New Directions for Student Services*, no. 95 (2001): 11.

18. Ibid., 12.

19. Parks, *Big Questions, Worthy Dreams*, 95.

20. Love, "Spirituality and Student Development," 14.

21. Bill Hettler, "Wellness Promotion on a University Campus," *Family & Community Health* 3, no. 1 (1989): 94.

22. Alexander W. Astin, "Student Involvement: A Developmental Theory for Higher Education," *Journal of College Student Personnel* 25 (1987): 301.

23. Ibid., 305.

24. Vincent Tinto, *Leaving College: Rethinking the Causes and Cures of Student Attrition*, 2nd ed. (Chicago: University of Chicago Press, 1987), 17.

25. Ibid., , 24.

26. Ibid., 48.

27. Patrick T. Terenzini, "A Review of Selected Theoretical Models of Student Development and Collegiate Impact" (Baltimore: MD: Association for the Study of Higher Education, 1987).

28. Ibid., 31.

29. Ibid., 32.

30. Nancy J. Evans, "Psychosocial, Cognitive, and Typological Perspectives on Student Development," in *Student Services: a Handbook for the Profession*, 4th ed., edited by Susan R. Komives (San Francisco: Jossey-Bass, 2003) 183.

3

Making It Better: Library and Student Services Collaboration at Harrisburg University of Science and Technology

Nancy E. Adams and Jennifer K. Olivetti

Adams and Olivetti share the story of a collaborative relationship that resulted in numerous joint programs. Their examples illustrate how such collaborations are mutually beneficial as the partners learn from and support one another while also strengthening outreach and services for students.

The published literature of academic librarianship yields increasing evidence of collaborations between librarians and student services professionals. Often such collaborations are well-defined projects involving the library and a single facet of student services, such as career services, orientation programs, or academic integrity initiatives.[1] Because of our unique situation at a new university, the authors were able not only to implement a student services/library partnership in all three of these areas and more, but also to integrate student services and library functions into a single organizational structure. This chapter explains how the student services/library integration at Harrisburg University came about, describes specific examples of projects and processes in which we collaborated, and reflects upon what the librarian and student services partners learned from each other.

A HISTORY OF THE COLLABORATION

In order to understand how this collaboration came about, it is important to recognize the peculiar institutional environment of the university.

Harrisburg University of Science and Technology (HU) is a private, not-for-profit institution founded in 2001 that offers undergraduate programs in integrative sciences, biotechnology, computer and information science, geography and geospatial imaging, and management and e-business, as well as graduate programs in learning technologies, project management, and information systems engineering and management.[2] Since a primary mission of the institution is to develop the central Pennsylvania region's STEM-related (science, technology, engineering, and mathematics) workforce, the institution emphasizes two important features: student learning is both experientially based, with a required internship and related independent projects, and competency-based—focused on discipline-independent skills such as ethical decision making, global awareness, and information literacy. These two features of the HU educational model would offer a crucial impetus for library and student services collaboration. The first students arrived on campus in 2005, when the university was housed in various leased spaces throughout downtown Harrisburg. The university then built a $73 million academic center in downtown Harrisburg in 2008 and achieved accreditation by the Middle States Commission on Higher Education in 2009. However, these numbers paint only a partial picture of the environment in which the library/student services collaboration was born. The institutional culture is distinct in that HU comprises a lean faculty and staff in a young, entrepreneurial institution that attracts a diverse student body, a large percentage of whom are first-generation college students. HU's organizational chart is quite flat, which encourages cooperation, boundary-spanning, and the wearing of multiple hats. Staff time is a precious commodity, which necessitates these same behaviors. The lack of legacy systems and processes results in very low barriers to innovation. Technology is a defining feature of the university, and its creative use in teaching, learning, and service delivery is encouraged. Teamwork is a necessary survival skill for coping with the constant pace of change and the heavy lifting associated with inventing processes and workflows in a brand-new organization. Indeed, teamwork and collaboration form a core competency that HU students are expected to master and on which they are evaluated.[3] This combination of cultural factors results in an institutional environment in which collaboration is encouraged and can flourish—one of the antecedent conditions important for the ultimate success of any joint endeavor.[4] Our student services/library partnership was situated in a fertile matrix for collaboration. HU's staff environment was definitely "lean" in the library and student services units. At the time our partnership developed, student services staff consisted of two individuals: a Vice President for Student Services and a Manager of Student Transition, one of the authors of this chapter. Library services were provided by a staff of one: the University Librarian, the other author of this chapter. Student services staff were responsible for academic and personal student advising, assisting with placement testing, administering the tutoring program, managing experiential programs such as required internships and projects, planning and teaching four required University Seminar courses, planning and supervising student events including orientation and graduation, and student discipline and advocacy. The University Librarian was responsible for all library-related tasks, both strategic and operational: collection development, information literacy instruction, copyright tasks, maintaining the library website, training faculty in the use of the streaming media system and the automated lecture capture system, interlibrary loan and document delivery, administering the integrated library system, and other administrative details such as vendor relations, purchasing, budget, policy development, and planning.

A major development in the relationship between the library and student services partners occurred when the Vice President for Student Services left HU in late 2009. At that point, what had developed informally and organically was formalized in a new organizational structure in which the University Librarian became also the Director of Student Services, with the Manager of Student Transition, as well as a Manager of Experiential Programs hired shortly thereafter, reporting directly to her. With this change in the organizational structure, the library and student services partners continued with the projects and programs we had already developed and continued to move forward with the partnership.

MAKING IT BETTER THROUGH RELATIONSHIPS AND PROXIMITY

In addition to the institutional environment favoring collaboration, our physical proximity was crucial to the development of the work relationship. This is one of the lessons learned from this collaboration: although social media and electronic communication have had a great impact on the workplace, we live in our bodies, and proximity enhanced our collaboration. Our partnership might not have developed as quickly nor resulted in as many tangible products had we not been physically situated as close as we were, with offices right next door to each other. Each of the authors could not help but notice the types of interactions that the other experienced with students and faculty, which led to increased understanding and appreciation of each other's job responsibilities. The librarian partner noticed that there was a constant parade of students seeking advising, guidance, and tutoring at the student service professional's door, and the student services partner noticed that the librarian's duties were heavily oriented towards instruction and technology. We soon found ways to work together to decrease each other's burden and work synergistically whenever possible.

Interestingly, the idea that collocation enhances collaboration is a hypothesis that being investigated in the growing science of team science (SciTS), a field that seeks to identify the communication, geographic, social, technological, and other factors that promote success in large-scale, cross-disciplinary scientific teams.[5] SciTS researchers find that although scientific papers published by large-scale, geographically distributed research teams garner the highest numbers of citations by other authors, physical proximity at a more local level is still positively associated, in certain contexts, with higher quality of research.[6] In our own partnership, our physical proximity led to the establishment of an informal relationship and very frequent communication and information transfer—important factors involved in collaborative success.[7]

The power of physical proximity has implications for the current movement in academic libraries and learning-support services towards the learning commons, a model of collaborative service delivery and space configuration—often reconfigured and repurposed space within the campus library—that collocates librarians with units such as technology and academic support services.[8] The desired end result is the academic success of the student, who is immersed in an intentional environment that emphasizes learning.[9] Spencer describes the learning commons concept well when she writes that "the academic library is transforming the typical university labyrinth of writing centers, career centers, tutoring services, computer labs and more into a logical and seamless suite of blended services for their constituents."[10] To achieve this integration, institutions that are considering moving towards a learning commons model for the delivery of library, IT, and student services would perhaps benefit from physical proximity of the concerned units even during the period while the collaboration is being planned. The more time spent working next to each other, the deeper the understanding of others' work processes and professional challenges. More opportunities for collaboration likely will present themselves.

One of the challenges in implementing collocation of services lies in yielding physical space to others, as ownership of physical space often equals power. For library staff, the idea of sharing the physical space of the library with other campus units may seem threatening; it could represent a loss of control and decreasing autonomy for the library. In the case of student services and libraries, power differentials may exist between these two units on many campuses—possibly an artifact of libraries' historic positioning within academic affairs while student services units have only recently begun aligning with academic affairs.[11] However, in order for any collaboration between campus units to be authentic and complete, these feelings of territoriality must first be acknowledged and then eliminated, as they threaten to destroy the trust essential to a true collaboration.[12] Mattessich, Murray-Close, and Monsey explicitly address this pitfall when they write, "Any imbalances of power among collaborating partners must be addressed openly. These imbalances should not be allowed to stop the group from developing a truly shared vision."[13]

At HU, we found that daily proximity between the library and student services cultures led to serendipitous, rich interactions; natural crosstraining; and a deeper understanding of each other's challenges, values, and strengths. This is interdisciplinary cooperation and the power of physical space at work: physical proximity led to increased respect between the two disciplines and unexpected opportunities for collaboration. Therefore, embrace physical proximity. Approach those around you as colleagues with the same goal in mind: the development of human beings and the best possible educational experience for students.

MAKING IT BETTER BY INTEGRATING INFORMATION LITERACY AND CAREER EXPLORATION

Our development of the I-Search assignment is a prime example of a collaboration that grew organically. Since the beginning of our working relationship, the librarian partner would often wax philosophical and passionate about the need for today's students to develop information literacy skills, while the student services partner would remark on her own passion for nurturing and facilitating the career exploration and development of university students. During preparation for the next semester's classes, these conversations melded into an exploration of how these two crucial needs of students—information literacy and career development—could be developed in tandem. The librarian partner had been exposed to the "I-Search" research and writing assignment, an intriguing way to motivate students to use information resources for the purpose of exploring a personally relevant research question and to encourage critical reflection upon the information search strategies employed in the process.[14] What more personally relevant research question could there be than a question related to one's anticipated career?

We decided to develop an I-Search assignment which would be used as a major vehicle for both career exploration and information literacy skills development for students in University Seminar 200. This required one-credit second-year course, managed by student services staff and with the student services partner as the instructor of record, prepares students for the internships and junior and senior projects that are important components of Harrisburg University's experiential learning program. Using a template found on a community college website,[15] we designed a career-focused I-Search, in which students would formulate and research a career-related question of personal interest to them. We formulated an evaluation rubric for the deliverables which included a research log where students recorded not only all of the successful and unsuccessful information-seeking strategies used throughout the research process, but also their personal reflections during each stage of the search process. The students were then instructed to transform the research log into a short paper, written in their own voice, telling the story of their search. Use of our campus's web-based student assessment and retention toolkit, which provides access to a career interest assessment, and conducting a personal interview with a subject expert were other required components of the activity. The librarian partner presented the assignment to the students and returned several weeks later to lead the students through a hands-on demonstration of how to use the Business Source Premier database and the library catalog to locate print and electronic resources such as local business newspapers that could be used to explore industries, companies, and other career-related topics. The student services partner answered students' questions and provided guidance throughout the learning activity. We then collaborated on assessing the students' final products; each partner viewed and made comments on student work according to the rubric we had jointly developed, with the student services partner, as instructor of record, assigning the final grade. Finally, to wrap up this project, we engaged in an honest follow-up discussion of features of the I-Search activity that each partner felt were successful and what each would like to change in future iterations of this learning activity.

The I-Search sparked the creativity and inquisitiveness of the Seminar 200 students. One student explored potential issues relating to midlife career change. Another investigated the skill sets and aptitudes necessary for web developers. Yet another explored the personal traits of successful entrepreneurs and gathered her friends' and family's opinions on her own entrepreneurial skills using a survey she designed herself; she later stated that she desired to continue her I-Search beyond the bounds of the course. Through this learning activity, learners engaged in meta-thinking about the information-seeking process; located and used a variety of information resources; built their personal networks and practiced interpersonal communication with subject experts; practiced their writing skills; and came several steps closer to finding an answer to a question of personal impact.

The design and implementation of the I-Search activity was one of the most successful products of our partnership and is illustrative of several powerful aspects of collaboration. Overall, when viewed through the lens of Monteil-Overall's theory of librarian/teacher collaboration, we see that the I-Search activity was a true collaboration in that it was created by "two or more equal participants involved in *shared thinking, shared planning* and *shared creation of integrated instruction* [emphasis in original]."[16] First of all, we began with *shared thinking;* this new idea was the result of wondering together about the intersections of career development and information literacy. We continued with *shared planning,* in which we identified a possible framework for a learning activity, the I-Search, and considered how this might fit into the Seminar 200 curriculum. It culminated in *shared creation of integrated instruction;* we each had unique expertise to contribute, but we also stood on the common ground, as educators, of our commitment to student development. The learning activity that resulted was more than the sum of the parts that each could contribute on her own. We jointly established the process, carried out the instruction, evaluated the student products, reflected upon the entire process, and decided upon improvements to be made in future iterations.

When examined according to the factors that influence collaborative success according to Mattessich, Murray-Close, and Monsey, it can be shown that a number of these factors were evident in our work on the I-Search project, most strongly those factors relating to mutual benefit, development of clear roles, concrete goals, good communication, and sufficient material resources.[17] First of all, in addition to the fact that the institutional environment was conducive to collaboration as described previously, the initiative was born in an atmosphere characterized by mutual respect and understanding between the two partners. Perhaps this is what allowed us to engage in the deep discussions that resulted in our realization of a shared "problem" that could be addressed in tandem. This particular project was also in the self-interest of each partner; the mutual benefits would offset any possible costs. The I-Search activity was a vehicle for us to address learning domains—career development and information literacy—in which not only was each highly invested and knowledgeable professionally, but these areas also brought us great personal satisfaction and enjoyment. Therefore, there was a level of fun present in this collaboration that was inspiring to each of us. It also addressed learning objectives that each of us knew were crucial to student development. For the student services partner, the possible loss of autonomy in her role as course instructor was balanced by the benefits of an enhanced learning experience for her students as well as a decreased work load since the instructional design and delivery were carried out jointly.

Process and structure factors refer to the "management, decision-making, and operational systems of a collaborative effort"[18] and include a clear understanding of the roles of each partner. In the I-Search project, we established clear roles for planning, instruction, division of tasks, evaluation, and grading and a structure and timeline for the project. The purpose of this collaboration was clear: we desired to develop students' skills and attitudes in our spheres of instructional responsibility and selected a concrete goal—design of a successful integrated learning activity—to achieve that end. Good communication occurred as we planned the project together, had frequent check-ins about progress during the project, and jointly evaluated success at the culmination of the project. Lastly, resources of all kinds are important to collaboration, and we had sufficient time, staffing, and materials to carry out the I-Search activity successfully.

Not only did the I-Search experiment enrich the Seminar 200 experience for the students, but it deepened our appreciation of each partner's strengths and the synergies possible between the library and student services. The success of our initial experiment and the flexibility of this learning activity led to the I-Search being incorporated into additional University Seminars with other foci including researching a potential internship site and exploring a question related to professional ethics in a chosen field. Other components of student services/library collaboration in the area of career services were developed as well. In partnership with the Manager of Experiential Programs, a collection of career and test preparation books was created in the Learning Commons, and a consultation with the University Librarian became a required component of the mandatory junior and senior projects—experiential components that were managed by student services staff. This consultation was a win-win situation for both students and staff, serving to guide students toward information resources to support their projects and to help inform decisions for development of the library collection.

MAKING IT BETTER BY TRAINING STUDENT WORKERS

When the university opened the new academic center in January 2009, library, IT, and student services relocated to offices adjacent to the university's learning commons. This space housed the library's print collection; offered group study rooms with digital displays and whiteboards along with open collaborative and quiet study space; and featured three service points. The physical configuration of the learning commons space provided the opportunity for the library and student services partners to move farther towards formalizing our collaboration. One way we did that is through training a cadre of student workers in tutoring skills, basic information technology troubleshooting skills, and use of library resources.

A background description of HU's student worker landscape is necessary. The Model Student program was one of the first student programs implemented at the university. Developed by the student services partner, it is a peer-led tutoring program in which exemplary students are identified by faculty and trained as tutors, then paid to attend core required classes in which they have already excelled and to lead study groups and offer individual tutoring by appointment in those subjects—a small-group approach that has been proven effective in increasing academic achievement and persistence of underrepresented minority students in science, technology, engineering, and mathematics.[19] The Model Student program had been in existence for several years by the time we moved to the new academic center, and we saw these students as a possible supplement to HU's lean professional staff in providing services in the learning commons.

In order to leverage this student workforce, we began crosstraining Model Students, along with two student workers employed by IT staff, in customer service and tutoring skills, basic information technology troubleshooting skills, and use of library resources based on a list of information commons baseline staff skills identified by Beagle.[20] Weekly student training meetings planned by the student services and librarian partners helped ensure that all students who worked in the learning commons had this common skill set. Collaboration in this training was a way to meet the professional goals of both partners: the student services partner used the training as a way to mentor and develop leadership skills in the students in the program; the librarian partner recognized an opportunity to improve the information literacy skills of these students. Model Students would then disseminate these skills to the rest of the student body, both as paid workers and through their own personal influence. Our Model Students training program is a clear example of an initiative that was in the self-interests of both the library and the student services partners, a factor which is shown by Mattessich, Murray-Close, and Monsey to influence the success of a collaborative enterprise.[21]

MAKING IT BETTER THROUGH SHARING PROFESSIONAL EXPERTISE

Student services professionals and librarians are natural partners because both are deeply invested in student success. Both groups seek better ways of reaching students, and ethics statements published by library and student services associations call for practitioners in each group to partner with other higher education professionals; however, as of just a few years ago, there were only a few instances of collaborations between student services and librarians published in the literature.[22] One of the best ways that librarians and student services professionals can begin a dance that may eventually lead to a collaborative partnership is to offer to share professional expertise with each other and to be open to receiving expert assistance from the other. This is one route to establishing the mutual respect, understanding, and trust that is required for a productive partnership according to the model described by Mattessich, Murray-Close, and Monsey.[23]

One of the expert domains that can be leveraged for partnerships between librarians and student services is technology. Technology has profoundly changed the teaching, learning, and service delivery landscape in higher education. A technology skill set is crucial to professional success in higher education today, and the student services profession is no exception.[24] Librarians have been at the forefront of integrating technology into service delivery in higher education, beginning in the mid-1970s with the move-ment toward converting library card catalogs and bound periodical indexes into electronic, networked databases.[25] A librarian's technology skill set can run the gamut from technical hardware and software skills (programming languages, networking, and administering the integrated library system), to the effective use of information resources such as bibliographic databases and data visualization tools, to the use of Web 2.0 tools, such as blogs, online chat, wikis, RSS feeds, podcasting, and social media such as Twitter and Facebook, in teaching and communicating with students. Therefore, one of the most important ways in which librarians can partner with student ser-vices staff is through technology training and consulting, sharing skills, and possibly even leveraging library technology resources so that student services staff, and ultimately the students we serve, can benefit.

In our collaboration at Harrisburg University, the seeds of technologi-cal skill sharing were actually planted by the student services partner, who shared knowledge of a new screencasting technology that the librarian part-ner then began using in all facets of library service delivery. Library resources were offered to be leveraged for the use of student services. LibGuides soft-ware, a commercially available content management system enabling easy creation of customized web portals, was used at HU as the platform for the library website, and student services staff were offered the opportunity to use LibGuides to create their own online subject guides in the areas of test prepa-ration, interviewing and job search skills, and career exploration. Later in the partnership, the library and student services partners also worked with IT staff to embed student success services into the shell of every course created in HU's course management system (CMS). Links to a 24-hour online tutor-ing service and to the student service professional's e-mail address became part of every course in the CMS, just as a search box for the library's data-base search system and online request forms for interlibrary loan service had been embedded previously. Other projects, such as student success–related messages tailored to individuals delivered through the student information system and the use of an automated e-mail tool for sending retention-related messages, were planned.

Librarians can also take initial steps toward partnering with student ser-vices professionals by offering to support their information needs.[26] Student services professionals comprise a professional "guild" that strives to base its practice upon research; therefore, they are often in search of information to support local decision making and to keep themselves updated in the literature of their field.[27] For example, during our partnership, the authors have collaborated on literature searches on topics such as peer-led tutoring programs, attracting women and minorities to scientific and technical fields, retention of first-generation college students, and best practices in student activity programs. Often the information gathered has supported proposal planning for student services–related grant applications involving these topics. Library outreach to student services professionals, perhaps through a liaison program, helps them become aware of the rich mix of resources that they can access through the library's collections, such as professional journals and video collections that could be used for project planning, research, and training in their departments.

Student services practitioners have a rich body of professional expertise to share with librarians. For example, librarians can learn from student services professionals about service learning, civic engagement, developmental stages of a college student, and designing outreach programs and messages that resonate with students. In our collaboration, the library partner learned from her student services partner about the importance of an immediate response to a student's request; when students become stressed, anxious, or overwhelmed (e.g., during the beginning stages of writing a research paper), just knowing that there is someone ready and willing to help may be enough to get them through the perceived crisis. The student services partner then included the library partner in a web-based communication and retention tool administered by student services. In their University Seminars, students were required to use the tool to complete self-assessments in areas such as their individual learning style, locus of control, and stress level. While completing the stress level measurement, students answered the question "What are you anxious about right now?" If they indicated that research and writing tasks were stressors, then the librarian was automatically notified by e-mail. The most crucial outcome of this notification was not that students received an exhaustive list of library resources, nor that they received an invitation to meet with the librarian; most importantly, they received a timely, personalized response that acknowledged their request and demonstrated that there was a real, live human being at the other end who was ready to help.

Much has been written in the library literature about integrating library services into a campus's course management system, but student services staff and academic advisors may utilize other systems and tools that could be leveraged by the library to reach students.[28] For example, learner analytics is a burgeoning field that applies data mining techniques to the huge stores of data collected by academic institutions through course management systems, student records, and other information sources to identify patterns related to academic success. Early detection of the learner behavior patterns that are associated with academic success or failure can enable appropriate and timely interventions for at-risk students.[29] Student services professionals who use these and more traditional types of retention tools can proactively approach librarians and explore ways to increase student success and retention by integrating the library into these systems—while adhering to professional standards that protect the privacy of library users

MAKING IT BETTER BY CLARIFYING GOALS AND SHARING A VISION

As stated by Walter and Eodice, finding partners with whom to collaborate is relatively easy, but "building models for substantive and sustainable instructional programs designed in collaboration and based on complementary interest … is more complicated."[30] When embarking upon a partnership between student services and the library, each partner must have a clear understanding of the other's professional culture, values, and strategic goals; together they must be able to develop a shared vision of joint mission and to agree upon a strategy to achieve it. As in any sustainable relationship, an ongoing dialogue must be established in which each describes what he or she can *give to* the other as well as what is *needed from* the other. Upon reflection, an area in which our collaboration could have improved was in clearly communicating our individual goals in all areas, including assessment, instruction, and student development. As explained previously, we had numerous in-depth conversations about our goals for student development in the areas of career exploration and information literacy; as a result, we were able to work in synergy to design a mutually beneficial and very successful student learning activity. However, institutional assessment of library and student services as a strategic goal was not discussed nearly enough, resulting in a lost opportunity for advancing the assessment goals of each partner and possibly embarking upon a mutually beneficial assessment project. Another factor that often negatively impacted our collaboration was related to resources; the ambitious agenda we had set for ourselves often was not realistic due to a lack of staffing and time.

We truly believe that collaboration does indeed "make it better"—better for students, better for university staff, and better for the institution as a whole. Our collaboration did not always have a perfect outcome; at times it was "messy" and sometimes required great effort to reconcile our professional goals; however, our greatest collaborative success occurred when we were able to keep a focus on the shared vision of creating the best possible educational experience for our students. We learned that leadership styles can sometimes clash; compromise can represent a solution that is both necessary and satisfying. Here, the partnership positively influenced Harrisburg University and provides an example that can be built upon by other individuals in many areas at the institution. The experience engendered within each of us the desire to continue our exploration of library/student services collaboration in the future. We urge student services professionals and librarians to reach out to others and explore the possibilities for partnership and learning together.

Notes

1. Christopher Hollister, "Bringing Information Literacy to Career Services," *Reference Services Review* 33, no. 1 (2005): 104–11; James G. Rhoades, Jr. and Arianne Hartsell, "Marketing First Impressions: Academic Libraries Creating Partnerships and Connections at New Student Orientations," *Library Philosophy and Practice* (August 2008), http://www.webpages.uidaho.edu/~mbolin/rhoades-hartsell.pdf; Pauline S. Swartz, Brian P. Carlisle, and E. Chisato Uyeki, "Libraries and Student Affairs: Partners for Success," *Reference Services Review* 35, no. 1 (2007): 109–22.

2. Harrisburg University of Science and Technology website, accessed May 2, 2011, http://harrisburgu.edu.

3. Ibid.

4. Paul W. Mattessich, Marta Murray-Close, and Barbara Monsey, *Collaboration: What Makes It Work?* 2nd ed. (Saint Paul, MN: Amherst W. Wilder Foundation, 2001), 12.

5. Northwestern University Clinical and Translational Sciences Institute, Science of Team Science website, accessed January 27, 2012, http://www.scienceofteamscience.org.

6. Kyungjoon Lee, John S. Brownstein, Richard G. Mills, and Isaac Kohane, "Does Collocation Inform the Impact of Collaboration?" *PLoS ONE* 5, no. 12 (2010), e14279, doi:10.1371/journal.pone.0014279; Koen Frenken, Roderik

Ponds, and Frank van Oort, "The Citation Impact of Research Collaboration in Science-Based Industries: A Spatial-Institutional Analysis," *Papers in Regional Science* 89, no. 2 (June 2010): 351–71; Daniel Stokols et al., "In vivo Studies of Transdisciplinary Scientific Collaboration: Lessons Learned and Implications for Active Living Research," *American Journal of Preventive Medicine* 28, no. 2 (2005): 202–13.

7. Mattessich, Murray-Close, and Monsey, *Collaboration*, 24.

8. Rebecca M. Sullivan, "Common Knowledge: Learning Spaces in Academic Libraries," *College & Undergraduate Libraries* 17, no. 2–3 (April–Sept. 2010): 130–48.

9. Scott Bennett, "Libraries and Learning: A History of Paradigm Change," *portal: Libraries and the Academy* 9, no. 2 (April 2009): 181–97.

10. Mary Ellen Spencer, "Evolving a New Model: The Information Commons," *Reference Services Review* 34, no. 2 (2006): 244.

11. Jeff A. Doyle, "Where Have We Come From and Where Are We Going? A Review of Past Student Affairs Philosophies and an Analysis of the Current Student Learning Philosophy," *College Student Affairs Journal* 24, no. 1 (Fall 2004): 66–83.

12. Mattessich, Murray-Close, and Monsey, *Collaboration*, 26.

13. Ibid.

14. Marilyn Z. Joyce and Julie I. Tallman, *Making the Writing and Research Connection with the I-Search Process. How-to-Do-It Manuals for Librarians* (New York: Neal-Schuman, 1997).

15. Sylvia G. Robins, "The I-Search Paper," last modified March 3, 2003, Delta College website, http://www3.delta.edu/sgrobins/I-Search.html.

16. Patricia Monteil-Overall, "Toward a Theory of Collaboration for Teachers and Librarians," *School Library Media Research* 8 (2005), http://www.ala.org/aasl/aasl-pubsandjournals/slmrb/slmrcontents/volume82005/theory.

17. Mattessich, Murray-Close, and Monsey, *Collaboration*.

18. Ibid., 18.

19. Leonard Springer, Mary Elizabeth Stanne, and Samuel S. Donovan, "Effects of Small-Group Learning on Undergraduates in Science, Mathematics, Engineering, and Technology: A Meta-Analysis," *Review of Educational Research* 69, no. 1 (Spring 1999): 21–51.

20. Donald Robert Beagle, Donald Bailey, and Barbara Tierney, *The Information Commons Handbook* (New York: Neal-Schuman Publishers, 2006), 173.

21. Mattessich, Murray-Close, and Monsey, *Collaboration*, 16–17.

22. Laura Urbanski Forrest, "Academic Librarians and Student Affairs Professionals: An Ethical Collaboration for Higher Education," *Education Libraries* 28, no. 1 (Summer 2005): 11–15.

23. Mattessich, Murray-Close, and Monsey, *Collaboration*, 14.

24. Alan Burkard et al., "Entry-Level Competencies of New Student Affairs Professionals: A Delphi Study," *NASPA Journal* 42, no. 3 (2005): 300–301, http://www4.ncsu.edu/~ladare/eac595/readings/burkard-cole.pdf.

25. OCLC, "In the Beginning … ," OCLC website, accessed January 27, 2012, http://www.oclc.org/us/en/about/history/beginning.htm.

26. Forrest, "Academic Librarians and Student Affairs Professionals," 13.

27. American College Personnel Association, "The Student Learning Imperative: Implications for Student Affairs," ACPA website, 1996, last modified September 10, 2008, http://www.myacpa.org/sli_delete/sli.htm.

28. Pamela A. Jackson, "Integrating Information Literacy into Blackboard: Building Campus Partnerships for Successful Student Learning," *Journal of Academic Librarianship* 33, no. 4 (July 2007): 454–61; John D. Shank and Nancy H. Dewald, "Establishing Our Presence in Courseware: Adding Library Services to the Virtual Classroom," *Information Technology and Libraries* 22, no. 1 (2003), http://www.ala.org/lita/ital/22/1/shank; David Cohen, "Course-Management Software: Where's the Library?" *EDUCAUSE Review* (May/June 2002): 12–13, http://net.educause.edu/ir/library/pdf/ERM0239.pdf.

29. EDUCAUSE Learning Initiative, "7 Things You Should Know About Analytics," EDUCAUSE website, April 2010, http://net.educause.edu/ir/library/pdf/ELI7059.pdf.

30. Scott Walter and Michele Eodice, "Meeting the Student Learning Imperative: Supporting and Sustaining Collaboration between Academic Libraries and Student Services Programs," *Research Strategies* 20 (2007): 221.

4

Plagiarism Education, Prevention, and Student Development: A Collaborative Approach to Improving Academic Integrity

Maria T. Accardi, Ruth Garvey-Nix, and Leigh Ann Meyer

As libraries and student affairs departments embark on collaborative efforts, it is helpful to identify not only shared programmatic interests, but shared values as well. In describing the development of a plagiarism prevention program, Accardi, Garvey-Nix, and Meyer show how the process was grounded in articulating their shared values, from the importance of cooperation to taking an educational approach to student judicial violations.

Imagine the following scenario: Students gather in a computer classroom and begin logging into the system without saying a word. The room is quiet except for the clicking of the keys.

As the start time of this new workshop gets closer, the instructors look at each other and wonder if this is a good idea. Facilitating this workshop is not something they had to do; it is not something that anyone had even talked about before on campus, so why go to all of this trouble and effort on a Friday morning?

As the librarian and writing center director begin talking, the students reluctantly turn to look, but the glaze stays over their eyes. After the introductions, the conversation moves to defining academic honesty, specifically plagiarism. The phrase *common knowledge* is mentioned, and one student comes to life and wants to talk. She says this issue got her "into trouble" and is the reason she had "to come to this workshop." The instructors didn't expect anyone to self-identify, having been careful not to mention that some students were required to attend as part of a sanctioning process, but her comment wakes up the rest of the students, who then have something to say. A young man talks about how his professor had mentioned the term *common knowledge,* but he did not know what she was talking about, and he felt too shy and intimidated to ask. Soon the discussions begin, and the instructors become facilitators instead of lecturers. The fears of the students seem to subside, and the purpose of the workshop crystallizes.

At this moment, the idea of collaborating to create a plagiarism prevention workshop for students begins to look like it may really offer the needed focus on this subject. The efforts of the Vice Chancellor for Student Affairs, Dr. Ruth Garvey-Nix, the Coordinator of Library Instruction, Maria Accardi, and the Writing Center Director, Leigh Ann Meyer, were a good idea after all. The inspiration for this idea came from an article by Swartz, Carlisle, and Uyeki, which describes a collaborative project between the dean of students and the college library at UCLA. In the Swartz, Carlisle, and Uyeki case study, the dean of student affairs and the library partnered to deliver educational programs concerning information ethics, including plagiarism, and students who had been sanctioned by the office of the dean of students for plagiarism were required to attend the plagiarism education workshops.[1] The successful model outlined in that article held promise for the shared goals of student affairs, the writing center, and the library at Indiana University Southeast, all of which seek to foster an environment that promotes student success. The library, which is particularly well-positioned to support student success and retention through campus partnerships,[2] initiated the collaboration.

The following case study outlines the successes and the challenges of the partnership. For a collaboration to be successful, all parties must have something valuable to contribute and all must share in the work and the outcomes, which describes the situation in this three-way partnership. The prevention of plagiarism and the cultivation of information literacy skills are primary goals of the IU Southeast library and its instruction program, and the plagiarism prevention workshop that was developed certainly helps the library achieve these goals. These goals also overlap with the philosophy of the student affairs division, where the value of congruence between personal values and one's actions is emphasized in the student conduct process. The motto of the writing center is "Stronger writers, not perfect papers," so this workshop supports the goal and learning outcomes in which the center strives to create stronger, more educated academic writers.

The three-part collaboration in the case study reflects a national trend, where academic librarians are pursuing ways to creatively collaborate on campuswide initiatives that promote student learning and development. Guided by the notion that student learning and development are interconnected, librarians and other academic units are connecting with students in more substantial and enriching ways by partnering with student affairs. This chapter describes a collaborative project between the IU Southeast library, the writing center, and the office of student affairs. The library and the writing center partnered to develop an educational, interactive workshop designed to teach students about plagiarism and ways to prevent it. Understanding that information ethics and the conventions of academic conduct are inextricably connected to student learning and development, the collaboration described in this chapter was created in conjunction with the Vice Chancellor for Student Affairs, who was very interested in including the workshop as a sanction requirement for students who had been found responsible via the student conduct process for violating the university's policy on plagiarism. The campus already employed a similar strategy for students who violated alcohol or drug policies, and the team believed an educational component of the sanction for plagiarism would be helpful for students.

The campus climate for collaborative, cocurricular projects is favorable at IU Southeast, and student success is a central focus for all campus entities. The campus has the following four core values: nurturing environment, holistic learning, integrity, and connectedness. This particular collaborative endeavor relates, in some way, to each of the four values. It is especially worth noting that these core values were developed via a campuswide process, wherein members of the campus community identified values that best exemplified our ethos and guiding principles. These values were not imposed on the campus community as rules to live by but were the guiding principles already reflected in its work. Indeed, the team was fortunate in that it did not experience any institutional barriers in developing or implementing the collaborative program.

The institution's profile might also be a factor in the ease of collaboration. Indiana University Southeast, one of eight regional campuses of

Indiana University, is a small-to-medium-sized institution of 7,100 students. Approximately 50 percent of the student body is comprised of first-generation college students, and the campus has approximately 30 percent nontraditional students. Both of those student groups tend to seek and benefit from academic support services.

SURVEYING THE LITERATURE: COMPLEMENTARY PERSPECTIVES

Examining the theoretical underpinnings of student affairs, information literacy instruction, and writing centers provides a helpful perspective on the shared goals and the importance of collaborative practices in each of these arenas.

Teaching information literacy is one of the key responsibilities of academic instruction librarians. *Information literacy* refers to skills required to "recognize when information is needed and have the ability to locate, evaluate, and use effectively the needed information."[3] Effective use of information involves observing legal and ethical conventions; educating students about plagiarism prevention and academic honesty is an important component of an information literacy instruction program. As Lampert notes, "The need to educate students about efficient and ethical ways to interact with information continues to grow with each entering class."[4] Indeed, librarian interactions at the reference desk and teaching faculty input confirm that plagiarism is a pervasive, complex issue on campuses today. Many institutions have turned to plagiarism-detecting software such as Turnitin.com, to which our campus subscribes. However, a more proactive approach is consistent with the ethics of academic librarianship and information literacy instruction.

The literature on information literacy and plagiarism education indicates that librarians can play an important role in helping students understand what plagiarism is and how to avoid it. In particular, the literature suggests that a collaborative approach to plagiarism education can be effective. Mundava and Chaudhuri note, "Organizing a campus-wide discussion forum that involves the students, the Writing Center, the office of Judicial Affairs, teaching assistants, librarians, and faculty could also be useful."[5] Lampert also addresses collaboration as an effective approach to plagiarism education: "depending on the academic environment and structure of the campus or university, those parties interested [in plagiarism prevention] outside the teaching faculty may include administrators, academic advisors, writing center staff, international student program administrators, and student affairs officers."[6] Lampert also points out that "collaborative partnerships forged beyond faculty-librarian boundaries not only increase efforts but also market and cement the library's commitment to the issue of student plagiarism across the entire campus population."[7]

In writing center literature, the idea of collaboration is addressed mostly as it pertains to a consultant and client working together, but another way that writing centers are collaborating is to reach out to other departments at the university. One reason that writing centers should reach out to other services is that this collaboration can provide an educational benefit to all participants. Many writing centers' missions may be misunderstood. These concerns about other university departments not understanding the missions of writing centers are correct as they apply to the standard writing consultation, and they have a part to play in the collaborative efforts a writing center must make with other entities of a university. As stated in "The Idea of a Writing Center" by Stephen North, "This is not always the case for the rest of the academic community in which a writing center exists: What makes the situation particularly frustrating is that so many such people will vehemently claim that they do, *really*, understand the idea of a writing center. The non-English faculty, the students, the administrators—they may not understand what a writing center is or does, but they have no investment in their ignorance, and can often be educated."[8]

The question is how and to whom to reach out in order to educate the academic community, which brought us to the place where the writing center wanted to collaborate with other departments, specifically the library and student affairs, to work together to not only help our students but also to raise awareness of the work of the center. After reading the article "Teaching Librarians and Writing Center Professionals in Collaboration: Complementary Practices," the instruction librarian and the director of the writing center knew this would be a good partnership to assist with their shared goals and closely aligned missions. As Hook states, "Writing center professionals and teaching librarians need to work more closely together because they are working with integrally related processes."[9] After several discussions, all parties agreed that their functional missions were closely connected, and they should find a way to work together. This type of collaboration outside of the writing center is one way that education regarding the mission can be achieved.

Writing centers as a whole have proven through studies and statistics that they should exist, but explaining the purpose for that existence may be more challenging. Molly Wingate states in her article "Writing Centers as Sites of Academic Culture" that "we have tied our successes with the missions of our institutions, and we have cultivated allies on our campuses."[10] This idea clearly points in the direction that libraries and writing centers need to work together. The two academic colleagues agree with this concept, and by bringing in student affairs an important partnership was formed to better assist students with their understanding of the benefits of academic honesty and the consequences of plagiarism.

A survey of related student affairs literature clearly supports out-of-class learning, academic affairs and student affairs partnerships, and the holistic development of students. In *Learning Reconsidered*, two leading student affairs professional associations make a case "for the integrated use of all of higher education's resources in the education and preparation of the whole student."[11] Nationally, student affairs staffs have always been committed to the development of the whole person. The holistic perspective and focus on the intellectual, social, cultural, physical, and spiritual growth of students are rooted in more than fifty years of college student development research. In the past fifteen years in higher education, learning has become increasingly understood as a more integrative process, one that incorporates in-class learning with out-of-class experiences.[12] "Student Affairs ... is integral to the learning process because of the opportunities it provides to students to learn through action, contemplation, reflection and emotional engagement as well as information acquisition."[13]

Partnerships between academic affairs and student affairs, as well as other areas of campus, provide a key context for helping students make the connections between their coursework and other educational experiences. The move from providing separate academic experiences to seamless, integrated educational experiences is evidenced via academic and student affairs collaborations such as extended orientation courses, internship programs, academic integrity processes, and service learning.

Some oft-cited desired student outcomes include "knowledge acquisition, integration, and application" and "interpersonal and intrapersonal competence," which includes dimensions of ethics and integrity.[14] None of those desired student outcomes can be fully accomplished in the classroom alone, nor can they be achieved without the classroom.[15]

COLLEGE STUDENTS AND PLAGIARISM

One doesn't have to look far to identify some of the causes of plagiarism today. The millennial generation, students born after 1980, are characterized by Howe and Strauss as having seven core traits: "special, sheltered, confident, team-oriented, conventional, pressured, and achieving."[16] The combination of being collaborative or team-oriented, pressured, and achieving provides a fertile context for academic misconduct to occur. With regard to being team-oriented, college administrators are now challenged to define for students the line between the often encouraged use of a study partner and the potential negative outcome of submitting similar work on assignments, which can be construed as cheating or plagiarizing. Bricault reported that several studies have considered the causes of academic dishonesty and included several reasons: "fear of failure, stress, time, workload, course difficulty, perceived low risk of getting caught, and ignorance."[17]

In addition to the causes, the methods for plagiarism have changed with improved technology. The abundance of information available at one's fingertips via the Internet presents a time-saving means to plagiarism. Students can easily copy and paste information from various sources, download an entire piece, or purchase a term paper online. The causes above, the interplay of characteristics of the millennial generation, and the ease of access provided by advances in technology have been evident and increasing in frequency in academic misconduct judicial cases in the past five years on our campus.

CREATING A PLAGIARISM WORKSHOP

Upon reading the Swartz, Carlisle, and Uyeki article, the instruction librarian sent it to the director of the writing center and asked if she was interested in developing an interactive, educational workshop on the topic of plagiarism education and prevention. The instruction librarian, who has a writing center background, knew that plagiarism education is part of the focus of writing center practice, so she knew that the writing center director would be a likely collaborator. The two approached the Vice Chancellor for Student Affairs, describing the workshop, stating that it was open to all students, and proposing that the workshop be a part of the sanction for students disciplined for plagiarism. The vice chancellor was receptive to the proposal, and the group met to work out the details.

The Indiana University Southeast Student Conduct Process Principles include, "Utilize an educational approach when interacting with students, parents, and University community members regarding student rights and responsibilities. Assign educational solutions to students whose behavior falls below the standards established by the University community."[18] Thus, the shared interests in student development and learning made the library/writing center/student affairs collaboration a logical one, as well as our mutual interests in providing educational interventions for students who need assistance with complying with university standards for academic performance.

The development of learning outcomes was essential to the process. At first, the focus was strictly on the idea of plagiarism, but as the workshop was developed, the need to discuss the idea of academic integrity as well became obvious because it has to do with whether a student will choose to plagiarize after he or she knows what it is. The following are the student learning outcomes:

Students who attend this workshop will be able to do the following tasks:

- Define plagiarism in all of its forms.
- Understand the implications of plagiarism and disciplinary procedures at IU Southeast.
- Demonstrate the ability to paraphrase and summarize.
- Access reliable sources on citation formats and know how to apply those formats.
- Recognize plagiarism in their own writing and the writing of others.
- Store and manage citations using free online tools.
- Use criteria to evaluate quality and reliability of information sources.
- Understand the importance of academic integrity as it applies to work in the university setting; i.e., participating in groups, reusing a previous paper, helping fellow students with course work, and/or allowing other students to use their papers or homework for their own classes.

The workshop facilitators developed a curriculum that made use of plagiarism education resources freely available online. The plagiarism tutorial on the Rutgers University Libraries website proved to be an engaging and effective tool to use during our session.[19] The director of the writing center also wrote a number of scenarios that described an instance where plagiarism or some other form of academic dishonesty could occur. This kind of problem-based learning provided workshop attendees with the opportunity to think about the various ways in which plagiarism might occur. An issue that comes up frequently in the discussion of the scenarios is personal responsibility. The emphasis on personal responsibility and autonomy is an important concern shared by librarians, writing center professionals, and student affairs professionals.

Another issue addressed in the workshop is the student conduct process and student rights and responsibilities. As Nimsakont notes, "If librarians are seen as people who can help explain the often-confusing rules and practices surrounding research and writing, rather than as disciplinarians looking to punish students, then they can increase their effectiveness in preventing plagiarism."[20] In our case, a librarian and a writing center professional explain not only the rules and practices of writing, but also the rules and regulations of Indiana University concerning academic misconduct.

SANCTIONING AND THE JUDICIAL PROCESS

The team held the workshop twice in the spring 2010 semester. The vice chancellor informed students of the required workshop attendance during the judicial process, and she copied the director of the writing center on the correspondence with the student so that the workshop instructors knew who to expect at the workshop. When the referred students attended, the director of the writing center notified the vice chancellor so that she knew the students had satisfied this requirement. In most cases, students are concerned when they receive a letter of notification of allegations of academic misconduct from the vice chancellor and attend the scheduled judicial conference meeting. Generally, most students admit the wrongdoing and accept responsibility readily.

At the first workshop, one thing that was not expected was that not all of the students who had been mandated to attend did in fact attend. This was rather surprising and confusing, and it truly underscores how imperative it is for students to learn about personal responsibility in all aspects of the college experience. One might imagine that being called to the vice chancellor's office to discuss an academic dishonesty violation might jolt a student into the realization that academic integrity is serious business and that perhaps it would be worthwhile to take responsibility and learn from his or her mistakes.

If a student does not attend the plagiarism workshop as sanctioned, a "hold" is placed on his or her academic record, preventing that student from registering, getting a transcript, and so forth. Students often cite schedule conflicts or simply forgetting about the workshop as the reason for not attending the workshop, and once they learn about the hold on their record, they inquire about other workshop dates.

The principal philosophy of our student conduct process is for it to be an educational and developmental experience for the student. The judicial conference includes a discussion that ensures the student understands what plagiarism is, that the campus has a writing center available to assist them with their writing, and the importance of academic and personal integrity. The required plagiarism workshop is also discussed and is included in the follow-up letter with the sanction to the student. Even though students take the judicial process seriously, some students do not carefully read the sanction letter and make a note of the workshop date, time, and place. Hence, they miss the workshop. While students might not be thrilled about a required two-hour workshop on a Friday, most of them are genuinely interested in becoming more confident in their writing, if for no other reason than avoiding further judicial action.

In one situation where the student truly was not able to attend any of the upcoming scheduled workshops and was sincere in her interest in completing the sanction, the director of the writing center engaged the student in a creative agreement for learning the material. The student's task was to make the information available in an electronic format. This unique arrangement served two purposes: (1) the student learned the material by reviewing all of the information from the workshop, and (2) a PowerPoint presentation was created that the workshop presenters could use in future workshops. The writing center now has an additional resource available to students, especially the few who are unable to attend a scheduled workshop.

INITIAL ASSESSMENT: EVALUATING THE IMPACT

The workshops have proven to be an effective educational opportunity for students. The instruction librarian developed brief web-based entrance and exit surveys to gain a sense of what students know about plagiarism and academic integrity before and after the workshop. On the entrance survey (see appendix A), students are asked to define plagiarism and make decisions about brief scenarios that involve academic dishonesty The workshop instructors display the anonymous results and lead the students in a discussion based on that feedback. For example, if students answer *False* to "Copying and pasting a few sentences from an article into a paper without citing your source can be considered plagiarism," then this topic will be covered in depth during the workshop. In addition, the exit survey (see appendix B) asks students to report what they will do differently now that they have attended the workshop. For example, some students report that they will no longer procrastinate, which is often cited as a reason why some students resort to plagiarism. Others report that their understanding of plagiarism has been clarified and improved. All students, to date, have complied with the sanction requirement by participating in the plagiarism workshop, and there have been no instances of repeat violations by those students.

LESSONS LEARNED: THE BENEFITS AND CHALLENGES OF COLLABORATION

Any new, collaborative endeavor requires ongoing evaluation. The team encountered a few minor challenges and also gained some insights regarding successful collaborations that may be transferable in other settings. One relatively minor challenge faced by the three colleagues is that of determining the optimal time to schedule workshops. On one hand, the goal is to inform students in an effort to prevent plagiarism. Using that objective as a guide, conventional wisdom would lead one to offer workshops early in the semester. The large majority of reported plagiarism incidences, however, occur toward the end of the semester. Students often cite time management, procrastination, and competing pressures around finals week led them to seek a shortcut in completing an assignment. The increase in reported cases near the end of the term also presents a challenge, as the possible hold on a student's record at that time could impede student persistence from one semester to the next. Collaborative efforts must, therefore, consider the mission, vision, and strategic plan of the institution when making decisions.

Another minor challenge involved determining the optimal number of workshops to offer. The workshop instructors began with two workshop dates in spring 2010, but with no-shows and new referrals coming at a time when a workshop was not scheduled, the three colleagues had to regroup. The team is flexible, without accommodating or enabling a student's lack of responsibility. Ultimately, a few more workshops than initially planned were offered; a couple of students were accommodated individually, and others had a hold on their record until they met the sanction requirement.

Truly collaborative efforts require all parties to seek consensus, often by sharing individual experiences as well as professional philosophies regarding best practices. The collaborative team is now in its second year of managing this program and process. While institutional factors identified earlier certainly lend themselves to this partnership, the team members' passion for assisting and educating students has also been an effective driving force.

For the instruction librarian, the opportunity to help students understand information ethics in this context is an invaluable approach to integrating information literacy, one of the eight General Education Student Learning Outcomes for IU Southeast, throughout the curriculum and into real-life contexts that have direct impact on students' lives. For the Vice Chancellor for Student Affairs, explaining to students in the judicial conference that the plagiarism workshop will ultimately help the student become a better, more confident writer has reinforced the operating philosophy that the student conduct process is developmental. For the writing center director, every opportunity to collaborate with other departments on campus has been welcomed because of the mission to create better writers at our institution and the knowledge that by working with others, this mission will be better understood and supported. In addition, the core values, mentioned earlier, are demonstrated in this collaboration. The writing center is very fortunate to operate within an academic setting where these efforts are encouraged, which in turn benefits the most important people in this equation, the students.

Faculty and students are seeing the benefits of this collaborative project. Both academic and student affairs benefit logistically from the efficiency of coordinated efforts to deliver student services. Rather than duplicating similar efforts, multiple parties team up to offer one service that fulfills the goals of each group. And when students see campus groups collaborating to help them achieve academic and personal success, they experience a seamless learning environment, where learning is not limited to one sphere or one classroom, but extends across departments, disciplines, and beyond.

Other campuses seeking to develop a plagiarism prevention partnership should scan the campus environment to ensure that collaborative initiatives are fostered and facilitated by the campus culture. The coordinator of library instruction, the writing center director, and the person in charge of student conduct are the key people to engage in a plagiarism prevention partnership, and buy-in from the library director should also be secured in the process. There are several central questions to consider when examining the campus environment: What are the key concerns of the campus administration? What goals does the campus seek to achieve? Is there a strategic plan, and what roles do the library, student affairs, and the writing center have in the plan? What collaborative efforts already exist on the campus, and what can be learned from their successes and challenges?

In exploring the answers to these questions, this IU Southeast collaborative project found purpose, direction, and institutional validation. The library, student affairs, and the writing center plan to continue the partnership, evaluating its impact and reflecting on its challenges and successes, and making modifications as indicated. The authors hope that the IU Southeast plagiarism prevention workshop model can serve as an example to other institutions seeking to achieve similar goals.

Notes

1. Pauline S. Swartz, Brian A. Carlisle, and E. Chisato Uyeki, "Libraries and Student Affairs: Partners for Student Success," *Reference Services Review* 35, no. 1 (2007): 114.

2. Cindy Pierard and Kathryn Graves, "Research on Student Retention and Implications for Library Involvement," in *The Role of the Library in the First College Year*, edited by Larry Hardesty (Columbia: University of South Carolina, National Resource Center for the First-Year Experience and Students in Transition, 2007), 155.

3. American Library Association, *Presidential Committee on Information Literacy: Final Report*, quoted in Association of College and Research Libraries, *Information Literacy Competency Standards for Higher Education* (Chicago: Association of College and Research Libraries, 2000), 2, ACRL website, http://www.ala.org/acrl/files/standards/standards.pdf.

4. Lynn D. Lampert, *Combating Student Plagiarism: An Academic Librarian's Guide* (Oxford: Chandos, 2008), 12.

5. Maud Mundava and Jayati Chaudhuri, "Understanding Plagiarism: The Role of Librarians at the University of Tennessee in Assisting Students to Practice Fair Use of Information," *C&RL News* 68, no. 3 (2007): 173.

6. Lampert, *Combating Student Plagiarism*, 106.

7. Ibid., 110.

8. Steven M. North, "The Idea of a Writing Center," *College English* 46, no 5 (1984): 433.

9. Sheril Hook, "Teaching Librarians and Writing Center Professionals in Collaboration: Complementary Practices," in *Centers for Learning: Writing Centers and Libraries in Collaboration*, edited by James K. Elmborg and Sheril Hook (Chicago: American Library Association, 2005), 21.

10. Molly Wingate, "Writing Centers as Sites of Academic Culture," *The Writing Center Journal* 21, no. 2 (2001): 7, http://casebuilder.rhet.ualr.edu/wcrp/ publications/wcj/ wcj21.2/ WCJ21.2_Wingate.pdf.

11. Richard P. Keeling, ed., *Learning Reconsidered: A Campus-Wide Focus on the Student Experience* (Washington, DC: American College Personnel Association, 2004), 3, ACPA website, http://www.myacpa.org/pub/documents/learningreconsidered.pdf.

12. American College Personnel Association, "The Student Learning Imperative: Implications for Student Affairs," ACPA website, 1996, last modified September 10, 2008, http://www.myacpa.org/sli_delete/sli.htm.

13. Keeling, *Learning Reconsidered*, 12.

14. Ibid., 18–19.

15. Richard P. Keeling, ed., *Learning Reconsidered 2: A Practical Guide to Implementing a Campus-Wide Focus on the Student Experience* (Washington, DC: American College Personnel Association, 2006).

16. Neil Howe and William Strauss, *Millennials Go to College*, 2nd ed. (Washington, DC: American Association of Collegiate Registrars and Admissions Officers, 2007), 59.

17. Dennis Bricault, *Academic Dishonesty: Developing and Implementing Institutional Policy* (Washington, DC: American Association of Collegiate Registrars and Admissions Officers, 2007), 10.

18. Indiana University Southeast, "Section 2A: Philosophy," *Code Procedures*, revised August 2010, IUS website, http://ius.edu/studentaffairs/pdf/IUSCode.pdf#2A. Philosophy.

19. Paul Robeson Library, "How to Avoid Plagiarism: An Information Literacy Tutorial," video, Rutgers University Libraries website, accessed October 1, 2010, http://library.camden.rutgers.edu/EducationalModule/Plagiarism.

20. Emily Dust Nimsakont, "How Can Academic Librarians Educate Students about Plagiarism?" *PNLA Quarterly* 72, no. 3 (Spring 2008): 11.

5
Promoting Collaborative LEADers in the St. John's University Community

Natalie Maio and Kathryn Shaughnessy

Collaborations thrive when all parties are able to bring their expertise to the table, a point Maio and Shaughnessy illustrate well in this next chapter. The authors developed a plagiarism workshop as part of St. John's University's Leadership Development Program and then expanded their collaborations beyond plagiarism education to other areas of the program. As part of their lessons learned, Maio and Shaughnessy share ideas for library and student affairs collaborations and suggestions for creating productive working relationships.

This case study addresses the collaboration between St. John's University's Office of LEADership Development and the libraries' Instructional Services office to improve an extracurricular program which enhances student leadership and communication skills and which facilitates student-faculty interaction on leadership topics. Collaboration between the librarian and the leadership development program director began when they worked together to improve a workshop on plagiarism and scholarly communications in the Leadership, Education, and Development (L.E.A.D.) program. Their initial collaboration transformed a "sage-on-the-stage" workshop into a workshop where students learn from each other through interactive games and role-playing to address plagiarism and copyright problems in a student-organization publication. Collaboration grew to include additional libraries and student affairs offices, with library faculty working with student affairs to champion a new workshop series promoting faculty mentoring of students, cofacilitation of workshops on leadership issues, and roundtables where faculty share insights into leadership from in their own areas of expertise and experience.

The type of collaboration employed in the case study focuses on Raspa and Ward's model of sustained, open communication among workshop developers and workshop participants and a willingness to learn from each other's academic and personal experiences during discussions with the student leaders.[1] The authors' "official" interdepartmental collaborations and subsequent collaboration with students led to an increased participation by the students in their own leadership development—both personally and programmatically. Establishing a willingness to listen to suggestions and to share both the successes and failures of individual workshops led to the development of an improved leadership program that fosters informal but meaningful extracurricular interaction between faculty and students—a prized part of the university experience. While these workshops and programs arose in the context of collaborations around the theme of leadership, similar types of programs might be developed in conjunction with libraries and student affairs programs around other themes which draw on academic research and personal experience, such as student wellness, active citizenship, academic service learning, and so forth.

ST. JOHN'S UNIVERSITY

St. John's University is a private Catholic university, based in Queens, New York, serving a widely diverse student population of approximately twenty thousand students from forty-six states and 111 countries. The university embraces the global character of our internationally diverse community and values the knowledge that each member brings to the community's learning environment. While various academic and student affairs units of the university address "global" aspects of learning and living together, the Division of Student Affairs Office of LEADership Development and the university libraries' department of Instructional Services collaborated to explore the scholarly and technical aspects of communication and leadership in our community. While the university has a robust Institute for Writing Studies with a very popular Writing Center Tutor Program, the center's efforts were geared primarily towards academic writing. The leadership office approached the libraries as a natural fit for facilitating both the academic parts of the leadership program—which addressed citation and plagiarism in the context of scholarly communication—and the extracurricular aspects of the responsible communication of accurate information in the context of leading a student organization in a culturally and technologically rich environment.

OUTLOOK ON COLLABORATION, LEADERSHIP, AND LEARNING

The L.E.A.D. program director, Natalie Maio, and the Instructional Services librarian, Kathryn Shaughnessy, recognized that the best way to instill values of collaboration and open, ethical communication in student leaders was to model it ourselves. Although Raspa and Ward's framework of collaboration is explicitly geared toward collaboration between librarians and teaching faculty, it was well-suited for collaboration on extracurricular and cocurricular goals as well. At minimum, Raspa and Ward's notion of collaboration requires recognizing common goals and working in a coordinated fashion to accomplish them (collegial phase); hopefully the collaborative relationship grows into one where the collaborators value each other's (perhaps unique) approaches to issues and interdisciplinary insights (interpersonal phase) and finally grows to the point where arbitrary distinctions between disciplines begin to blur and collaborators primarily see the interconnectedness and overlaps between issues and potential solutions (syncretic phase).[2] Raspa and Ward's five principles of collaboration—"Passion, Persistence, Playfulness, Project, Promote"—also served as a recurring model, both in building the particular workshops and in promoting collaborative leadership in our students. Particular attention was paid to the essential "playfulness" principle, which asks interlocutors to suspend judgment about what they "think they know" in discussions and to participate in a type of listening that assumes "not-knowing."[3] This principle was taken to heart, not only in terms of the creation and execution of workshops, but also between the workshop directors and the students in the program, who listened each other as people who offer a valued perspective on the topics at hand.

Playfulness in collaboration was bootstrapped by the notion of playfulness in learning. We noted especially the work of English professor and collaborative learning proponent Kenneth Bruffee, who lamented that the games/icebreaker sessions, which met with such success in campus orientation, were abandoned when students walked into the classroom, especially when such types of collaborative learning could be easily employed to introduce concepts throughout disciplines in low-stakes learning exercises.[4] On a more literal level, Gee and Levine take note of the rise of play within gaming cultures and the potential that games have for collaborative learning and libraries.[5]

This approach of playful communication and active participation (rather than passive reception of information in learning) gels well with a constructivist approach to learning, where a workshop "isn't so much to lecture at students but to act as an expert learner who can guide students into adopting cognitive strategies such as self-testing, articulating understanding, asking probing questions, and reflection."[6]

Finally, both the libraries and the leadership development office recognized ACRL's move to broaden the scope of information literacy, with an emphasis on contextual learning in regard to the issues of access to and evaluation of reliable information, the incorporation of information into knowledge, and an understanding of the legal and social issues surrounding information and communication. Again, while most literature at the time of initial collaboration dealt with integrating information literacy into the academic curriculum[7] and within the context of specific disciplines,[8] we were also seeing the opportunity to address information literacy and ethical uses of information and communication technologies in a way that transcends specific curricula or disciplines.[9]

COLLEGIAL PARTNERSHIP

When Shaughnessy joined the libraries' faculty in 2005, the libraries had already been involved in the L.E.A.D. program by facilitating the required workshop on plagiarism, which was part of the Emerging Student Leader track. The initial L.E.A.D. program developers included this workshop in the early 2000s in response to the growing trend of plagiarism on campuses, compounded by the use of Internet resources, which facilitated copy-and-paste plagiarism. At the same time, Student Government, Inc., had established a student honor code and wanted a more effective way for student leaders to recognize and understand the consequences of plagiarism. The plagiarism workshops evolved a bit in response to the rise in use of *Wikipedia* in 2001, but by 2005, when the academic pitfalls of *Wikipedia* were pretty well-known, interest in the plagiarism workshops waned, and workshop evaluations reflected a middling level of student interest.

Shaughnessy had taught some L.E.A.D. sessions her first year, and when she first met with Maio, who had taken over as director of the L.E.A.D. program, it was in the vein of "collegial" collaboration. The two shared a common goal that both were *passionate* about: wanting student leaders to know the importance of ethical, effective communication, both in the classroom and outside, and wanting to make grappling with this important topic interesting and engaging.

Upon review of the plagiarism workshop evaluations for the prior three years, it was clear that students felt that the workshops offered only information they "already knew" and that the topic lacked any relevance for "leaders." While we sympathized that a session on plagiarism might seem boring, we suspended for the moment "what we thought we knew about the students" and as well as "what the students thought they knew about plagiarism" and worked together to come up with some reasons why we thought our student leaders should care about a session like this. Ultimately, we thought they needed to understand the impact that technology could have on organizational communications, not only in terms of both the commission and the discovery of plagiarism, but in the quick dissemination of ill-researched information or misinformation. We also thought they needed to be aware that the "remix/mashup" mentality among students could have ethical and legal ramifications for organizational leaders who have official publication venues.

Although students might have wanted to eliminate the workshop or make it optional, and although the libraries were trying to move away from one-shot library instruction sessions in favor of direct collaboration with professors, both Maio and Shaughnessy felt that this L.E.A.D. workshop offered an unique opportunity to move beyond the traditional single-session library workshop. A revamped workshop would hold the possibility of a more in-depth conversation about plagiarism and the role that Web 2.0 information and communications technologies (ICTs) play in copyright violations—all within the context of leadership.

INTERPERSONAL PARTNERSHIP

Maio and Shaughnessy had passion and persistence in sticking with the important topic, and as collaborators, they were moving away from mere collegial partnership towards Raspa and Ward's "interpersonal" stage of personal interdisciplinary collaboration. Maio and Shaughnessy discussed how the workshop fit into the whole scheme of the L.E.A.D. program, and drawing on Maio's education background and Shaughnessy's philosophy/library background, they explored the principle of playfulness to come up with some of the hands-on, problem-solving approaches for this session. The revised version of the plagiarism workshop used a game approach to test participants' actual knowledge of plagiarism and proper citation by asking them to break into teams and answer questions in a *Jeopardy*-like format. Questions regarding proper citation, plagiarism, Web 2.0 publication, and mashup tools, as well as questions regarding the relationship between plagiarism and copyright infringement, were posed; teams competed to answer questions correctly. While no actual prize money could be offered, the game approach allowed participants to find out how much they actually did know in a low-stakes environment. The game also generated lively discussion about the some of the specifics of plagiarism versus copyright and how leaders could prevent citation and plagiarism problems in their organizations, all in a way that encouraged collaborative learning. To address the desire for problem solving in a way that explicitly addressed leadership issues, workshops also included discussions and role-playing where leaders thought through an organization's selection of publishing venues and possible procedures for writing, fact checking, and publishing information in an organization venue. Discussions about the need for rapid dissemination of important organization information were balanced by discussions about editorial and level permissions in a publishing venue to avoid rapid redistribution of plagiarized work, miscited information, and unresearched or misinformed communications, which would then be attributed to an organization.

The project, which arose as the result of the simple revamp of these sessions, led to a number of positive outcomes.

- The most quantifiable outcome was that subsequent evaluation scores indicated a positive change in student assessment of the workshops. More favorable reviews indicated that students saw the workshop as helpful to them as leaders, in addition to being helpful to them for "personal development."

- The interactive element had the beneficial effect of making students feel enough at ease to ask for follow-up help with research on personal and organizational matters. Students contacted the librarian for follow-up information on resources referred to in the presentation, and several asked to use the *Jeopardy* format for other student organization training programs.

- Success with these initial sessions led to Shaughnessy being asked to mentor student leaders and cofacilitate the plagiarism workshops with them. Planning for these student-led sessions fostered the students' reflection on and engagement with plagiarism issues from their own experiences and from the viewpoint of their disciplines. For example, student leaders worked with Shaughnessy to research the negative impact plagiarism had for students in the pharmacy and business schools, from both academic and postschool perspectives. This led to more robust discussion among session participants regarding parallels or dissimilarities in other disciplines and whether the problems transcended disciplines.

- In reviewing the workshops in the context of the whole L.E.A.D. program, we saw some overlaps with workshops being provided for the first-year-experience course, Discover New York (DNY). We saw that if we held combined sessions of library and L.E.A.D. workshops that met the needs of DNY students too, DNY students would be exposed to the L.E.A.D. program, which might pique their interest in attending other L.E.A.D. sessions or in joining a certificate track program. This, in turn, led to subsequent conversations about which new or potential library workshops might work well in the L.E.A.D. program, which naturally led to crosspromotion of library, L.E.A.D., and DNY academic workshops and increased participation for all involved.

- Maio and Shaughnessy's collaborative approach to revamping and evaluating the success of this workshop was introduced into the libraries' workshop development program, which in turn, led to more robust discussions about creating interactive library workshops and the use of Maio's evaluation form by the Instructional Services department to evaluate extant workshop series.

PASSION, PERSISTENCE, PLAYFULNESS, PROJECT, PROMOTE

Long-time colleagues can often find a "tipping point" that turns collegial collaborators into interpersonal collaborators—and it generally revolves around both parties extending themselves just a little more than is required out of an appreciation for the other. One particularly busy spring, towards the end of the semester, an excited L.E.A.D.-certificate candidate entered the last Track 1 workshop of the semester. Before the workshop started, she indicated that she needed this last workshop to qualify for the L.E.A.D. certificate, but her attendance conflicted with the opportunity to give a speech in her bid for class treasurer—her goal in being a "real leader." Not wanting to undermine the L.E.A.D. track requirements, Shaughnessy counseled the student to make the decision she thought best and to be sure to contact Maio to let her know that decision either way. The student left the workshop in time to make the speech; because she did not remain until the end, she was unable to sign the workshop participation sheet.

Shaughnessy and Maio consulted after the workshop. This candidate was not the only student in the position of being one workshop shy of L.E.A.D. certification, and the authors both expressed concerns about time management and commitment elements of being involved in the LEADership program and in leadership positions. Would making an exception to requiring one last workshop send the wrong message, or would it reward students who worked through most of the program and actually wanted to put the training to good use in a leadership position? Since the last workshop conflicted with this pre-election student organization meeting—which had been scheduled independently—Shaughnessy volunteered to host another "unscheduled" session as a library workshop for this student and others in her position; if the student attended this session, it would count as the last L.E.A.D. credit. While this might have been considered a "natural solution" from a librarian's perspective, Maio saw it as a demonstration of Shaughnessy's commitment to the L.E.A.D. program goals. Maio was touched, and as a small recognition of this effort on behalf of the L.E.A.D. students, she nominated Shaughnessy for honorary membership in Omicron Delta Kappa, the national leadership honor society. And while this might have been considered a "natural token of appreciation" from a leader's perspective, Shaughnessy saw it as recognition of how much they shared in their commitment to young leaders and was touched to be included among them. The aforementioned student was elected treasurer and received her L.E.A.D. certificate; both Maio and Shaughnessy were delighted. In retrospect, the authors refer to this incident as the tipping point because it has so many of Raspa and Ward's principles in one story: *passion* about the common goals of promoting responsible leaders, *persistence* in analyzing and overcoming surmountable obstacles, *playfulness* in listening to the student and each other, commitment to the *project* as a whole, and *promotion* of the program and of each other as collaborators.

SYNCRETIC PARTNERSHIP

After the "tipping point," Shaughnessy and Maio's conversations about leadership and communication expanded to include other leadership projects that Maio coordinates. Maio extended an invitation to Shaughnessy to step outside the "plagiarism zone" and facilitate another type of workshop for the Student Leadership Conference organized by the Office of Campus Activities. While no workshop topic was a clear match for an academic library discipline, Shaughnessy knew she could draw on experiences from university committees to facilitate a session on Robert's Rule of Order in order to help students conduct collegial and efficient meetings. Although many students indicated that they found Robert's Rules a bit cumbersome, they appreciated his general guidelines for conducting deliberations in a fair, dispassionate way, and they worked together to propose "up-to-date versions" of the rules to deal with distractions or delays and to rein in overly talkative members. Shaughnessy's participation marked the first time that any faculty member had acted as a facilitator in the Student Leadership Conference, and student participants seemed to appreciate faculty involvement. Positive evaluations of the sessions led to Shaughnessy being asked to serve as a faculty advisor for the conference to be held the following year and to her serving as a liaison to get other faculty more involved.

Successful participation in the Student Leadership Conference led to Maio requesting that Shaughnessy facilitate a breakout group for LEADership Development's Women in Leadership Conference. Shaughnessy was unavailable, but she referred Maio to the libraries' Outreach Librarian, Caroline Fuchs, who drew on her experiences as a legislative advocate to create a shared leadership breakout session. Positive evaluations of this session led to Fuchs being asked to develop and facilitate shared leadership workshops for the L.E.A.D. and Women in Leadership programs.

Including library faculty in workshops on leadership topics which were outside their library discipline also led to discussions about cosponsoring library programs that were outside of the LEADership program. The Outreach Librarian and Student Engagement administrators collaborated in crosspromotion of Fuchs's academic-enrichment programs, including a "Read-It-

See-It Book & Film Discussion" series, a graphic novels discussion group, and her ongoing great books discussion group. Subsequently, Fuchs and Student Engagement worked together to develop two new book discussion programs; the Reading Memoirs series and the Freshman Read book discussion groups were included as academic engagement activities in Student Engagement's MVP Student Rewards Program.[10]

LEAVE NO PARTNER BEHIND: WHEN COLLABORATION HITS A BUMP

The authors do not want it to appear as if everything in this case study on collaboration was smooth sailing; this is the part where they admit to a fiasco—but because of a solid foundation of successful collaborations and a commitment to the principles of passion and persistence, the partnership remains intact.

As the coordination deadline for the 2010 Campus Activities Student Leadership Conference approached, Shaughnessy reached out to her faculty colleagues in the libraries and faculty collaborators in various schools to generate interest among faculty in cofacilitating workshops with students. Despite the meticulous directions of Maio and the conference coordinator (a wonderfully organized and active Ebony Calvin), Shaughnessy's initial e-mail to her colleagues contained some misinformation that effectively generated more confusion than collaboration due to an onslaught of misdirected e-mails. Additionally, once the respondent e-mails reached their proper recipients, belated responses led to a series of scheduling conflicts so that most faculty volunteers were unable meet with either the conference coordinator or the student facilitators prior to the August conference date. As a result, in 2010, no faculty could cofacilitate sessions at the Student Leadership Conference.

The silver lining to this rather dark cloud was that the passion that Maio and Shaughnessy had for helping these young leaders was kindled in other faculty members as well. The total number of faculty colleagues who expressed a willingness to participate was unprecedented. Rather than waiting a year and taking advantage of this goodwill at the 2011 summer conference, Maio asked Shaughnessy to join her and her supervisor, Jodi Cox, the director of Campus Life, in a late summer meeting dedicated to finding ways to increase faculty involvement in school-year programs sponsored by the Division of Student Affairs and to get a new student-faculty engagement series off the ground.

COLLABORATION REGAINED: LESSONS LEARNED

The best elements of the collaborations between the libraries and student affairs crystallized in this late summer meeting. When the instruction librarians made a collaborative shift in 2005 to work directly with faculty to incorporate information literacy and library resources at point of need in the classroom, it also meant that they had developed a rich faculty colleague network extending far beyond departmental liaison work and committee membership. This extended network included collaboration-oriented faculty partners from across all schools (DNY and core professors, Title III participants, fellows in the Center for Teaching and Learning, fellows in the Vincentian Center, etc.), and librarians knew that these were colleagues who shared in a passion for developing well-rounded students.

By continuing to collaborate with student affairs, instruction librarians were given a chance to reconnect directly with students in academically relevant and engaging ways, but beyond the confines of the typical library instruction session or reference interview.

Making the most of both of these types of collaborative connections enabled Shaughnessy, Maio, and Cox to connect classroom faculty facilitators to Campus Activities' extracurricular engagement efforts and to offer insights into what sorts of activities might appeal to faculty—including library faculty who worked behind the scenes or had less flexible schedules which deprived them of opportunities to engage with students. The late summer meeting produced a list of qualities for faculty-student engagement opportunities that would likely appeal to a variety of faculty: variable time commitments, scheduling flexibility, and the ability to set their own topics or share their extracurricular experiences.

The most recent invitation extended by student affairs offered three types of extracurricular student-engagement opportunities for all faculty. Maio extended the invitation to those library and teaching faculty members who had expressed interest in the August Campus Activities Student Leadership Conference, and Shaughnessy extended it to additional faculty colleagues in a carefully edited e-mail; the authors await the results with justified hope.

IMPLICATIONS FOR OTHER INSTITUTIONS

While the authors' collaborations initially developed around the theme of leadership, similar types of programs might be developed in conjunction with library and student affairs programs around other themes which draw on academic and personal experience, such as student wellness, active citizenship, and academic service learning. At the most basic level, other institutions might seek out ways to promote "collegial collaboration" between libraries and student affairs to ensure that workshop and outreach efforts are being not duplicated in separate programs (as the DNY, libraries, and L.E.A.D. workshops had been at St. John's).

Going to the next level in their collaborations, the authors recognized that the LEADership Development office and the libraries both had a core mission of expanding students' intellectual horizons outside the classroom. While not every student affairs activity will be a natural fit for library collaboration, the fact that academic librarians often hold subject masters' degrees in addition to their LIS degrees makes them likely collaborators for those activities which hold an intellectual appeal for students, for example, discussion groups based on books and movies, poetry slams, or a debate on a timely topic.

In terms of sustained collaboration, campus activities organizations might benefit from specifically recruiting librarians for student engagement or mentoring opportunities, assuming varying levels of time commitment and schedule flexibility. For example, are librarians asked to volunteer as club moderators for campus activities? Although this is the most time-intensive type of collaboration, the fact that library faculty are on campus nearly every day can make this a good option for library faculty who would otherwise be unable to be involved with student groups. Campus activities might also find librarians to be helpful collaborators with single-session workshops or roundtable discussions with students in an informal setting throughout the year; these are often perfect for subject specialist librarians or any faculty members who wish to share their excitement for the research that inspired them to get an advanced degree in their discipline.

The authors' collaborations have bloomed in five years, and they remain a work in progress. By being advocates of each other's individual efforts, the authors have been able to make good workshops better. By being advocates of each other's department-level programs, the authors have been able to include a wider array of faculty and student collaborators in academically and personally relevant programming for the university community. The authors gratefully acknowledge their department heads and departmental colleagues who have allowed them the time and space to undertake such collaborations, to foster creative thinking, to make mistakes, and to generate

fruitful solutions—including making lemonade out of lemons when necessary. The authors wish readers luck, and success, in their collaborations as
well.

Notes

1. Richard Raspa and Dane Ward, *The Collaborative Imperative: Librarians and Faculty
Working Together in the Information Universe* (Chicago: Association of College and
Research Libraries, 2000).

2. Ibid., 11.

3. Ibid., 9.

4. Kenneth A. Bruffee, "Cultivating the Craft of Interdependence: Collaborative
Learning and the College Curriculum," *About Campus* 7, no. 6 (2003): 17–23.

5. James Paul Gee, *What Video Games Have to Teach Us about Learning and Literacy*,
1st ed. (New York: Palgrave Macmillan, 2003); Jenny Levine, "Gaming &
Libraries: Intersection of Services, Introduction," *Library Technology Reports* 42,
no. 5 (2006): 5–9.

6. Diane F. Halpern, et al., "Learning Theory," in *Encyclopedia of Education*, 2nd
ed., edited by James W. Guthrie (New York: Macmillan Reference USA, 2002),
1458–69.

7. Ilene F. Rockman, *Integrating Information Literacy into the Higher Education
Curriculum: Practical Models for Transformation*, 1st ed. (San Francisco: Jossey-
Bass, 2004).

8. John Budd, *The Changing Academic Library: Operations, Culture, Environments*
(Chicago: Association of College and Research Libraries, 2005).

9. Patricia Senn Breivik and E. Gordon Gee. *Higher Education in the Internet Age:
Libraries Creating a Strategic Edge*, rev ed. (Westport, CT: Praeger Publishers,
2006).

10. The Most Valuable Participant (MVP) Student Rewards Program is sponsored
by the Division of Student Affairs and is designed "to increase school spirit and
tradition while also creating excitement and attendance at athletic events and
University-wide programs and activities" (http://www.stjohns.edu/campus/
queens/studentlife/activities/mvp). Student affairs' extensive student network
allowed students to be more aware of and involved in attending these programs
and offered an opportunity for students to lead these libraries programs.

6

Posters, Programs, and Perspectives on Democracy

Chad Kahl and Janet Paterson

Kahl and Paterson provide an example of collaboration around a specific, one-time program that both units were interested in bringing to their university, in this case an art installation on the theme of democracy. Although the authors spearheaded the program, they tapped the expertise of colleagues in their units and across campus in order to accomplish their goals. Kahl and Paterson's work also serves as an example of combining active programming, in this case three lectures by campus faculty, with passive programming, an approach where professionals create exhibits or educational displays in a centrally located venue for students and others to browse and absorb at their convenience.

Milner Library and Student Affairs collaborated at Illinois State University to offer passive programming, in the form of the exhibit *Thoughts on Democracy: Reinterpreting Norman Rockwell's Four Freedoms Posters*. The exhibit, originally curated by Florida International University's Wolfsonian museum, ran from February 1 to May 7, 2010, and displayed graphic works expressing ideals at the core of American democracy by sixty contemporary artists. A related lecture series and exhibit website were also created.

In this chapter, the authors use Dr. Dick Raspa and Dane Ward's "Five Ps of Collaboration"—passion, playfulness, project, persistence, and promotion—to examine what proved to be a truly collaborative relationship.[1]

The collaboration worked well because the librarian and student affairs official took advantage of complementary skills, joint interest in offering cocurricular resources by nonacademic units, and shared desire to support the campus's American Democracy Project (ADP) that promotes civic engagement.

OVERVIEW OF THE COLLABORATION

In FY2010, Milner Library and Student Affairs collaborated as part of Illinois
State University's American Democracy Project (ADP). ADP is a cooperative
campus effort with a goal of promoting civic engagement—one of five core
values of the university's strategic plan, Educating Illinois.[2]

The collaboration was the exhibit *Thoughts on Democracy: Reinterpreting
Norman Rockwell's Four Freedoms Posters,* located on the library's main
floor. The exhibit, originally curated by Florida International University's
Wolfsonian museum, displayed graphic works expressing ideals at the core
of American democracy by sixty contemporary artists. A related lecture series
by three resident faculty attracted over 220 people and was rated excellent in
forty-seven of fifty-six evaluations. An exhibit website provided information
on the artists, access to podcasts of the three lectures, and additional online
resources.

This partnership between student affairs and the library is an example
of passive programming. In this case, the developmental concept of student/
environment interaction was bringing an art exhibit into a student study space
where it was not expected. The lecture series, opening reception, and inclusion of the exhibit in coursework helped students make meaning of the art.

A working relationship had developed between the exhibit co-coordi-
nators—the Dean of Students, Jan Paterson, and a social sciences subject
librarian, Chad Kahl—due to their interaction in ADP. There was also joint
interest in offering cocurricular resources by nonacademic units. It worked
well because it merged the skills of the librarian—institutional experience
with exhibits and academic lectures and disciplinary focus—and the student
affairs official—experience with programming for students, contracting, and
vendor relations. Both participants also had access to grant funding opportunities that were successfully utilized.

ILLINOIS STATE UNIVERSITY

In 1857, Illinois State Normal University was founded as the first public
institution of higher education in the state. Established as a teacher education institution, Illinois State has developed into a multipurpose, comprehensive university with degree programs at the bachelor's, master's, and doctoral levels.

The university is one of twelve public universities in Illinois. Its academic
departments offer more than two hundred major/minor options in the colleges

of Applied Science and Technology, Arts and Sciences, Business, Education, and Fine Arts, and the Mennonite College of Nursing. The Graduate School coordinates forty-nine master's, specialist, and doctoral programs. Most of Illinois State's 1,136 faculty members hold the highest degrees in their fields. The university enrolls students from throughout Illinois, forty other states, the District of Columbia, and over sixty other countries. Students are mentored by a faculty that includes numerous teacher-scholars recognized at national and international levels, and all are dedicated to superior teaching.

The fall 2011 enrollment was 20,762 of which 18,254 were undergraduates. Students from groups traditionally underrepresented in higher education account for thirteen percent of all students.

Milner Library's mission is to serve university constituents, including the citizens of Illinois. Milner is a member of the Alliance Library System and the Consortium of Academic and Research Libraries of Illinois. Milner has a staff of eighty-five, materials budget of $3.6 million, and a collection of more than 1.6 million volumes, fifty-four thousand electronic journals, and thirty-two thousand multimedia items. The library instruction and information literacy program offered over seven hundred instructional sessions in the past academic school year, and the library assisted patrons with over twenty-seven thousand reference transactions in the 2010–2011 academic year.

The mission of the Division of Student Affairs at Illinois State University is to influence the campus culture to achieve student engagement, inclusion and pride in the University. To realize that vision, the division serves as an umbrella organization for twelve departments that offer services, programs, and facilities to augment the formal education of students and promote their growth as citizens and leaders.

PASSIVE PROGRAMMING

Passive programming is planned programming that does not necessarily require a specific meeting time. Instead, this type of programming has the ability to reach people over a longer period of time as well as reaching those students who, on their own, might not choose to attend a program being offered. Passive programs convey information in a manner in which active participation is unnecessary and is often done in the form of displays. Placing the exhibit where students already congregate takes advantage of existing traffic patterns, thus reducing the need to direct people to the display. "A good passive program will attract patrons to the activity and, while it may require planning, does not require a huge amount of staff time day to day. Passive programming can give visitors something to do without dedicated staff time," and therefore can be very cost-effective.[3] If what is provided is educational, most students will instinctively learn something and this approach has the ability to reach a different audience than formal programs.

These programs have the potential to be more effective than active programs by allowing greater amounts of information to be presented because students are able to absorb the information at their own pace. Passive programming—visual or auditory—provides information and keeps the environment interesting.

THE EXHIBIT

The exhibit contained over eighty graphic works created by contemporary artists and designers that responded to the invitation of Florida International University's design museum, the Wolfsonian, to express ideals at the core of American democracy. Each artist was asked to consider Norman Rockwell's visually moving paintings that conveyed the meaning of Franklin Delano Roosevelt's Four Freedoms speech to Congress and the American people—*Freedom of Speech, Freedom of Worship, Freedom from Want,* and *Freedom from Fear.* The paintings originally appeared in four consecutive issues of the *Saturday Evening Post* in 1943.

Images were reproduced as two-by-three-foot posters and displayed for twelve weeks on the main entry floor of Milner Library during the spring academic semester of 2010. The main floor of the library consists of the circulation desk, reference desk, reference collection, current periodicals, computer lab, new books, browsing collection of best sellers, microfiche and microfilm readers, computer workstations, and a considerable amount of open study space.

The culture allows for conversation on this floor. The images were hung on the walls of two adjacent but separate spaces. A display case with original copies of the *Saturday Evening Post* and two large posters describing the exhibit were placed at the entrance to one of the spaces. Although the opening reception allowed for the display of all eighty-three pieces, the ongoing display allowed for only a third of the collection at a time. The artwork was rotated three times throughout the semester.

From the outset, the *Thoughts on Democracy* program was an art exhibit. It was determined that displaying the works in the main floor study area of the campus library had multiple benefits. First, the hanging equipment was already in place, which would reduce additional costs. The library was open for more hours than any other building on campus. The area was monitored whenever the building was open by existing library staff. It was space that all patrons to the library, at a minimum, passed through when utilizing the building. The traditional use of the space was as a study lounge with moveable furniture and tables. These furnishings can be easily reconfigured to support the use of the space at any given time. The use of the space allows for high turnover between classes, guaranteeing an ever-evolving audience for the display, and served as excellent space for the passive programming aspect of the program.

THE LECTURES

A lecture series was developed to accompany the art exhibit. The three speakers were carefully chosen to examine three different aspects: an exploration of the political themes raised in the images, a historical background of the Four Freedoms speech, and an examination of the visual culture significance of the images.

The lecture "The Impact of Fear on Contemporary Political Dialogue" was delivered by Dr. Robert Bradley, a full professor in the Department of Politics and Government at Illinois State University, on February 18, 2010. The presentation examined the parallels that exist between the warnings about fear of Presidents Roosevelt and Obama in their addresses to the nation. Both presidents were confronting substantial domestic and foreign challenges to the nation, and both were trying to appeal to the nation not to surrender to fear but instead pursue a course of hope. Also included was a discussion of actions undertaken by both presidents that appear to contradict their messages on fear.

"A Manifesto of Power and Ideals: FDR's Four Freedoms Speech in Historical Perspective" by Dr. Ross Kennedy, an associate professor of history at Illinois State University and author of *The Will to Believe: Woodrow Wilson, World War I, and America's Strategy for Peace and Security*, was delivered on March 3, 2010. Dr. Kennedy's contention was that Franklin Roosevelt's Four Freedoms speech had a profound impact on international affairs, directly contributing to Hitler's decision to attack the Soviet Union. The speech also provided a framework for America's national security strategy for the next fifty years.

"Visual Culture and American Modernism in the 1930s and 1940s: Figuration and Abstraction" was presented by Dr. Melissa Johnson, assistant professor of art history at Illinois State University and coordinator of the master's program in Visual Culture Sequence, on April 6, 2010. Her presentation examined Norman Rockwell in the context of American art in the thirties and forties and the interdisciplinary field of visual culture. She also addressed the change in scholars' evaluation of Rockwell, who has historically been seen as "illustrator" rather than an "artist."

WEBSITE

A website was created that included information about the lecture series; curricular teaching resources available online related to FDR's Four Freedoms speech; contact information for tours; and online resources related to the exhibit artists, Four Freedoms speech, and Franklin Delano Roosevelt.[4] The lectures were recorded and made available as podcasts from the site.

THE COLLABORATIVE EXPERIENCE

The authors would like to examine their efforts through the lens of Dr. Dick Raspa and Dane Ward's book, *The Collaborative Imperative: Librarians and Faculty Working Together in the Information Universe*, which describes a truly collaborative relationship, as opposed to mere coordination of efforts. Raspa and Ward highlight their "Five Ps of Collaboration": passion, playfulness, project, persistence, and promotion.[5]

The first two elements, *passion*, and *playfulness*, defined as the "capacity to engage an enterprise deeply—mind, heart, and spirit—all parts of us brought into the action of the moment" will be examined first.[6]

The exhibit grew out of a passion shared at a conference. Kahl and Paterson attended the American Association of State College and Universities' American Democracy Project (ADP) National Meeting in June 2009. The annual conferences focus on efforts by campuses nationwide to encourage the development of civic and political engagement among students. It is a very inspirational environment that focuses on all types of collaborative efforts by faculty and students; campus and community groups; academic and student affairs; and so on.

The conference displayed visually striking, movie-sized posters from the *Thoughts on Democracy* exhibit. ADP's executive director saw the posters during his travels to Florida. ADP contacted the Wolfsonian and found that the images were available for licensing. At a lunch, the authors began discussing how much they enjoyed the posters.

The authors also shared a passion for providing opportunities to students—through academic affairs services and events for Paterson and public library services for Kahl. Furthermore, both understood the importance of offering cocurricular resources by nonacademic units. They both believe colleges and universities should be intentional in creating environments that assist students in their intellectual and personal growth.[7] They shared a commitment to the developing civic engagement skills in our students that were also important to the university. Civic engagement is one of five core values of the university's strategic plan, Educating Illinois:

> Illinois State University prepares students to be informed and engaged citizens who will promote and further the collective goals of society. The University promotes active learning experiences through which students will gain an awareness and understanding of civic engagement as a lifelong responsibility. Furthermore, the University encourages faculty and staff to serve as engaged civic leaders and role models promoting the quality of life for all citizens through collaborative and individual action.[8]

Raspa and Ward's third *P* is the *project* where "participants may contribute their ideas and energies."[9] Both authors wanted to bring the posters to campus. But they quickly realized much more could be offered. They discussed a speaker series that would focus both on artistic themes of the exhibit, as well as the historical and political significance of the works. Previous efforts by the ADP on campus had primarily appealed to the humanities and social sciences. There had not been any programming relating to the fine or performing arts.

The project built upon institutional and personal expertise. The Dean of Students office offers extensive programming, so a student affairs official such as Paterson has experience with program planning, contracting, and vendor relations.

Milner Library had hosted exhibits previously, such as the National Endowment for the Arts' *Forever Free: Abraham Lincoln's Journey to Emancipation*, *Alexander Hamilton: The Man Who Made Modern America*, and *John Adams Unbound*. These exhibits included speakers, curricular materials, and opening receptions. In addition to the exhibits, Milner had been offering extensive speaker series for over a decade and has also displayed pieces from the International Collection of Child Art, housed at ISU.

When Paterson and Kahl sat down at the conference lunch, they knew each other through their work with ADP, but had not worked together professionally in any other context. Despite a similar commitment to helping students and the sharing of a plaza between their two adjoining buildings, there had been little interaction between Milner Library and the Dean of Students office. The two units' limited dealings in the past had not included programming, but centered on the Passages orientation weekend that welcomes students to campus. Milner had provided classroom space and tours to support newly arriving students.

Despite the lack of previous experiences to draw on, Kahl and Paterson's shared passion to bring this exhibit to campus provided an opportunity for the two units to closely work together for the first time. In doing so, they encountered the fourth of Raspa and Ward's five Ps, *persistence*. Raspa and Ward noted that "our institutions are not typically organized to promote collaboration beyond our disciplines."[10] So academic collaborators have to push beyond disciplinary isolation by having "the desire and commitment to find others with whom you can talk and collaborate."[11]

The project required a committed collaborative effort. This collaboration extended beyond Kahl and Paterson by relying on the skills of Milner Library faculty and staff. Milner librarians and staff provided guidance on poster production, the existing library picture hanging system, and outreach to K–12 classes.

The opening reception had a welcome by President Al Bowman and the Dean of University Libraries, Cheryl Elzy, displayed all the posters, and offered forties-themed food and music. The authors relied on the expertise of the Milner Library Public Relations Committee. The committee selected and arranged the catering, music, and equipment rental.

The opening reception and poster production incurred significant expenses. Both authors were able to secure funding through ADP and Friends of Milner Library.

The engaging exhibit and accompanying lectures were examples of the fifth *P, promote*, because they were "initiatives that enhance internal and external communication."[12]

Promotion relied heavily on the expertise, once again, of the Milner Library Public Relations Committee. The committee has been active since

1994 and has developed a well-organized process. An initial planning meeting occurred, and a marketing plan was developed. The meeting reviewed options for marketing and events. The marketing plan highlighted the various options for exposure, including posters, mailings, flyers, signs, digital signage, invitations, and so on. The exhibit website was discussed.

Communication was done both on and off campus. The Public Relations Committee has a mailing list that sends out press releases to campus, Friends of Milner Library members, library staff retirees, local media outlets, and so forth. The exhibit also collaborated with the Teaching with Primary Sources department, whose mailing list reaches over five hundred community K–12 teachers. Announcements were sent via campus Listservs, such as ISU-Teach, which facilitates discussion on teaching and learning, and ISU-CIVICENGAGEMENT, which offers a forum for sharing information about civic engagement. In addition to campus- and community-wide marketing, special attention was paid to inviting target audiences to different portions of the overall program.

The promotion of the event led to an unexpected opportunity. A teacher from a local elementary school read about the exhibit and contacted Kahl. The school had recently asked students to write essays on two of the Four Freedoms. The essays were evaluated by ISU's ROTC cadets, who had been working with the school's students as part of the Cadets Helping Kids program. The winning essays were scanned and displayed on a poster for the last month of the exhibit. The poster was presented to the school at an assembly honoring the essay winners.

LESSONS LEARNED

Based on experience, the following suggestions may be useful to others interested in similar efforts.

- Utilize everyone's expertise. Kahl had a disciplinary background in political science and a lifelong interest in military history, knew the library resources, and had witnessed Milner Library's successful hosting and marketing of exhibits and lecture series. Paterson had the experience reviewing and negotiating contracts and working with local vendors to produce the posters. Librarians and library staff—especially Judy Bee, Maureen Brunsdale, Sarah Dick, Jan Johnson, Kathleen Lonbom, and

Toni Tucker—shared their expertise about exhibits, poster displays, public relations, and working with K–12 classes.

- Determine target audiences and develop marketing materials accordingly. This program was designed to reach multiple audiences—students, faculty, staff, and the Friends of the Milner Library association. It also was being promoted under the auspices of the ADP, which provided some additional marketing opportunities.[13] To reach these various constituencies, a variety of marketing mediums were utilized to capture attention and participation.

- Widely share the program concept with others, and additional ideas and resources will come to you. The unsolicited contact by the elementary teacher concerning her students' essays resulted in the added feature to the exhibit.

- Allow for plenty of lead time for program modifications and enhancement opportunities that emerge. The original program was designed as a poster exhibit. The opportunity to add lectures by faculty and the website with additional information and podcasts and involvement were possible because the exhibit was planned for the following semester rather than rushing to offer it as soon as school started in the fall. Even with this additional planning time, supplementary program ideas, which included having art and composition classes create responsive pieces to the exhibit, taking the exhibit out into the community, and creating a auditory self-guided tour of the exhibit, did not happen because time ran out.

Following the first submission of this chapter, the editors posed the question "Was it truly the luck of sitting next to each other at a lunch and realizing you had a shared interest that resulted in the idea for (and commitment to) a joint program?"

The question is a good one. For many colleagues across the country, this type of collaboration might not have been nearly so easy. Rather than looking to leverage each other's strengths, the authors might have instead been territorial and worried about who would do the work and who would get the credit—or worse yet, not been willing to initiate the conversation at all: a "them versus us" mindset.

Instead, the question reminds the authors that Illinois State University has developed a campus culture of Student Affairs and Academic Affairs frequently collaborating and consistently recognizing each other as partners in the educational process. So whereas on many campuses a joint effort between student affairs and the library may not come to mind automatically or occur easily, at Illinois State it does, and the American Democracy Project framework provided the impetus for this particular collaboration.

Notes

1. Richard Raspa and Dane Ward, *The Collaborative Imperative: Librarians and Faculty Working Together in the Information Universe* (Chicago: Association of College and Research Libraries, 2000).

2. "Educating Illinois," Illinois State University, accessed September 30, 2010, http://educatingillinois.illinoisstate.edu.

3. Abby Johnson, "Passive, Not Aggressive," *Abby the Librarian* (blog), August 12, 2009, http://www.abbythelibrarian.com/2009/08/passive-not-aggressive.html.

4. *Thoughts on Democracy: Reinterpreting Norman Rockwell's Four Freedoms Posters* Exhibit, Milner Library, Illinois State University, accessed January 27, 2012, http://www.mlb.ilstu.edu/tod.

5. Raspa and Ward, *The Collaborative Imperative*, 8.

6. Ibid., 9.

7. Arthur Chickering and Linda Reisser, *Education and Identity*, 2nd ed. (San Francisco: Jossey-Bass, 1993).

8. "Educating Illinois."

9. Raspa and Ward, *The Collaborative Imperative*, 9.

10. Ibid., 8.

11. Ibid.

12. Ibid., 11.

13. "American Democracy Project," Illinois State University, accessed September 30, 2010, http://americandemocracy.illinoisstate.edu.

7
Living, Learning, and Libraries: A Cross-Campus Collaboration

Kathryn M. Crowe, Mary L. Hummel, Jenny Dale, and Rosann Bazirjian

Many colleges and universities have significant numbers of students living in on-campus housing. In addition to overseeing physical facilities, residential life staff provide programming that creates community and supports students' academic, social, and cultural development while living in the residence halls. In this chapter, Crowe, Hummel, Dale, and Bazirjian show the variety of programs that can be developed through a collaboration between residential life and the library and discuss some practical considerations for those interested in initiating a similar collaboration on their own campuses.

The University of North Carolina at Greensboro (UNCG) established one of the first Living Learning Communities (LLCs) in the country, the Warren Ashby Residential College, in 1970. UNCG now hosts eight LLCs, and the university's 2009–14 strategic plan identified expanding LLCs as a means to enhance the educational experience for students. Like most academic libraries, the UNCG University Libraries had a long-standing liaison program with academic departments and programs. In order to communicate more directly with students, the libraries also established formal liaisons to many of the LLCs in 2007. In 2009, UNCG's Student Affairs Division merged with Academic Affairs to report to the Provost. These administrative changes offered new opportunities to enhance the partnership between the libraries and the LLCs.

This chapter functions as a case study that describes an approach in which librarians and student affairs staff successfully collaborated to achieve the goal of expanded LLCs across campus. This collaborative effort began with the strategic planning process, continued with team participation in a national learning communities workshop, and established a variety of services tailored to meet individual program goals. It illustrates the development of best practices through a highly collaborative process. The challenges of applying theory in a practical setting are discussed, including the theoretical framework, staffing models, and specific programmatic efforts. The examples, including those of negotiating these processes in a changing environment, may be generalized to other campuses working toward similar goals.

THE UNIVERSITY OF NORTH CAROLINA AT GREENSBORO

The University of North Carolina at Greensboro, one of seventeen campuses of the University of North Carolina, is a publicly supported Research University with High Research Activity and an enrollment of 14,300 undergraduates and 3,225 graduate students. The Carnegie Corporation also granted UNCG its "Community Engaged Classification" in 2008. With 1,064.50 FTE faculty, UNCG's student /faculty ratio is 17:1. At the present time, 81 percent of freshman and 31 percent of the total undergraduate student body live on campus. Currently, 721 of these students are members of Living Learning Communities. Future plans for the university call for doubling the number of students living in residence halls with a special emphasis on LLCs. The University Libraries at UNCG collaborate actively with Housing and Residence Life and the LLCs to provide and support both academic and cocurricular programming. UNCG librarians also serve on campuswide committees engaged in planning future residence halls and LLCs. Through these partnerships, the University Libraries and Housing and Residence Life have successfully integrated libraries' services and resources with LLC student residents' course work and other activities.

Institutional leaders selected living-learning programs as a means to develop partnerships between academic and student affairs and as a vehicle to create greater student engagement with the institution. Living-learning programs are defined as involving undergraduate students who live together in a discrete portion of a residence hall or the entire hall; having staff and resources dedicated for that program only; and offering participants special academic and/or extracurricular programming designed especially for them.[1] In recent years, a number of national studies were published that highlight the importance of engagement. One is the National Survey of Student Engagement (NSSE), based on the simple premise that the more students do something, the more proficient they become. All of the benchmarks in the study (such as student/faculty interactions and supportive campus environment) can be enhanced through academic/student affairs partnerships in the residence halls.[2] In addition to the NSSE, there is a body of research that discusses how universities create environments to enhance student success.[3]

While these studies describe the ways universities can encourage opportunities for academic achievement and success, living-learning programs in particular are excellent microcosms of these larger principles. The seminal study which illustrates the effects of living-learning programs is the National Study of Living/Learning Programs conducted by principal investigator Karen Inkelas. This study examined multiple typologies of living-learning programs and multiple outcomes on a number of campuses across the country. One key outcome noted that because there is no "one size fits all" model for a campus, different types of programs excel in different ways.[4] UNCG used this finding as the basis to develop multiple models of living-learning programs to meet a variety of needs.

LIVING LEARNING COMMUNITIES AT UNCG

For forty years, UNCG has housed campus LLCs and through them, fostered a strong collaboration between academic and student affairs. The Warren Ashby Residential College (WARC), established in 1970, was among the first of its kind in the nation. It pioneered collaborations by providing on-site classes and faculty offices in the residence hall, academic advising, and a small student-faculty ratio. This coordination was represented in a unique way with a staff position, the Residential College Coordinator (RCC). The coordinator not only teaches several classes in the residential college, but is also responsible for the housing and community-building aspects of the residence hall. These collaborations formed the basis for additional types of linkages through the future partnership with the libraries' services and resources.

In the 1990s, as colleges and universities nationwide increased these types of learning opportunities, UNCG added several new LLCs. While they all share a residential requirement, each has varying degrees of curricular and cocurricular involvement. For example, Cornelia Strong College, modeled on the Harvard University Houses, offers students the chance for more informal interactions with faculty. Grogan College is designed around small groups of first-year students who share common interests and take courses together. More recently, additional programs have emerged spanning the range of transition programs, leadership, community service, and international education. The Reynolds First Year Experience (FYE) Program provides an introduction to the university and social support activities for a group of approximately 140 students living together in a residence hall. UNCG currently hosts a total of eight LLCs, and more are in the planning stages for fall 2011. UNCG adopted a definition for LLCs that includes having an academic component to the program as well as living in contiguous space. Another type of program at UNCG is defined as themed housing, where students live together and focus on developing leadership, communication, and social awareness skills focused on a particular area of interest such as sustainability, entrepreneurship, or health and wellness. These programs help students connect to the academic and cocurricular experience of the university and the greater community.

Expanding LLCs is part of an overall Strategic Housing Plan, adopted by UNCG in 2009, which outlines a philosophy and strategy for doubling on-campus housing over the next ten years.[5] Key strategic directions focus on increasing campus living opportunities, becoming the first-choice living environment of undergraduates at all levels, building on the special attribute of being a strong residential community of common purpose in an urban setting, and enhancing the learning potential of residence hall life. From these directions, four goals were established for housing , two of which relate directly to this collaborative work between LLCs and the libraries. First, because 81 percent of first-year students live on campus, Housing and Residence Life should serve as the "gateway" experience for them. Creating a powerful gateway experience for first-year students and outstanding subsequent experiences for students at all class levels is a critical component of the plan. A second goal is to enrich community life and student learning by providing connections to programs of student engagement and experiential learning. The plan also identifies several core characteristics for all residentially based learning communities:

- Each program is a joint partnership between an academic unit or department and Housing and Residence Life.
- Each program has a unique identity.

- Core learning outcomes are established with active faculty involvement.
- Connections with academic support services such as advising, tutoring, and study groups are established.
- Adequate administrative and financial support is provided.
- Assessment is an integral part of the model.[6]

This plan is based on research that indicates campus living has a positive impact on student retention. At UNCG, there are higher rates of persistence by students who lived on campus their first semester than by their cohorts who lived off campus. This finding is consistent with national data stating the retention impact of residence hall living.[7]

CHANCELLOR'S VISION FOR LIVING LEARNING COMMUNITIES

The Strategic Housing Plan is based on the university's strategic plan. Shortly after Chancellor Linda Brady arrived in fall 2008, UNCG embarked on strategic planning for 2009–14.[8] Writing the new plan was an inclusive, university-wide process with numerous committees structured around specific themes and strategic areas. Much of the plan was based upon the vision of the UNC Tomorrow Commission,[9] created by University of North Carolina then-President Erskine Bowles in the effort to make the university system more responsive to the needs of North Carolina citizens.

UNCG's new strategic plan focuses on the importance of student success with an emphasis on student retention and graduation rates. This dynamic document also stresses the importance of creating more meaningful connections between learning inside and outside of the classroom and collaboration. One strategic area, education and leadership, includes the goal "Implement first-year learning communities for all first-time UNCG undergraduate students to encourage integration of learning across courses."[10] The university defines a learning community as a curricular and interactive entity that enhances student success (learning, development, retention, and persistence) and also assists in recruiting quality students. It brings faculty, students, and staff together in a focused academic community organized around a thematic central thread that is intellectually attractive to all participants. The chancellor views the development of LLCs as a partnership between academic, business, and student affairs. She also recommended that UNCG consider adding one in-residence faculty or postdoc for each new residence hall. To accomplish this goal, a broadly representative committee was appointed to establish additional LLCs across campus. That committee included two faculty members from the libraries.

As noted in the Strategic Housing Plan, the chancellor also calls for UNCG to increase the number of students living on campus and plans to add several new residence halls in the coming years. As the university embarks on these construction projects, as well as the renovation of older residential halls, she sees the opportunity to integrate living and learning by challenging the campus community to think creatively about defining mixed-use spaces. She wants to be certain that plans for new and renovated housing facilities include models for LLCs and stresses the impact of LLCs on retention and graduation rates. She encouraged the committee to think about programming such as theme-based residence halls, where upper-class students in different majors could live and study around an interest in a specific theme— for example, sustainability, entrepreneurship, music and performing arts, or global business. Learning communities should also include integrative learning assignments, cocurricular activities, and faculty engagement beyond the classroom.

It is the chancellor's vision to provide a campus environment where as many students as possible belong to a community and where all first-year students are part of a learning community. Combining the benefits of learning communities with the academic path of students expands their educational experience and furthers their sense of belonging. This vision also provides for an enhanced role for faculty and academic affairs to participate in housing and residence life and is part of an overall university restructuring. In January 2010, Academic Affairs and Student Affairs combined to report to the provost in the effort "to better ensure the work of faculty within Academic Affairs and the work of Student Affairs professional—supporting the success of our students as partners—is better integrated to enhance services for our students."[11]

THE STRATEGIC PLAN AND THE SUMMER INSTITUTE

The University Libraries were heavily involved in the strategic planning committee tasked with establishing LLCs across campus. All the academic deans were required to chair planning committees and the libraries' dean served as cochair of this one along with the dean of undergraduate studies. The libraries' First-Year Instruction Coordinator was also a member of this planning committee. In regular meetings throughout 2010, this committee engaged in planning for the practical implementation of the chancellor's vision for LLCs across campus.

An integral part of this process was UNCG's participation in the Washington Center's 2010 National Summer Institute on Learning Communities, an intensive four-day institute during which campus teams develop an action plan for creating new or enriching existing learning community programs.[12] An eight-member team was appointed to represent UNCG, with members from various campus units. The libraries' First-Year Instruction Coordinator was part of the team and played a role in the development of the action plan, further strengthening the libraries' role in the initiative. The action plan developed at the institute and revised upon consultation with the larger strategic plan implementation committee includes a learning community proposal plan for interested faculty, a timeline for implementation and assessment of learning communities on campus, and a series of workshops to engage faculty and staff in discussions about learning community development.

While action plan development was the primary goal of the National Summer Institute, large-group discussions and breakout sessions were also an integral part of the experience. Topics covered ranged from student learning to faculty development, with a recurring theme being integrative learning and its place in learning community models. Integrative learning can take place within the curriculum, as interdisciplinary work or integrative assignments across linked courses, or in a cocurricular setting, with learning experiences outside of the classroom or the campus.

The Association of American Colleges and Universities (AAC&U) and the Carnegie Foundation for the Advancement of Teaching issued a statement on integrative learning in 2004, encouraging educators to "work together to build knowledge about integrative learning in its many varieties, and about how it is best encouraged and assessed."[13] AAC&U provides a rubric for assessing integrative learning, with criteria including making connections between academic content and experience, making connections across subject or disciplinary lines, applying knowledge in different settings or situations, "integrated communication," and self-reflection.[14] The AAC&U and the Carnegie Foundation statement recognizes learning communities as one type of space in which integrative learning can take place, and there has been significant talk on UNCG's campus about the importance of integrative learning experiences for students participating in planned LCs and LLCs. The libraries are uniquely positioned to support integrative learning in both curricular and cocurricular settings. In their more traditional public service and information literacy role, librarians assist students with integrative assignments and interdisciplinary work by providing instruction sessions, research assistance, and in-depth consultations. As liaisons to student affairs units, librarians can also have a presence in the cocurricular aspects of learning community life.

UNIVERSITY LIBRARIES AND THE LIVING LEARNING COMMUNITIES

Having library liaisons to academic departments is an established model in academic libraries. In 2007, the UNCG libraries applied this concept to other units on campus and developed a liaison program that assigns librarians to student organizations and offices as part of its Student Affairs Connection program, which also includes a Student Libraries Advisory Council and special events. The goals of the liaison program are to market libraries' services and resources directly to students, improve communication, and learn about particular student needs. The program fulfills one of the libraries' established public services goals, "connect with UNCG student, academic and administrative units to integrate the Libraries with the curriculum and student life."[15] Because of this goal, the liaison program has strong support from the libraries' dean and the Associate Dean for Public Services. Liaisons work with their units in a variety of ways, with involvement depending on the organization. They communicate with leaders and directors, meet with key staff, and attend lectures, meetings, and social events. New libraries' services and resources are advertised through e-mails sent to liaisons' contacts, who then forward them to their students. Several liaisons provide relevant programming, some of which is academic in nature, such as plagiarism workshops or information literacy sessions for courses in the LLCs. Others offer informal informational sessions such as presentations to student athletes or student government about libraries' services and resources. Liaisons also make presentations to staff of units such as the Student Success Center and Residence Life so that they are aware of appropriate times to refer students to the libraries. The Student Affairs Connection program provides many opportunities for collaboration within the libraries and across campus. Academic libraries' traditional student interactions are through information literacy sessions and research assistance, but

Student Affairs Connection has enabled UNCG librarians to reach students in new and different settings and promote resources and services more effectively. Getting to know students better and being a part of their organizations is an added bonus. The program has also enhanced the libraries' collaboration with colleagues in student affairs and student services offices.

Since the liaison program began, the libraries were especially active with Housing and Residence Life and the LLCs, providing both academic and cocurricular programming. Some librarians provide introductory library sessions for UNS 101, UNCG's one-hour transition to college course, as well as information literacy sessions for upper-level courses. Two librarians taught a semester-long section of UNS 101 reserved for students in the First Year Experience LLC during fall 2010. Librarians also participate in House Calls, a program where each first-year residence hall student is visited by a faculty or staff member during the first week of the fall semester to welcome him or her and provide a bag of resource materials. One librarian was a faculty fellow in Strong College for many years and built on that relationship through the liaison program. Liaisons provide satellite reference service in the residence halls as well as individual consultation services. On a lighter note, they've served as judges in various contests and attend social events to get to know students and other faculty in the community.

The libraries saw the increased emphasis on LLCs in the 2009–14 UNCG strategic plan as an opportunity to augment their relationship with the LLCs. Liaison assignments were expanded to all LLCs, and liaisons met in summer 2010 to set specific outcomes for the following academic year:

- Library liaisons to the LLCs will increase contact and embed further with their communities in order to establish closer communication and to ensure that students utilize the libraries' resources and services. Contact may be whatever is appropriate for the community and may include, but not be limited to, office hours, information literacy classes, UNS 101–type courses, training student peer mentors, and general programs.

- Liaisons will gather data such as number of questions asked, hours on site, classes, program attendance, and student feedback.

- Data will be collected at the end of the academic year and a report developed. We might hold a summit with the LLCs or participate in a program already happening to report our results.

CAMPUS COLLABORATIONS: LLC CASE STUDIES

The Warren Ashby Residential College (WARC) appointed a new director beginning in fall 2010 who is very enthusiastic about strengthening its relationship with the libraries. The libraries' liaison to WARC established regular office hours in the residence with an average of four hours a week and more during peak times. She also joined regular staff meetings and worked to integrate information literacy into the curriculum. A WARC student assistant was identified as the Ashby Residential College Library Representative to serve as a peer consultant and is funded by the libraries for ten hours a week. The representative was trained by the libraries' liaison to WARC. Training included shadowing at the reference desk and liaison office hours as well as one-on-one instruction in basic library resources. The goal for the peer consultant is to embed in the LLC and to serve as a primary communication link between WARC students and the libraries. She also serves as the "first responder"—she can be in-house for those 2:00 a.m. paper panics! To track her work and help assess the success of a peer consultant, she recorded her work and the questions received in a Google form. This pilot program had a successful start and will serve as a model for future LLCs.

A new LLC established in 2010 was a residential component of the Lloyd International Honors College. The honors program was established in 1947 and the honors college in 2006. In fall 2010, 150 honors students moved into a newly renovated residence hall. A specific office space was identified for the libraries' liaison to hold regular office hours of one to three hours a week depending on the time of the semester. The liaison also worked with the eight UNS 101 sections called Proseminars. Also, a libraries' touch screen is installed in a common area of the LLC with access to the library catalog, AskUs, hours, and other information.

The libraries have a long history of supporting first-year student success at UNCG. This support has traditionally been academic and has been the role of the First-Year Instruction Coordinator, who coordinates outreach and instruction efforts for traditional first-year classes like English 101 and University Studies 101. While the creation of the First-Year Instruction Coordinator position predates the Student Affairs Connection program by over ten years, the increased focus on outreach expanded this position's role to include partnerships with campus units beyond the traditional academic departments. First-year LLC programs were a logical place to expand library services, with their academic and cocurricular components. The First-Year Instruction Coordinator serves as liaison to two first-year LLC programs on our campus: Grogan College and First Year Experience. To provide research and academic support, the First-Year Instruction Coordinator holds office hours on-site in the residence halls housing the First Year Experience and Grogan LLCs during peak research times. She also works closely with the University Studies courses (UNS 101 and UNS 105) associated with these programs, providing tours and research instruction. With the increased focus on learning communities for first-year students on UNCG's campus, the liaison to first-year LLC programs is currently working with coordinators of these programs to increase outreach. More office hours and research clinics are also planned with both of these first-year programs. In addition to these academic pursuits, the libraries hosted a "library mystery night" with Grogan College, which required creative use of library resources to solve a mystery.

GUIDING PRINCIPLES

Through this work with several program initiatives, overarching guiding principles were created which provide a framework for institutions considering these types of collaborations. These principles provide important checkpoints at the beginning of a collaboration and at key points along the way:

- Partners must commit staff time to work on a collaboration in a unique arrangement. With the variety of demands on both student affairs and librarians' time, each partner's supervisor must value the work and see it as a productive use of time. In addition, embracing the differences in work setting, hours, and delivery methods is a critical aspect of success.

- Senior leadership's support of and commitment to collaboration between student and academic affairs in key messages to the campus community and through reward and recognition systems is important for a sustained collaboration to continue to thrive. Inclusion in strategic plans, keynote addresses, and marketing materials are examples of this type of commitment.

UNCG exhibited a strong commitment to LLCs by appointing a director of LLCs during the 2010–11 academic year.

- While resources between and among units can be pooled to create opportunities for new programmatic efforts, it is both an important message and statement of ongoing commitment to provide specific funds for staff, programs, and operation needs for collaborative projects. For example, specific internal grants can be established and request-for-proposal processes created to encourage new programs to develop. It will be important to be creative and consider different revenue streams to provide funds for these programs.

- In considering the ongoing efforts, it is important to put systems in place so that the collaborations can grow and be sustained beyond an individual's passion for the particular projects. This integration into the culture of an institution is perhaps the most challenging of the principles to put into practice

- The programs and resources created should complement the student experiences in ways that are consistent with the university's mission, academic goals, and cocurricular opportunities. Involving students and faculty in the program development of these collaborations is key to the sustainability of the efforts.

- Clear learning outcomes should be established at the beginning of the project. A method of assessment should also be outlined at the outset and a timetable for measurement detailed.

LESSONS LEARNED AND RECOMMENDATIONS FOR THE FUTURE

Much has been documented in the literature about the differences in culture between academic and student affairs. For example, faculty are rewarded for independent work, with strong allegiance to their discipline, and allowed to be institutional critics with the protection of tenure. Student affairs staff often enter the field to work with a student community and get involved with the larger campus and value collaboration with less allegiance to a discipline. They are not protected by tenure and therefore can appear to be more accepting of the status quo. With limited resources and potentially competing needs, these different cultures could lead to challenges. However, what is emerging is a new interest in student learning and collaboration focused on an emphasis on undergraduate education and retention. At the same time, residence halls are no longer thought of as just facilities. Instead, they are now considered part of the educational experience by combining academic and cocurricular activities. When faculty and staff from different professional cultures come together, there are always lessons to be learned!

As the University Libraries developed the liaison relationships with campus LLCs through the Student Affairs Connections program, it became apparent that there is no one-size-fits-all approach to providing outreach to learning communities. For instance, the relationship with WARC changed significantly with the appointment of its new director and her keen interest in working with the libraries. The WARC liaison saw an increase in opportunities for involvement with the community and is now considered an integral part of its staff. The libraries were also involved in the new residential program for the Lloyd International Honors College from the early planning stages, which helped cement our collaboration with it. The initial semester provided some good lessons and fine-tuning for the future. It turned out, for example, that the office hours scheduled both in WARC and Honors College were not convenient for students, so they were revised.

This close involvement, however, is not as good a fit for some of the other learning communities. For instance, liaisons to the first-year LLCs have learned that office hours in the residence halls met with varied success. Timing plays a critical role in these cases—office hours should be established at times with plenty of traffic in and out of the residence hall, but also must be planned at points in the semester when students tend to be working on research and writing assignments. Library tours and research instruction tend to be more consistently successful with first-year LLCs. Newer initiatives, such as the library mystery night and more structured research clinics provided as part of the existing LLC programming structure, will include opportunities for student and LLC staff evaluation and feedback.

Because UNCG's strategic plan calls for a learning community program that permeates campus life, the libraries' role will likely expand and change. Assessment data from current initiatives will inform plans and decisions. As the number of communities increases, a reevaluation of the liaison structure may be necessary and discussions of scalability of programs will certainly be needed. As mentioned above, we hope the peer consultant pilot with WARC will prove to be a successful model that can be adapted for other learning communities. It may also be necessary to hire or designate a learning communities librarian to coordinate outreach efforts. Whatever the future holds, a collaboration has been established between an academic and student affairs unit that has contributed to enhancing student success at UNCG, and we look forward to building and growing this important partnership.

Notes

1. Karen Kurotsuchi Inkelas, "Living and Learning Together: Results from the 2004 National Study on Living-Learning Programs," (plenary session, 8th Conference on Living-Learning Programs and Residential Colleges, Indiana University Bloomington, November 15–17, 2004), 2, http://www.livelearnstudy.net/images/LLRC_plenary_address.pdf.

2. National Survey of Student Engagement, "Summary Statistics—National Benchmarks of Effective Educational Practice," in *Converting Data into Action: Expanding the Boundaries of Institutional Improvement,* annual report (Bloomington: Indiana University, Center for Postsecondary Research and Planning, 2003), http://nsse.iub.edu/2003_annual_report.

3. See, for example, Alexander W. Astin, *What Matters in College? Four Critical Years Revisited* (San Francisco: Jossey-Bass, 1993); George Kuh et al., *Student Success in College: Creating Conditions That Matter* (San Francisco: Jossey-Bass, 2005); Ernest T. Pascarella and Patrick T. Terenzini, *How College Affects Students: A Third Decade of Research,* vol. 2 (San Francisco: Jossey-Bass. 2005).

4. Karen Kurotsuchi Inkelas and Susan Longerbeam, "Working toward a Comprehensive Typology of Living/Learning Programs," in *Learning Initiatives in the Residential Setting,* First-Year Experience Monograph Series no. 48, edited by Gene Luna and Jimmie Gahagan (Columbia: University of South Carolina, National Resource Center for the First-Year Experience and Students in Transition, 2008), 29–42, ERIC document ED503178.

5. Department of Housing and Residential Life, *UNCG Strategic Housing Plan 2020* (Greensboro: University of North Carolina at Greensboro, 2009), http://hrl.uncg.edu/about_us/pdfs/housing_plan_2020.pdf.

6. Ibid.

7. Pascarella and Terenzini, *How College Affects Students,* 422–23.

8. "Strategic Plan, 2009–2014," University of North Carolina at Greensboro,

September 29, 2009, http://uncgtomorrow.uncg.edu/plan/UNCG_
StrategicPlan_2009-2014.pdf.

9. University of North Carolina Tomorrow Commission, *Final Report* (Chapel Hill, University of North Carolina, 2007), http://www.northcarolina.edu/nctomor-row/reports/commission/Final_Report.pdf.

10. "Strategic Plan," 3.

11. University of North Carolina at Greensboro, Minutes of the Faculty Senate Meeting, October 7, 2009, 2, http://facsen.uncg.edu/Content/Minutes/y-%20%20%20Faculty%20Senate%20Mintues,%20Oct%207,%202009.pdf.

12. See "2010 Summer Institute on Learning Communities," Washington Center for Improving the Quality of Undergraduate Education, http://www.evergreen.edu/washcenter/eventInfo.asp?eid=447.

13. "A Statement on Integrative Learning," Association of American Colleges and Universities and The Carnegie Foundation for the Advancement of Teaching, March 2004, http://www.aacu.org/integrative_learning/pdfs/ILP_Statement.pdf.

14. "Integrative Learning VALUE Rubric," Association of American Colleges and Universities, 2009, http://www.aacu.org/value/rubrics/pdf/integrativelearning.pdf.

15. "Public Services Mission Statement and Goals," University of North Carolina Greensboro University Libraries, accessed July 21, 2011, http://library.uncg.edu/services/public_services.aspx.

8

Career Center and Library Collaborations: Preparing Students for Employment in the Twenty-First Century Workplace

Connie Scott and Cindy Price Verduce

One benefit of collaboration is that both partners improve their understanding of what the other department has to offer. Scott and Verduce illustrate how collaborative work between a library and a career center resulted in improved collections and valuable programming as well as an increased awareness of one another's resources and services that has fostered crossreferrals of students.

Long before CareerBuilder.com or Monster, libraries and career centers have been indispensable departments for job seekers on college campuses. At Indiana Tech, the McMillen Library and the Career Planning and Development Center have partnered to prepare learners at various career levels for the global future, helping students gain important career-information-literacy skills based on the Association of College and Research Libraries (ACRL) *Information Literacy Competency Standards for Higher Education.*[1] Students use these skills for career planning and exploration, during the job search process, and to gain an understanding of the importance and use of information in their chosen career.

Leading this trend at Indiana Tech's Fort Wayne campus, McMillen Library director Connie Scott and career center director Cindy Price Verduce have developed and grown their collaborations over the past two years, institutionalizing the work between the departments and reaping benefits for both. Both Scott and Verduce recognize that today's employers desire information-literate graduates—employees who can competently navigate knowledge in its various forms. This chapter will focus on how Scott and Verduce have begun to redefine each of their respective units through collaboration and synergy.

INDIANA TECH AT A GLANCE

Founded near downtown Fort Wayne in 1930 and located on 42 acres, Indiana Tech is a private, independent, and nondenominational university. Its mission is to provide learners of all ages with a career-focused, professional education in the areas of business, computer studies, engineering, criminal sciences, and general studies. The mission is tied directly to preparing students for the world of work, where career-information-literacy skills are essential for success in all arenas. Indiana Tech's mission is also focused on preparing students for active participation in the complex global society of the twenty-first century, and again, information literacy skills are necessary if students are going to succeed in the global marketplace. The university offers diverse programs for the student populations, which include traditional, adult professional, and military students. Indiana Tech also has campuses in Elkhart and Indianapolis, with additional sites throughout the state.

The career center, established in 2004 with support and assistance from the Lilly Endowment, provides advising, programs, and activities related to self-assessment, career exploration, and job search preparation. The McMillen Library, originally built in 1962, offers over thirty thousand volumes of resources with twenty-one computer workstations and two study rooms. Both departments are located in the state-of-the-art two-story Andorfer Commons, which was erected in 2004, and both departments operate with small staffs and employ student interns and workers to assist them in reaching their goals.

CAREER INFORMATION LITERACY AND ITS IMPORTANCE

Information literacy, as defined by the ACRL, "is the set of skills needed to find, retrieve, analyze, and use information."[2] ACRL provides five standards with performance indicators and learning outcomes. In brief, these standards are to know how to access, evaluate, use, and understand the ethical, legal, and social issues of information; these standards can be applied across a broad range academic disciplines.

But why is information literacy so important, especially to collaborations between the libraries and career centers? Career center professionals, like their library counterparts, recognize that these basic skills are essential to the job search and on-the-job success. So how can libraries collaborate with career centers to assist our students in developing these needed skills for success? In "Working with Wisdom: Collaboration between Career Services and University Libraries," Paula Quenoy and Elizabeth Orgeron sum up the consensus they see in the professional literature: succinctly outline the dominant theme found in the literature: "Collaboration between career services and libraries strengthens the quality of services for each entity and provides greater access to information for students."[3] At Indiana Tech, Scott and Verduce have created programs and opportunities for Tech students to develop career-information-literacy skills, both in the job search process and on the job.

As many academic libraries incorporate information literacy skills within the curriculum or as part of instructional services, career centers are beginning to see the implications for their students in this growing practice. How can our students steer through an immense volume of information in the career exploration and job search processes? How can they find accurate information on salary ranges in a given field or the latest trends in emerging technologies? How can they ascertain the true financial health of a potential employer or the impact of current affairs on certain sector job markets (e.g., available jobs on Wall Street after the banking bailouts)? All in all, there is a vast amount of information available to our students for career-related decision making.

Many institutions are joining the cause for career-related information literacy. In its "Five Reasons Why: Information Literacy throughout the Curriculum," Woodbury University Library lists three reasons why information literacy is necessary in the workplace:

- Information literacy is one of six essential functional skills identified by the US Department of Labor Secretary's Commission on Achieving Necessary Skills (SCANS) report.[4]

- Employees without adequate information skills have negative impacts on business.[5]

- Peter Drucker says so: "The data users, whether executive or professional, have to decide what information to use, what to use it for and how to use it. They have to make themselves information-literate."[6]

CREATING THE RAY BROSHAR CAREER RESOURCE CENTER

In order to prepare students for employment in the twenty-first-century workplace and help them develop career-related information literacy skills, Verduce and Scott have coordinated several services and events. Their first collaboration was organizing a combined career resources collection in the library. The library's initial collection was small and spread throughout the library according to classification designation. There were a small number of resume and interview books, along with a few personality assessment titles, but no graduate school materials.

When Verduce initially approached Scott about creating a separate career resources section, Scott was hesitant. As a thinker working in a lean, fast-paced institution, Scott needed to step back and ascertain the obstacles and options of such a request. Scott also needed to communicate to Verduce the impact of rearranging shelves and reallocating space to create a separate "pocket collection," similar to those found in retail bookstores. Logistics, manpower, and cataloging changes would also affect the arrangement. In addition, there was limited funding to build a collection. What helped Scott change her mind was the acquisition of the career center's existing collection and seeking donors and grants to help sustain the collection.

When all the career-related materials formerly held in the career center merged with the library's collection, thereby eliminating duplication of resources, the collection grew from a few dozen titles to nearly one hundred volumes. In spring 2008, Ray Broshar, a 1968 civil engineering alum and engaged advocate for the career center, generously donated the needed funds to get the project off the ground. Scott's seeming indecisiveness was not a stalemate or ego-driven issue, but an opportunity for her and Verduce to further learn one another's personalities and management styles, an important element in creating such partnerships. Both were committed to the project and operated from complementary perspectives. Efficiency coupled with effectiveness resulted in a collection that jumpstarted student interest and campus community awareness of the collaboration.

Although the collection is housed in the library, the two departments continue to collaborate on developing and supporting the collection. The career center supplies and maintains a variety of handouts, articles, publications, and job search guides. For example, the National Association of Colleges & Employers' *Job Choices* annual magazines are available for students to take home for their own personal use. In addition to print titles, the library subscribes to two electronic book databases and five journal databases that offer career-related links. Armed with a vast array of information on every aspect of career exploration and job search skills and strategies, the career center has a great deal of content for student use, and it uses the Ray Broshar Career Resource Center as a vehicle to push this content to students.

FOSTERING INTERDEPARTMENTAL KNOWLEDGE AND REFERRALS

One unintended but valuable spin-off of this particular collaboration has been the reciprocal referrals both departments have seen in the past few years. Taking advantage of being located in the same building, the library and career center staffs have the ability to direct students to the resources of both departments. Career center staff members have made it a priority at the end of advising sessions to literally walk students down to the library to introduce them to the Ray Broshar Career Resource Center and suggest particular resources for use. They may recommend a certain book, give out graduate school guides, or in general introduce students to the resources available to them in the library.

In turn, as library staff members are approached by students for information on career-related questions, they direct students to the career center for additional assistance beyond what is available in the library. In addition, as librarians use the reference interview to explore a variety of inquiries, these interactions have uncovered needs such as information about time-management skills, personality type, and internship opportunities that are best handled by a referral to the career center professionals.

Next in the process, Verduce and Scott sought to educate and train both of their staffs on the services offered by both. Quenony and Orgeron write, "The consensus among all of the literature is that the presence of career service literacy among library personnel and career professionals well versed in library services may be 'the key component in service provision for career and job seekers.'"[7] Seeing the benefits, each staff gained a better understanding of the work of the other and came to the understanding that students, uneducated on the resources or services of either department, might be better served when each department shares not only its own resources, but also those of the other department as well. To do this, we had to be innovative, open-minded, and nonterritorial. Both departments were pleased to engage the students and direct them to the other department for additional assistance, a win-win for both departments and students alike.

In part because of these reciprocal referrals, both departments have experienced an increase in student traffic. In the 2009–10 academic year, the career center experienced a 47 percent increase in the number of one-on-one student appointments and a 55 percent increase in the amount of e-mail correspondence, the primary method of contact by students on many of Tech's satellite campuses. The McMillen Library has also shown significant increases in public services and database usage. Overall, comparative statistics for the 2009–10 academic year have shown a 58 percent increase in one-on-one reference assistance. Electronic book usage has increased by 92 percent, and database usage, including the popular databases EBSCOhost and ProQuest, have shown an 18 percent increase. Although circulation statistics have decreased by 66 percent, online, walk-in, and phone services numbers demonstrate the value of professionals in a seemingly highly technological and self-service environment.

PARTNERSHIP: PROGRAM DEVELOPMENT AND GROWTH

As the collaboration continued to grow, Scott and Verduce expanded their interactions to develop several unique programs. Some of the programming efforts have included hosting psychology internship presentations in the library café area and holding mock interviews in the library meeting rooms; the departments have plans for cosponsoring Breakfast with Santa, where career center personnel have an opportunity to educate student-parents on their services while their children enjoy breakfast with Santa. Holding these events has acquainted students with the library, and they have become more familiar with career center–sponsored events, again, a win-win for both departments.

In addition, the departments have collaborated to promote events sponsored by the career center, including American Business Women's Day, Mock Interview Days, Graduate School Club, and the biannual Etiquette Dinner.

Library staff members create displays of materials related to the event, resulting in publicity for the event and increased awareness of books, periodicals, and other materials related to the subject. For example, the American Business Women's Day luncheon display included a significant number of books and magazines on the topic of women in business, the glass ceiling, women as entrepreneurs, and women as managers, to name just a few. By continually promoting relevant programming, the library can highlight materials in its collection while supporting and partnering with the career center.

Another way the two departments collaborate is through crosspromotion of printed materials, including newsletters and flyers. Having career center materials available to students in the library means that students who visit the library for academic resources can be engaged unintentionally or introduced to some of the services offered in the career center. As students visit the career center, staff members are able to update students on the most recent additions to the library, especially new databases, books, and other resources highlighted in the library's newsletters, e-mail communications, and online resources. Through their shared resources, the development of joint programs, and an emphasis on career information literacy, these two departments are helping students prepare for active participation in the complex global society of the twenty-first century.

TAKING IT TO THE NEXT LEVEL
While the traditional emphasis has been on reciprocal sharing, the two departments together recently created activities for students to actively engage in career information literacy. During the career center's Career Leadership Institute weeks, students were led through a weeklong set of activities geared toward learning more about the skills necessary in the job search process and opportunities to practice those skills, including career information literacy. In addition to career information literacy, topics focused on varying aspects of career preparation, such as professional dress, resume reviews, mock interviews, and etiquette.

As part of the week's activities, McMillen Library reference librarians provided sessions on various aspects of career information literacy, including researching companies (for the College of Business); investigating graduate school resources (for the College of General Studies); and researching industry trends (for the College of Engineering and School of Computer Science). These activities also served to introduce students to the various databases and research options. Completion of the assignments was not the goal of these sessions; rather, the goal was to raise students' awareness and foster those "aha" moments in which students understand why they need career information-literacy skills in hopes that they will follow up with library or career center staff members for more information. It is through these types of collaborations that we hope our students will come to see the value of career information-literacy skills and seek more information as to how to gain these skills.

BENEFITS OF THE COLLABORATION: COOPERATION AND UNDERSTANDING

A final benefit to both departments has been increased understanding of one another's field. Library staff have shared information on the ever-changing field of library science. Scott has provided the career center with postings for library job openings and helped career center staff understand the characteristics of the "new librarians of the twenty-first century." Library staff have assisted the career center staff in better understanding how the field of library and information science continues to change and how to identify which personality types might be drawn to the field, and provided information on scholarships and fellowships, which allows career center staff to have the most current and up-to-date information available. With this information, the career center staff are better able to advise students on the various career paths offered to those with MLS/MLIS degrees.

Career center staff have also shared their expertise of the field and presented tours of their department. This exchange has helped the librarians and staff to become more familiar with career professional resources such as journals and association materials. Collection development librarians regularly review for career-related acquisitions along with those for the standard academic programs, often with suggestions from career center staff. It also has been an opportunity for library staff to discover that there is another department on campus that serves all students, including the military and international populations. Finally, the partnership gave staff a firsthand view of the process of departmental alignment that supports the mission and vision of the university.

LESSONS LEARNED

Scott and Verduce initially connected through a shared love of reading and research. In Indiana Tech's atmosphere of continuous improvement and relationship-based education, the authors found it easy to cooperate around ideas that embraced student success. At the same time, the authors have identified qualities beyond personal traits and this setting that led to their successful collaborative process and that can be emulated by others interested in a similar collaboration.

In order to work collaboratively, professionals in libraries and career centers need to demonstrate

- flexible thinking
- commitment
- motivation
- a positive attitude
- identification of complementary leadership skills
- a defined plan of action
- open communication
- creative brainstorming
- passion connected to a shared mission

The following tips will also assist in forming an authentic career center and library collaboration:

- Discuss roles and define expectations of each unit so that each is aware of the other's situation. In this collaboration, both parties were aware of their overall responsibilities; however, discussion about specific roles helped determine how to function in those roles. To foster clear communication, openly discuss any concerns, such as Scott's aforementioned hesitation related to managerial issues.

- Discuss similarities, perceived differences, and mutual benefits. Verduce's high energy level proved indispensible when describing the departments' similarities, while Scott identified differences, both of which helped to create mutual change.

- As the collaboration grows and involves others, develop a communication network so that others have an opportunity to share ideas openly and implement change effectively and efficiently. In order to work as a team, each department demonstrated

respect for the other's profession and remembered the importance of listening skills; these built trust so that misunderstandings or differences were addressed for the benefit of students.

- Think outside the box and take calculated risks. Both authors
  had prior experience working in organizations that encouraged
  vision casting and risk taking, so they were enthusiastic about
  trying new tactics in their current positions.

- Get buy-in from administrators and other stakeholders by telling your story well. Both authors freely and informally shared
  information with faculty and staff, but it was only after receiving the initial alumnus donation that the story began to unfold.
  Verduce, along with the university's Institutional Advancement
  Office, planned a public relations event that was attended by
  key personnel. The addition of university publications, print
  and electronic, also helped promote visibility.

- Plan strategically and realistically for budget, resources, and
  services. In retrospect, Scott and Verduce admit there was little
  planning in their collaborations. While the lack of a formal
  plan was not a deterrent to initial success, as the collaboration
  expands, a formal strategic plan is highly recommended.

- Record, evaluate, and assess collaborative efforts!

FUTURE OUTLOOK

The process of collaboration came about because both Scott and Verduce
are natural collaborators and actively seek out opportunities in the midst of
innovative change. Both departments provide services to the entire university
and are part of the academic team, with both reporting to the Vice President
of Academic Affairs. The authors easily connected through a shared love
of reading and research, and in Indiana Tech's atmosphere of continuous
improvement and relationship-based education, Scott and Verduce found it
easy to cooperate with an ideas-oriented mindset that embraced student success. Opportunities may present themselves to identify more formal learning experiences as this collaboration grows and influences other departments

to the benefits of collaboration. Assessment and evaluation will help create future programs and a bright future at Indiana Tech for continued collaborations between the library and career center.

Notes

1. Association of College and Research Libraries, *Information Literacy Competency Standards for Higher Education* (Chicago: ACRL, 2000), accessed December 9, 2009, http://www.ala.org/ala/mgrps/divs/acrl/standards/standards.pdf.

2. "Introduction to Information Literacy," Association of College and Research Libraries, accessed October 30, 2010, http://www.ala.org/acrl/issues/infolit/overview/intro.

3. Paula Quenoy and Elizabeth Orgeron, "Working with Wisdom: Collaboration between Career Services and University Libraries" (paper presented at the, ACRL 11th National Conference, Charlotte, NC, April 10–13, 2003), 1, http://www.ala.org/acrl/files/conferences/pdf/orgeron.pdf.

4. Deborah Whetzel, "The Secretary of Labor's Commission on Achieving Necessary Skills: ERIC Digest," ED339749, March 1992, accessed January 31, 2011, http://www.eric.ed.gov/PDFS/ED339749.pdf, cited in "Five Reasons Why: Information Literacy throughout the Curriculum" Woodbury University Library, accessed December 4, 2009, http://web3.woodbury.edu/library/infolit/five_reasons_why.pdf.

5. Bonnie Cheuk Wai-Yi and Arthur Anderson, "Information Literacy in the Workplace Context: Issues, Best Practices and Challenges" 2002, cited in "Five Reasons Why: Information Literacy throughout the Curriculum" Woodbury University Library, accessed December 4, 2009, http://web3.woodbury.edu/library/infolit/five_reasons_why.pdf.

6. Peter Drucker, "Be Data Literate," *Wall Street Journal*, December 3, 1992, http://online.wsj.com/article/SB113208395700897890.html#mod=2_1194_1, quoted in "Five Reasons Why."

7. Quenoy and Orgeron, "Working with Wisdom," 2, quoting Dominique Mikulec, "Career Information Centers in Libraries: Measurement of Services Awareness" (master's research paper, Kent State University, 1999).

9

A Stress-Free Collaboration: The University of Lethbridge Students' Union and the University Library Partner to Deliver a "Stress-Free Zone" to Students during Final Exams

Nicole Eva and Jeremy Girard

Many institutions struggle with tight financial resources, and libraries may abandon ideas for student-oriented programs due to budgetary concerns. Student affairs departments typically have funds designated for student-oriented programming and may be able to use those funds to support the work of outside departments. In this article, Eva and Girard describe the creation of a "stress-free zone" to support students during exams and show how libraries and student affairs can pool financial resources in support of innovative programs and services.

The University of Lethbridge Library partnered with the University of Lethbridge Students' Union to provide a "stress-free zone" for students during exam times. The pilot project occurred during the December 2009 final exam period and was a resounding success, leading to its recurrence during the April 2010 final exams. The zone was a room in the library in which students could take a study break, have a coffee and snack, play games, watch movies, and "chill out." It was open from 7:00 to 11:00 p.m. for the duration of the final exam period. The students' union supported the venture with a cash donation towards healthy snacks, which the library used to purchase fruit and granola bars. The zone was well-used by students, and many comments of appreciation were received. Other partnerships across campus were utilized: coffee and tea was donated by food services, the campus massage therapist donated his time on a couple of evenings, and the health, counseling, and writing centers provided stress- and exam-writing–related information. This successful collaboration between the students' union and the library builds on past successes between the two organizations and ensures a continued model of working together in the future.

BACKGROUND—THE UNIVERSITY OF LETHBRIDGE

The University of Lethbridge (U of L) is located in Lethbridge, Alberta, a city of about eighty thousand people in southwest Alberta, Canada. The U of L is a comprehensive public university of approximately 8,200 students—the smallest of three such institutions in Alberta. As such, it has a history of being known as a university with a more personalized, individualized touch than larger universities. Traditionally, class sizes have been smaller and students have had easier access to their professors than they might have at bigger institutions. While the university has been growing and expanding into more areas of postgraduate studies, the faculty and staff have tried to maintain an environment of caring and community. This is reflected in the recently adopted 2009–2013 strategic plan, which focuses on five main strategic directions:

- Confirm our place as a comprehensive university
- Enhance the student experience
- Build internal community and enhance relationships with external communities
- Promote access to quality post-secondary education
- Enhance the environmental sustainability of the University[1]

The emphasis on student experience and community is evident in both the plan and many of the initiatives undertaken on campus. Every unit on campus, from the president's office to caretaking, is expected to govern itself according to the strategic plan and ensure all activities fall into at least one of the categories.

The university library has recently undergone a leadership transition, with a new University Librarian in July 2008 and two new Associate

University Librarians in July 2009. Library units were also restructured, and renewed focus on library outreach and public relations has been emphasized. Librarians are encouraged to try new ideas, and no reasonable proposal focusing on student engagement is turned down.

The University of Lethbridge Students' Union was established with the University of Lethbridge in 1967. The organization is managed by the executive council—consisting of the presidents and vice-presidents—who are annually elected student representatives and also full-time employees of the students' union. The executive council manages the organization on a year-round basis, and internal proposals and external applications for funding are often vetted through this group.

The students' union's purpose is to provide an avenue for the student perspective to be heard wherever needed; so, naturally, the students' union has a history of collaboration with the university. This includes advocating for students to the university, to the city of Lethbridge, to the provincial government, and to the government of Canada. Further, the students' union appoints student members for university governance structures such as the Curriculum Coordinating Committee, the General Faculties Council, the university senate, and the university board of governors. This engagement of students in the governing of their university provides them with valuable opportunities for involvement in strategic planning and decision making as a whole. This often results in more frequent and stronger relationships between members of university administration, faculty, staff, and the students.

In 2005–2006, the students' union and the university worked together to create a funding framework for future collaborations. The Quality Initiatives Proposal (QIP) fund was set up as an account, accessible by both the students' union and the university with the other party's approval, to forward initiatives to benefit students. The university board of governors approved the QIP fund, which was created by apportioning a percentage of tuition increases into the central account. As the students' union is governed by a new general assembly on annual terms, there is a constant influx of new ideas for student outreach initiatives, events, and services which closely reflect student needs. The students' union is thus able to provide many proposals for funding from the QIP fund, on a continuous or one-time basis.

A HISTORY OF COLLABORATION

The university library has a history of collaboration with the students' union, which provides a great opportunity for both the involvement of the library in student affairs and the involvement of students in their library.

One of the first major projects between the two groups was the Library Laptop Program. The students' union's 2007–2008 general assembly, under the recommendation of past students' union Vice-President Administration, Adam Vossepoel, had the opportunity to support library services in a substantial way by using money from the Quality Initiatives Proposal (QIP) fund to provide the library with an increased number of laptops which would be available to lend out to students. It was recognized at the general assembly meeting where approval was granted that the circulation statistics for the laptops purchased by the library in 2006–2007 indicated many students were utilizing this service. Further, it was reported at the meeting that a lack of computer availability was a perennial student issue. As a result, the Library Laptop Program was created to enhance the academic lives and experience of the students at the University of Lethbridge, which was in line with the mission of the students' union.

Along with increasing student quality of life, the increased visibility of the students' union through this program was seen as an effective promotional tool. One of the authors spoke with Kelly Kennedy, 2007–2008 president of the students' union, who observed that while students could have lobbied the library and administration for the laptops, QIP allowed the students' union to expedite the process of providing tangible improvements to the service offerings of the university library. With the executive council recommendation to use QIP fund monies to support the program, the general assembly voted unanimously to provide $7,312 to purchase additional laptops for the Library Laptop Program.

The Fines Amnesty program—also known as Food for Fines—was started by the library's Public Relations and Promotions committee in November 2007. For every donation of a nonperishable food item, the library will waive five dollars of the patron's fines—as long as the overdue books are returned in good condition and the entire fine is paid, either with food items or a combination of food and money at the time of the donation. This campaign benefits students in two ways; not only does it offer immediate financial relief from library fines, but all food donated is then given to the food bank on campus, which is run by the students' union. This approach is eagerly welcomed by students, and often additional food items are donated even where fines have not been incurred. The program has run for the past three academic years, always at random times so that patrons cannot anticipate its arrival and thus "save up" their fines for the event. Over the past three years, the project has benefited the students' union's food bank substantially, as it has a significant portion of its stock provided by donation from within the university.

The students' union and the university library had created a great platform of collaboration, and this continued when librarian Nicole Eva proposed a new, exciting collaboration in the academic year of 2009–2010.

THE PROJECT

The librarian-author of this article, Nicole Eva, started at the university library at the same time as the library was undergoing a leadership transition, and student engagement and outreach activities were welcomed and encouraged. A recent MLIS graduate with a background in marketing, she was interested in new ways of bringing students into the library and was quickly recruited to the library's Public Relations and Promotions team, of which she was shortly thereafter appointed cochair. Being an enthusiastic "newbie" librarian, she often read the library literature on a variety of topics, including marketing and public relations as it relates to libraries. One such article caught her attention: about the creation of a "stress-free zone" for students during final exams.[2] This type of event fits nicely into two areas of the university's newly adopted strategic plan: to enhance the student experience and to build internal community and enhance relationships with external communities. Eva asked library administration if she could organize a pilot project for the December 2009 final exam period; her request was met with an enthusiastic approval and a small budget to help cover costs.

Once given the go-ahead from library administration, Eva began contacting other units in the university she thought might make good partners in this project. She was able to get coffee, tea, and water donated by campus food services, as well as information on stress relief, study tips, and exam-writing skills from counseling services, the health center, and the writing center. She also secured giveaways from counseling services and the campus bookstore, a time donation from one of the campus massage therapists, and, most importantly, a financial donation from the University of Lethbridge Students' Union.

The article had mentioned having video games, such as a Wii, available for students in the room as one of the activities to do while "destressing," and a colleague on the library's Public Relations and Promotions committee suggested the students' union might have such a gaming console which the library could borrow for this event. Eva contacted Jeremy Girard, then the president of the students' union, to see if they could use the console.

While the unit was not available, Girard was excited by the event and thought the students' union could be involved in some way. He vetted the proposal through the executive council, and a $50 donation was offered towards the purchase of healthy snacks, as the students' union tries to promote healthy lifestyle choices to students and saw this as an opportunity to enable them to eat nutritiously during long studying sessions for finals. Eva readily agreed and used the money provided, along with the budget provided by library administration, to purchase apples, oranges, and granola bars, along with cookies. Other supplies purchased out of the library budget included board games, cards, puzzle books, Play-Doh, and jelly beans for a "jelly bean guess" game (the winner received the candy for guessing closest to the correct number of jelly beans). Jigsaw puzzles were brought in from the stock in the library staff room.

The stress-free zone was scheduled to run for the entire duration of final exams: December 12–21, 2009, from 7:00 to 11:00 p.m. each night. All of the partners provided useful information and supplies for the event, including essay-exam–writing tips from the writing center, information brochures from the health center, and pamphlets advertising the students' union food bank from the students' union. Counseling services sent over a variety of items, including fun and serious stress-relief tips and exercises, as well as information on how to obtain counseling if needed, and puzzles and stress balls with the counseling services logo as giveaways. The bookstore donated a t-shirt with the school's athletic team's logo as a drawing prize. The campus massage therapist agreed to come for two of the ten evenings and donate fifteen-minute chair massages to stressed students. Campus food services delivered the coffee, tea, and water at 7:00 p.m. each night and came to pick up the empty carafes the next morning.

A room in the corner of the top floor of the library, not a silent study floor, was reserved for the entire period. It was desirable to have a room in which some of the supplies and posters could be left for the ten days of final exams so as to minimize set-up and tear-down times each day. This room is normally used as a small classroom and meeting room, but during exam times it is mainly used as a study space by students. While not especially large, it is big enough to set up tables for the refreshments and games along one wall and has enough additional tables and chairs to seat approximately twenty people. The room is equipped with an overhead projector, DVD player, and projection screen; a wide variety of movies were selected from the library's collection and left in the room for students to enjoy as they wished. Students were still welcome to study in the room during the day, but signs were posted to let them know that as of 7:00 p.m., they might be joined by others seeking relaxation and refreshments.

Student assistants working evenings in the library regularly monitored the room to ensure there were no noise or messiness issues. Remarkably, no problems were reported. For the most part, students were observed coming into the room for a brief time, sometimes just to get a coffee and snack and take it back to their study area (food and drink—in covered containers—is allowed throughout the library). Some sat and chatted quietly with friends, and others took a more extended break to play a board game or work on a jigsaw puzzle or crossword. Overall, students were extremely respectful of the space and showed their appreciation by abiding by the rules posted regarding noise and tidiness. Caretaking staff had also been notified ahead of time, and they were very supportive of the event, cleaning up any additional mess and placing larger bins for garbage inside and outside the room. Their only request was to discontinue the use of Play-Doh in subsequent years as it got stuck in the carpet—a request with which the program readily complied.

One possible downside of the choice of room was its out-of-the-way location in the corner of the top floor of the library; however, it was the largest meeting room in the library that was available to book for the duration of the event. Staff on the library's Public Relations and Promotions committee posted signage throughout the library directing patrons to the room. One unforeseen benefit of the location was that the room was directly outside the library offices, which made it extremely convenient for set-up and tear-down of the room each evening.

PROMOTION
Avenues used by the library's Public Relations and Promotions committee to promote this event were the same vehicles used to promote most library notices and events. These include screensavers on all public computers in the library;[3] signage beside public access terminals as well as posters throughout the library and in campus dormitories; a notice on the library's website in the What's New section, which also feeds into the library's Facebook page and Twitter account; and additional Facebook and Twitter posts by staff. The

student newspaper was notified, and Eva was interviewed for a story which ran in this publication just prior to the event.

Eva also contacted University Communications, which publicized the event on the digital signage running throughout the university; they also posted a notice on the campus electronic notice board and included the message in the weekly e-mail update to faculty and staff sent by the communications office. The university's Communications Officer also thought the story merited a press release, which he wrote and sent to local media outlets. The story generated quite a bit of interest; Eva was interviewed by two local television stations as well as the city's newspaper, and the release was picked up by other regional papers and radio stations. University Communications estimated that the story generated approximately $13,000 worth of publicity for the university and reached up to 435,000 people in the region. This is always good news for the university, which tries to get its name out in the larger southern Alberta community as much as possible—especially with such "good news" stories such as this one.

The Outcome

Besides the positive promotion the event generated for the library and the university as a whole, the stress-free zone was really meant to benefit the students. And it would appear to have been a success in that respect, as well. Students repeatedly commented to staff how much they appreciated the refreshments and the space; remarks sent to the Comments and Suggestions section of the library's website included

> I LOVE THE STRESS FREE ROOM! Seriously. Who ever [sic] came up with this idea should win a prize. It helped with the stress of studying … right when i [sic] got to the point of wanting to throw things, I would go up to this great little room, get some coffee, eat a snack, watch a little bit of a movie … and feel great about my life again. THANK YOU, THANK YOU, THANK YOU!!"

> Keep it going … nice to have during finals

> The stress-free zone is an awesome idea! I often find myself needing a break from studying but I don't want to aimlessly walk around the library or the school. This provides a nice place to go and regain my sanity!!

Staff reported students waiting in the room at 7:00 p.m. for the refreshments to arrive, and many employees fielded questions about the time and place of the event.

Library administration took notice of all the positive feedback, and readily agreed to run the event again for the spring 2010 exam period, this time with an increased budget. Eva contacted the same partners, and all agreed to participate again with the exception of the massage therapist, who had other commitments. The students' union was so pleased with the outcome of the pilot project that it increased its donation from $50 to $150, again towards the purchase of healthy snacks. Once again, the event ran smoothly and garnered positive comments, and the zone was eagerly anticipated by students; before the first night, several library staff members were asked if the library was going to have a repeat of the stress-free zone for exams.

THE FUTURE

The stress-free zone is expected to be a regular event during exam periods. For a relatively small budget, the event generates a large amount of goodwill with students and is seen very positively throughout the university and the community. The continued support of sponsors such as the students' union is key to generating the positive perception.

In today's age of increasing electronic access and decreasing circulation, finding new and innovative ways to bring students into the library is vital. The increasing trend of the emphasis on library-as-place is evidence of that—catering to other student needs besides access to physical information resources. This means providing comfortable spaces for study and collaboration as well as access to food and beverages, new media and technology, and other campus resources such as writing centers, tutoring, and career services. This move towards a learning commons model is becoming the norm in universities and is one way for academic libraries to remain a vital hub of the campus. The University of Lethbridge Library has been working toward addressing more of these needs by creating more group study rooms and spaces for collaborative work, relaxing food and beverage rules, and creating different noise-level tolerance areas. The stress-free zone is another way to address student needs other than those which are purely academic—needs such as space, sustenance, and sanity. The library will continue to strive to improve all areas of student service, and it is through collaboration with other campus groups such as the students' union that it expects its biggest gains to be made.

Through their collaboration on the Library Laptop Program, the Fines Amnesty event, and the stress-free zone, the University of Lethbridge Students' Union and the University Library have seen mutually beneficial results. Student service is improved, and the library is positioned more firmly as a positive, welcoming space which has products and services that students want. The two groups will continue to look for projects which can utilize the expertise and experience of both parties to improve student life at the University of Lethbridge.

Notes

1. University of Lethbridge, *Strategic Plan 2009–13*, (Lethbridge, Alberta, Canada: University of Lethbridge, 2009), 12–16, http://www.uleth.ca/strategicplan/sites/ all/files/strategicplan_09-13_web.pdf.
2. Elizabeth M. Karle, "Invigorating the Academic Library Experience: Creative Programming Ideas," *College & Research Libraries News* 69, no. 3 (2008): 141–44.
3. Nicole Eva and Donna Seyed-Mahmoud, "Screensavers as a PR Medium: A Simple Idea with a Lot of Power," *Feliciter* 56, no. 2 (2010): 72–73.

10

Common Ground: UBC Library and Student Development in the Chapman Learning Commons

Julie Mitchell and Margot Bell

Many colleges and universities have created learning commons that bring together library, computing, and other campus services to support students' academic work. Mitchell and Bell describe the creation of a learning commons that became not only a place to access academic services, but also a focal point for student leadership and holistic support. Mitchell and Bell show how UBC's work is grounded in student development theory and cuts across traditional unit-based structures to be truly collaborative. The authors also provide advice and reflective questions to guide those who would like to undertake similar collaborations.

The University of British Columbia (UBC) is a public, multicampus university with more than forty thousand students at its main campus in Vancouver, British Columbia.[1] As a comprehensive, research-intensive university, UBC offers bachelor's through to doctoral degree programs. The Chapman Learning Commons, a branch of UBC Library, is a collaborative learning environment at the UBC Vancouver campus that offers a range of services to support learning, research, writing, and the use of technology. Located in the Irving K. Barber Learning Centre, the Chapman Learning Commons provides integrated and coordinated learning support for students across faculties, offering a suite of programs that foster academic success. Since 2001, UBC Library and Student Development have partnered in the delivery of services and programs in the Chapman Learning Commons, shaping a unique campus environment that supports student learning.

The following chapter examines the impact of student development philosophies on the Chapman Learning Commons, with particular emphasis on engaging students as program leaders. The chapter begins with an overview of the historical foundations that shaped the relationship between Student Development and UBC Library and provides details of the collaborative infrastructure. Next is an exploration of the framing models and theories that guide the partnership and the approach to working with students, including Keeling, Underhile, and Wall's concept of horizontal and vertical structures; Astin's Theory of Student Involvement; and Sanford's principle of challenge and support.[2] A discussion of challenges and opportunities in the partnership between Student Development and the library provides strategies and questions for other institutions to consider around staffing, managing space, and involving students. Ultimately, what guides the collaboration between UBC Library and Student Development is a trust in the expertise that each partner offers and a commitment to investing in student leadership.

HISTORICAL FOUNDATIONS OF PARTNERSHIP

One of the three oldest buildings on campus, the former main library at the University of British Columbia (now the Irving K. Barber Learning Centre) featured vaulted ceilings, beautiful stained glass windows, and marble floors in the main concourse of the building. In 2000, the once lively concourse of main library sat dormant with rows of dusty card catalogues that were no longer in use. Senior administrators from UBC Library, Student Development, and Information Technology (IT) Services began conversations about how the heritage core of the main library could be reimagined as a dynamic learning space and academic support center for students. At the time, information commons were emerging on campuses across North America and partnerships between libraries and IT departments in these facilities were common.[3] UBC, however, wanted to go beyond the traditional information technology orientation of an information commons and provide a broader focus on learning.

Prompting the collaborative conversations to develop a learning commons on campus were results from two influential documents: the Boyer

Commission report *Reinventing Undergraduate Education: A Blueprint for America's Research Universities* and the Canadian Undergraduate Survey Consortium's (CUSC) *Study of First Year University Students.*[4]

The Boyer Commission report called for a new model of undergraduate education at research universities to address major inadequacies in the quality of education delivered to the undergraduate student population. Of particular relevance to the learning commons environment, the Boyer Commission report emphasizes the creative use of information technology to support learning and the importance of fostering a sense of community for undergraduate students, particularly commuter students.[5] With UBC's large commuter student population, such findings were particularly relevant.

A significant finding from the CUSC report, which surveyed 5,548 first-year students at UBC, was the importance of the first-year student transition to university on their overall success. The survey indicated that some of the key areas adjusting to campus life at UBC were using the library, finding help with questions or problems, getting academic advice, and having a sense of belonging.[6]

The key themes from both reports were highly influential in shaping the program focus for the Chapman Learning Commons. United by the common interest to develop programs and learning support models to address the issues identified in the Boyer Commission and CUSC reports, the idea of a learning commons at UBC was developed and implemented through a collaborative initiative between the library, Student Development, and Information Technology Services. In September 2000, a learning commons proposal was prepared by the University Librarian and Library Development Office, which outlined how UBC's main library could be transformed into an "exciting centre of learning, cultural appreciation and academic discourse."[7] The proposal emphasized peer learning support, technology, tutoring, and the creation of an innovative library environment focused on welcoming and integrating first-year students. This proposal was presented by the university president to Kay and Lloyd Chapman, who were strong supporters of UBC Library with a history of annual giving dating back to 1975. The Chapmans supported the proposal, providing a gift of one million dollars to support the development of the learning commons. The university agreed to provide matching funds in the form of an endowment, 6 percent of which would be guaranteed and available for annual program support in the learning commons.

In fall 2001, the Chapman Learning Commons Working Group was formed and included representatives from UBC Library, Student Development, and Information Technology Services, a delegate from the UBC Fund Development Office, two undergraduate students, and two graduate students. As reflected by the composition of the working group, it was a priority to involve each partner in the planning process as well as include a strong student voice in decision making. As part of the planning process, responsibilities of the key learning commons partners were collaboratively developed, documented, and posted on the learning commons website.[8]

With funding secured by the Chapmans' generous gift and the collaborative efforts of the working group underway, construction began to transform the central concourse of the main library. On February 18, 2002, only a year and a half after the original proposal for the learning commons was submitted, the Chapman Learning Commons opened its doors.

COLLABORATIVE INFRASTRUCTURE

UBC Library is one of the largest university libraries in Canada, with over 350 staff members and twenty-one branches/divisions.[9] The campus Student Development unit includes fourteen professional staff who work collaboratively with the library and various faculties across campus to provide academic support, leadership and involvement opportunities, and orientation and transition programming for all students. Common to both the library and Student Development is the important liaison role with faculties and the commitment to support student academic success.

The full-time staff in the Chapman Learning Commons currently includes the coordinator (a librarian), a student affairs professional, and an administrative assistant. A team of fifteen students, ranging from undergraduate to doctoral level, staffs the Learning Commons Help Desk and the team is jointly supervised by the coordinator and student affairs professional. Notably, the student affairs position is jointly funded by UBC Library and Student Development. The primary reporting structure for the student affairs position is to the coordinator of the Chapman Learning Commons, with strong strategic direction from Student Development to ensure the library-based student affairs staff member remains part of a strong community of practice on campus.

The commitment within Student Development to joint training, mentoring, and sharing best practices and current research helps shape effective crossfunctional approaches to supporting students. This approach is evident in the Chapman Learning Commons through coordinated training of staff in both library and student affairs philosophies. The staff of the learning commons also develops interdisciplinary expertise through attendance at both library and student affairs workshops and conferences. This knowledge base helps in guiding daily decision making in the learning commons, working with the team of student assistants, and developing learning-centered programs.

In addition to Student Development and the library, other key partners in the collaborative infrastructure of the Chapman Learning Commons are represented on the Program Advisory Committee and Student Advisory Committee. The Program Advisory Committee consists of staff representatives from UBC Library; Student Development; the Centre for Teaching, Learning and Technology; the Writing Centre; and the School of Library, Archival and Information Studies. The Student Advisory Committee is comprised of ten students, including students at large, student senators, and other representatives from the undergraduate student government. Both groups meet quarterly and advise learning commons staff on how to best support student learning and help shape strategic directions.

The Chapman Learning Commons is tremendously popular with students, as both a vibrant study space and a place to access essential programs and services. Fundamental to the success of the learning commons is the leadership from student assistants, combined with the expertise of staff from UBC Library and Student Development. Guiding the collaborative efforts are key student development theories that challenge the learning commons to expand the realm of support traditionally emphasized by academic libraries from "cognitive development and scholarly pursuit" to a more holistic approach to student growth and development.[10]

FRAMING THEORIES AND PROGRAM DEVELOPMENT

Since the official opening in 2002, the programs and services in the Chapman Learning Commons have grown and continually transformed to meet student needs. The current suite of programs includes (1) learning technology and multimedia support at a central help desk, (2) tutoring in math, physics, economics, and chemistry, (3) writing support, (4) peer academic coaching, (5) learning-focused workshops and events, and (6) access to a variety of technologies. The help desk is staffed by tech-savvy, academically focused student assistants, and there is a strong commitment to referral to other library and student services.

The array of programs and services offered in the Chapman Learning Commons are intentionally shaped and guided by student development theories that address the multiple dimensions of student growth. While there are numerous student development theories applied in the Chapman Learning Commons, three influential models and theories include Keeling, Underhile, and Wall's concept of horizontal and vertical structures; Astin's Theory of Student Involvement; and Sanford's challenge and support principle.[11] There was no formal process of bringing forth each theory and reaching agreement between partners in terms of which models and philosophies would be most relevant. Instead, there is an inherent trust in the expertise of the student affairs professional in the Chapman Learning Commons to bring specialized knowledge in developing student-centered programs to an academic environment.

Keeling, Underhile, and Wall's Horizontal and Vertical Structures

Current thinking driving approaches to support student learning at UBC and other institutions is to challenge the vertical structures and consider a more horizontal approach. As noted by Keeling, Underhile, and Wall, higher education needs to think about creating horizontal structures to more accurately reflect how students experience the university environment. The shift represents a movement away from silos based on disciplines, schools, departments, or administration to an approach that cuts across these vertical structures, shifting thinking to concepts like first-year experience, student development, or advising.[12]

The horizontal approach is particularly relevant when considering the benefits of collaborating in a learning commons environment. Library staff, for example, could be working effectively with students with little awareness of initiatives underway in student services or, more importantly, of how partnering with staff in these units might provide stronger resources to students. Similarly, student services staff could be working to support students without considering how they might collaborate with other campus partners to make more accurate referrals and facilitate a more seamless experience for students.[13] Both areas may be providing strong service, but to the student the experience may feel fragmented and disconnected. The vertical approach results in a unit focusing more on the advancement of "internal goals and objectives than on adhering to, elucidating, or accomplishing broader institutional purposes."[14] An intentional effort is made in the learning commons partnership between Student Development and the library to keep each other informed in a timely manner of work happening in other departments and to identify opportunities to collaborate.

When applying this approach to the collaborative decision-making process in the Chapman Learning Commons, a question often asked is, "What makes the most sense for students?" In many cases, what is easiest for each unit may not be the best solution for students, but a joint commitment to authentically listen to student concerns and move beyond unit-based challenges to find solutions will lead to innovative outcomes. By committing to this perspective, the Chapman Learning Commons chooses a horizontal approach in designing programs and services, combining the knowledge and expertise of librarians, student development staff, and student leaders to create a seamless campus environment that supports student growth.

Astin's Theory of Student Involvement

Astin's Theory of Student Involvement guides practices in the Chapman Learning Commons and is applied to the collaborative decision making around programs and services, as well as how work is approached with students. Of particular relevance in shaping a learning commons environment, Astin notes that "the amount of student learning and personal development associated with any educational program is directly proportional to the quality and quantity of student involvement in that program."[15]

The Chapman Learning Commons continually strives to offer a variety of programs to meet student needs and encourage involvement. The majority of programs offered through the Chapman Learning Commons are delivered by trained student staff who provide peer-to-peer assistance. Many workshops are also student-initiated and student-led. Through tutoring, coaching, and other student-led programs, over three hundred involved student leaders are shaping the culture in the Chapman Learning Commons. The diversity of activities, workshops, resources, and learning support programs that result promotes students' "*social inclusion* in a college or university as member of a *community of learning.*"[16] [emphasis in original]

Astin's student involvement theory also provides useful guidance when working with the student team at the Chapman Learning Commons Help Desk. The team is jointly supervised by library and student development staff. A strong emphasis is placed on team building and engaging students in their work in a meaningful way. In addition to working shifts on the help desk, student leaders develop programs, participate in committees, and drive the content on the website. Every year, student leaders report the profound impact the position had on their student experience. In the words of Chapman Learning Commons Assistant Samuel Wempe, a fourth-year student in the Faculty of Arts:

> Working as a Learning Commons Assistant has not only made me a better student, it has also brought me closer to my university and enriched my sense of belonging in its community. I have become a transmitter of information about programs, support services and general help the university has to offer to my social network (many who frankly had never considered asking for help) and anyone I see in need of a helping hand around campus.[17]

The knowledge student assistants gain not only benefits the peers they help in the Chapman Learning Commons, but also contributes to their overall academic success and engagement with the campus community. Through effective collaboration, intentional planning, and investing in student leaders, learning commons can facilitate student involvement. According to Astin's theory, "the greater the student's involvement in college, the greater will be the amount of student learning and personal development."[18]

Sanford's Challenge and Support

According to Sanford, optimal learning and development in college results from a balance of challenge and support. He argued that when faced with the tension of the collegiate environment, students are continually trying to restore a sense of equilibrium. If challenged too much, a student may revert to "primitive responses" that have been effective in the past.[19] If challenged too little, the individual may become complacent and fail to develop. In order to promote individual development, an institution must present the student with "strong challenges, appraise accurately his [or her] ability to cope with these challenges and offer him [or her] support when they become overwhelming."[20]

To collaboratively train, mentor, and support the team of student leaders who work in the Chapman Learning Commons, Sanford's theory of balancing challenge and support is particularly valuable. The insight used most frequently in the joint supervision of the student team is the idea of lessen-ing the tension produced by the university environment and providing the support necessary to allow student leaders to succeed. In other instances, it may mean challenging students to push beyond their comfort zone and take on activities that will allow them to develop professionally and personally. The impact of this approach allows for tremendous growth of the team and results in outstanding, student-driven programs and services.

Relevant to Sanford's model, Student Development has mapped out a detailed monthly schedule of the student academic cycle, and this influ-ences the timing of programs and services offered in the Chapman Learning Commons. The cycle can also help supervisors understand the demands a student is experiencing at certain times of the academic year, which can guide decisions around expectations from staff. This does not eliminate the fact that the student assistants have a job to do and need to be accountable, but important skills can be mastered with the understanding of challenge and support. The benefits of applying this concept in the joint supervision of the student staff is a skilled, engaged, and capable team who demonstrate con-tinuous growth, learning to push themselves professionally to achieve the goals of the Chapman Learning Commons.

CHALLENGES AND OPPORTUNITIES

It is important to emphasize that the pathway to authentic partnership is not always easy—work cultures may vary, approaches to working with students differ, and approval paces or budgeting processes may be out of sync. Due to differences, there may be situations when getting the work done can seem easier without the involvement of partners or students. But it is critical to take the time to understand different work contexts and have open, trusting lines of communication. The results for students will be strengthened by this common understanding. Three key areas of challenge and opportunity in the collaborative partnership between UBC Library and Student Development are staffing, managing space, and involving students.

Staffing

Over the years, the Chapman Learning Commons has explored several differ-ent staffing models, some prompted by changes in organizational structure and others in response to shifts in student needs. Collaboratively shaping and supporting staffing models can present a unique set of challenges, particularly around hiring processes, funding, payroll procedures, and supervision. Based on the experience of Student Development and the UBC Library, some important questions for institutions to consider with respect to staffing a learning commons include these:

- Who will write the job descriptions for both student and staff positions?
- Are the positions funded by one unit or jointly?
- Who is part of the interview process?
- Who does the training and evaluation?
- What library committees should student affairs professionals participate in, and what student affairs committees should librarians be part of?

A greater willingness to work outside of functional frameworks, aligned with Keeling, Underhile, and Wall's horizontal approach, creates a greater understanding of how services can work more effectively together and will have a positive impact on students and staff alike.[21]

Managing Space

In many cases, the space that houses a learning commons is within a library, and with that can come an inherent set of challenges when partnering with an external unit in the management of programs and services. Although UBC Library is responsible for the space and daily operations of the Chapman Learning Commons, essential to the successful partnership with Student Development is creating a climate of shared ownership and management of the space and its programs. To do so, there is a joint creation of mission, vision, and values as well as greater flexibility and shared development of use polices around the space. Ultimately, student affairs professionals must be more than guests or tenants in the space with the mandate of bringing services in for students. Issues of control and traditional management structures must be examined in order to create student-centered space and a genuine place for student-led initiatives.

In managing space in the learning commons, some questions to consider include these:

- How are shared values reflected?
- How do the mission, vision, and values of the learning commons align with strategic plans of the institution as well as unit areas?

- Who is part of your team to create the shared vision?

Considering these questions and shaping the answers in partnership can provide key direction when impasses and differences of opinion occur throughout planning, implementation, and evaluation stages.

Involving Students

A core principle that grounds much of the decision making between UBC Library and Student Development is adopting a student-centered approach. This does not imply simply programming for students or asking them about their needs, but in line with Astin's theory, it means actively involving students in solutions. With a campus filled with bright student minds, the Chapman Learning Commons strives to use every opportunity to engage students in decision-making processes and encourage student-led initiatives. Involving students at this level, however, requires trust in their abilities, a willingness to allow students to drive programs, a commitment to mentoring students, and an acceptance that mistakes will be made along the way.

When operating a branch within a large library system where not all staff members may place the same trust in students, it may be challenging for all student-led initiatives to thrive. There are examples where program ideas were fully supported by all partners in the Chapman Learning Commons; however, when backing was required from larger units, the support was not there. Often the issue is finding the comfortable balance between staff expertise and student peer-led initiatives. Some questions to consider in authentically involving students include these:

- What education can be done with staff around the benefits of peer-led initiatives?
- Is the student voice represented at committee tables?
- What opportunities exist for students to help shape strategic direction?
- What mechanisms exist to get feedback from students?
- What role do students play in program and service delivery?

In order for the partnership between UBC Library and Student Development to be successful and enhance the student experience, it was imperative to understand what is important and valued by each partner, to respect one another's interests, and to work together to find collaborative solutions that benefit all partners involved. Whether the issues considered concern staffing, managing space, or involving students, one partner cannot be seen to have the final say on decisions but instead understand that solutions are reached through a collaborative approach.

CONCLUSION

Since opening the Chapman Learning Commons at UBC, there has been tremendous growth, change, and innovation. While there have been shifts in the collaborative infrastructure between Student Development and UBC Library, what remains constant is the common goal of supporting and enhancing student learning. Through a crossfunctional approach to training and professional development, student affairs models and theories are deeply ingrained in how learning commons staff work with students and develop programs. Keeling, Underhile, and Wall's model of horizontal and vertical structures; Astin's Theory of Student Involvement; and Sanford's concept of challenge and support are just some of the student development frameworks that guide practices. While the focus of this chapter is these three frameworks, equally important is research exploring the role of colleges and universities in the development of identity that further broaden the understanding of the student experience.[22]

Applying student development theories in the library environment represents a fundamental shift in perspective from information and resources at the center to students at the center. By offering diverse programs and services for students and also actively involving them in service delivery and program development, one can encourage students to engage with their university community and empower them to shape their academic experience. As noted by UBC's former Vice-President of Students Brian Sullivan, "Students, as individuals and in groups, are not only the recipients of our services but also critical partners in the achievement of institutional goals."[23]

By challenging those dichotomies with collaborative partnerships among librarians, student affairs professionals, and beyond, the Chapman Learning Commons strives to bring together programs and services that address the holistic student experience and meet the call for "new organizational structures in higher education … that incorporate innovative learning methods that do not reflect or reinforce the traditional dichotomies of student/academic affairs."[24] The approach requires mutual trust in the expertise that each colleague lends to the process as well as in students' abilities and potential. By letting go of apprehension around control of staffing, space, programs, and services and being flexible about the approach to working with students, creativity and innovation can flourish as the learning commons leverages a campuswide network of knowledge to enhance the student experience.

Notes

1. Planning and Institutional Research, University of British Columbia, "Full-Time and Part-Time Enrolment UBC Vancouver 2009/10," accessed January 29, 2012, http://www.pair.ubc.ca/statistics/students/students.htm.

2. Richard P. Keeling, Ric Underhile, and Andrew F. Wall, "Horizontal and Vertical Structures: The Dynamics of Organization in Higher Education," *Liberal Education* 93, no. 4 (2007): 22–31; Alexander W. Astin, "Student Involvement: A Developmental Theory for Higher Education," *Journal of College Student Personnel* 25, no. 4 (1984): 297–308; Nevitt Sanford, *Self and Society: Social Change and Individual Development* (Oxford, England: Atherton Press, 1966).

3. Maria T. Accardi, Memo Cordova, and Kim Leeder, "Reviewing the Library Learning Commons: History, Models, and Perspectives," *College & Undergraduate Libraries* 17 (2010): 310–29.

4. The Boyer Commission on Educating Undergraduates in the Research University, *Reinventing Undergraduate Education: A Blueprint for America's Research Universities* (Stony Brook: State University of New York, 1998); James L. Walker, *Survey of First-Year University Students: University of British Columbia Edition* (Canadian Undergraduate Survey Consortium, 1998).

5. Boyer Commission, *Reinventing Undergraduate Education*, 25, 34–35.

6. Walker, *Survey of First-Year University Students*, 14.

7. Martha C. Piper, *Main Library Learning Commons Proposal* (Vancouver: University of British Columbia, 2000).

8. "The Chapman Learning Commons: Vision Statement," 2002, UBC Library, archived on Internet Archive Wayback Machine, http://web.archive.org/web/20020616093003/www.library.ubc.ca/chapmanlearningcommons/vision.html.

9. UBC Library, "Facts & Figures 2009/10," 2010, http://www.library.ubc.ca/pubs/factfig.html.

10. Lisa Janicke Hinchliffe and Melissa Autumn Wong, "From Services-Centered to Student-Centered: A 'Wellness Wheel' Approach to Developing the Library as an Integrative Learning Commons," *College & Undergraduate Libraries* 17 (2010): 214.

11. Keeling, Underhile, and Wall, "Horizontal and Vertical Structures"; Astin, "Student Involvement"; Sanford, *Self and Society*.

12. Keeling, Underhile, and Wall, "Horizontal and Vertical Structures," 24.

13. George D. Kuh, "Guiding Principles for Creating Seamless Learning Environments for Undergraduates," *Journal of College Student Development* 37 (1996): 135–48.

14. "Learning Reconsidered: A Campus-Wide Focus on the Student Experience," National Association of Student Personnel Administrators and American College Personnel Association, January 2004, 22, http://www.myacpa.org/pub/documents/learningreconsidered.pdf.

15. Astin, "Student Involvement," 298.

16. Donald Robert Beagle, Donald Bailey, and Barbara Tierney, *The Information Commons Handbook* (New York: Neal-Schuman Publishers, 2006), 35.

17. Samuel Wempe, e-mail message to authors, September 22, 2010.

18. Astin, "Student Involvement," 307.

19. Sanford, *Self and Society*, 45.

20. Ibid., 46.

21. Keeling, Underhile, and Wall, "Horizontal and Vertical Structures."

22. For example, Arthur W. Chickering, *Education and Identity* (San Francisco: Jossey-Bass, 1969), 367; N. J. Evans and V. A. Wall, *Beyond Tolerance: Gays, Lesbians and Bisexuals on Campus* (Alexandria, VA: American Association for Counseling and Development, 1991); Jane Goodman, Nancy K. Schlossberg, and Mary L. Anderson, *Counseling Adults in Transition: Linking Practice with Theory* (New York: Springer, 2006).

23. Brian Sullivan, "Organizing, Leading and Managing Student Services," in *Achieving Student Success: Effective Student Services in Canadian Higher Education*, edited by Donna Gail Hardy Cox and Charles Carney Strange (Montreal: McGill-Queen's University Press, 2010), 179.

24. "Learning Reconsidered," 21.

11

The University of Nebraska at Kearney Learning Commons: Persistence in Partnership

Ronald L. Wirtz and Keri A. Pearson

Collaborative programs and services typically need a physical space in which to exist. Although it may be easy to find a place on campus to host a one-time program, finding the space to house an ongoing service can be challenging since it may require one or both partners to give up existing space. Wirtz and Pearson describe the creation of a learning commons to colocate services and focus on the space issues that accompany such a project, including the creation of both temporary and permanent spaces.

At the beginning of the fall semester of 2010, the Calvin T. Ryan Library, Academic Peer Tutoring, and the UNK Writing Center introduced a new, collaborative project to the University of Nebraska–Kearney community: the UNK Learning Commons. The project was launched in temporary quarters on the west half of the library's upper floor, but an upgraded, custom-designed space to house these programs, along with other resources for student collaboration and study, is projected to open in mid-year 2011. The new space—now under construction—includes a floor plan specifically designed by program managers especially for writing center and peer tutoring activities. It will feature flexible seating, group meeting and study areas, additional computing resources for student and tutor use, automated scheduling and management tools, and architectural features and custom colors that both define the learning commons space and link it to other student-centered functions of the library.

As the result of a deliberate partnership between the divisions of Academic and Student Affairs, the UNK Learning Commons originated from a clearly identified need to provide defined, unified space to academic support programs. The basis of this partnership was a formally defined strategic effort to bring together diverse campus entities to "establish collaborative mechanisms, enabling units to cooperate across organizational boundaries to enhance student retention, graduation, and career placement results."[1] It was planned from the beginning with a deliberate student-centered focus, providing for individual students as learners with unique needs, abilities, and learning styles, while at the same time contributing to increased institutional success in terms of student retention and graduation.

THE DEVELOPMENT OF THE UNK LEARNING COMMONS

Over its two-year development phase, the UNK Learning Commons blossomed from a simple relocation project to a precedent-setting collaboration, highlighting the effectiveness of simple networking and mutually respectful conversation, as well as the need for flexibility, persistence, and patience in demolishing mental "silos" and working across traditional departmental and divisional lines. Throughout this extended process, those involved never wavered from the ultimate goal of providing better service to more students in the UNK higher learning community. The journey was not without challenges, however, including unforeseen tightening of budgetary resources as well as unexpected and abrupt staffing changes.

Several pre-existing conditions contributed to the eventual success of the project. The first of these was the previously noted strategic commitment of the university to the development of a culture of partnership and sharing among colleges and departments. The second was the desire of both library and student affairs personnel to accept, and sometimes instigate, substantial changes to the status quo in the interest of better service to student clients. The third was the common goal among the three major partners in the learning commons project to enlighten, educate, engage, and empower UNK students to succeed academically.

INTRODUCING THE UNIVERSITY OF NEBRASKA AT KEARNEY

The University of Nebraska at Kearney is primarily an undergraduate institution with strategic focus on student research and academic contribution.

UNK offers 170 undergraduate degrees, as well as twenty five preprofessional programs and thirty-four graduate programs, and boasts a 17:1 student-to-faculty ratio for more than 6,700 students. Although UNK is located in a rural section of a Midwestern state, it draws students from all ninety-three Nebraska counties, forty-nine states, and fifty countries, with international students accounting for 8 percent of the student body population—the highest proportion of any unit of the state university system.[2] Many campus entities fall under the leadership of the Senior Vice Chancellor for Academic and Student Affairs, which includes the Calvin T. Ryan Library and the Division for Student Affairs.

The Calvin T. Ryan Library provides extensive traditional print and microform materials to the UNK community while offering increasing accessibility to electronic resources, including ten thousand e-books, 160 databases and electronic reference works, and more than sixty-one thousand full-text electronic journals. The original Calvin T. Ryan Library building was constructed in 1963. An addition in 1981–1982 doubled the size of the building, providing accommodations for more than eight hundred users. The building includes six group study rooms, an AV production and practice room, two classrooms, two multipurpose computer labs, a dedicated university staff training lab, and several large open seating and study areas. The growing focus on electronic resources is intended to meet the rapid expansion of the university's presence, which includes more than 1,100 distance-only students.[3] Under the direction of the library dean, the working goal of the library's ten librarians, three professional staff, and thirteen support personnel is to assist UNK students to succeed in their academic careers.

The Division of Student Affairs at UNK houses nine departments and includes combinations of offices, programs, and services that function together synergistically: Academic and Career Services, Academic Success, Admissions, Counseling and Health Care, Financial Aid, Multicultural Affairs, Undergraduate Recruitment and Admissions, and Residential and Greek Life. The division offices are in several locations on the UNK campus, including the Memorial Student Activities Building (MSAB), the Nebraskan Student Union, and Conrad Hall, one of the university residence halls. In accordance with the mission statement of the division to "Engage. Educate. Empower," the personnel of the division strive to meet the developmental and personal needs of students, develop leaders within the context of the campus learning community, and promote personal and academic success for UNK students and graduates. The Division of Student Affairs was under the direction of Dean Gail Zeller when the UNK Learning Commons project began and at the present time is under the leadership of Dean Joseph Oravecz.

DETAILS OF COLLABORATION

The development of the UNK Learning Commons was prompted by two incidents. The first was the development of a draft statement of core work-place values by library faculty and staff in the course of a summer 2008 planning retreat. The second was an administrative program review (APR) of the Academic Success Learning Strategies department in April 2009.[4] The first item among the library's core values was an expression of commitment to cooperation, collaboration, and open communication, both within the library and with other departments and individuals on the UNK campus, derived in part from the university's 2007 strategic plan.

At the time of the Academic Success review, Academic Peer Tutoring, one of several programs functioning within Academic Success, was located in an alcove of a hallway in the Memorial Student Affairs Building (MSAB). While centrally located and physically connected with Academic Success, the alcove was small and overcrowded for the growing tutoring program, which had increased the number of students it served by 20 percent in three years.[5] In conjunction with the review, satisfaction surveys indicated that the program was greatly valued by students but was also limited by deficiencies in its facil-ities.[6] In other words, the program was not challenged by failure, but rather by growing success that was pushing it beyond available resources.

Three recommendations from the Academic Success Learning Strategies' review team coalesced into a need for significant action. The first noted the potential strength of uniting the writing center and Academic Success into a "one-stop" service. However, no particular location was suggested for the partnership, mostly because of the limitations of space already in MSAB and the apparent lack of additional space in the library. Second, the review team suggested that Academic Success "initiate more connections with the library to include more resources and references for Learning Strategies,"[7] perhaps by designating a specific area for such a collection or adding or highlight-ing databases rich in learning resource content. Finally, the review team sup-ported the creation of more space for the Academic Peer Tutoring Program. While many review team members supported the idea of keeping peer tutoring within MSAB in order to maintain its proximity to other Academic

Success programs, acquiring additional space within that facility was not possible without significantly reducing that of other student affairs departments.

Like peer tutoring, the writing center was already a very successful and continually growing program in spring 2009. According to the writing center's self-study in its spring 2010 APR, the program consistently generated more than three thousand annual visits.[8] Like that of Learning Strategies, the writing center APR also revealed the program's positive reputation with students.[9] Furthermore, as it was already housed within the library, the writing center certainly benefitted from its proximity to the physical resources needed for research and writing—in particular, librarian assistance, computers, and printed book, journal, and document collections. In other words, the writing center was thriving with the library, a sign that collaboration between student and academic affairs was not only possible but also successful.

In a spring 2009 meeting of the UNK Deans' Council, the Interim Dean of Student Affairs discussed the peer tutoring program's growth and needed partnership with the writing center and library with a colleague at the meeting—the Dean of the Library. In response, the library dean, Janet Wilke, shared her interest in getting more students to physically utilize library space, as research could now be accomplished online from other locations and students were not visiting the library. Immediately following the council meeting, deans Zeller and Wilke reviewed and discussed the merits of forty-eight hundred square feet of underutilized study space as a potential site for peer tutoring. At the time, it and other areas within the library were no longer needed because of the increased availability of online collections and presented significant opportunities for the library to evolve its functionality for students. Serendipitously, moving the peer tutoring program would also help fulfill the need of peer tutoring to partner more directly and deliberately with the writing center. An office suite large enough to accommodate managers for both programs was located adjacent to the repurposed space on the library's second floor. It had been vacated by another academic program and was already slated to become the writing center's new home.

DEVELOPING THE PHYSICAL SPACE

With collaborative relocation in mind, the library dean, the interim dean of student affairs, and personnel from the library, writing center, and peer tutoring began a series of meetings to discuss and plan for the development of this shared space. These ranged from frequent informal discussions involving the director of the writing center and the coordinators of peer tutoring and library services to more structured formal project coordination meetings that were chaired by the dean of the library or of student affairs. The latter normally included one or both deans, the library and peer tutoring coordinators, the director of the writing center, and the campus architect. As planning progressed, meetings included all of the above in addition to a partner in a local architectural design firm, his assistant, the contractor and his foreman, and the director of facilities for UNK.

Both the library dean and the dean of student affairs also conducted informational and planning meetings with their respective staff and faculty members on a regular basis as well as inviting open discussion of the project in scheduled divisional meetings. In addition, student peer tutors and writing consultants were invited to participate in planning meetings and to provide critiques of proposed architectural features. As an example of the level of student participation, the university architect had envisioned the use of a number of glass partition walls to create three group-study rooms and to divide the main open area into a number of glass-walled cubicles. The student tutors and consultants liked the study rooms but objected to the other glass partition walls because they felt that the partitions would inhibit communication. As a result, the glass partitions were removed from the final blueprints while the study rooms were retained.

Eventually, the term *Learning Commons* was adopted for the project, based on the library dean's extensive research into tutoring and library partnerships. As conceptualized, a learning commons "emphasizes a range of programs and services to support students in their learning tasks."[10] Among the literature reviewed by Dean Wilke and shared with other project participants, two articles in particular provided the directions that would fulfill needs on the UNK campus. Mahaffy presented efforts by library reference groups and writing centers to collaborate in order to expand services beyond their traditional domains.[11] Even closer to the type of collaboration envisioned by the library dean was Love and Edwards's examination of ways in which libraries and several types of student services units could work together to "equip students with tools and resources needed to succeed in their studies and with their evolving personal, social, emotional and academic endeavors."[12]

Certainly, the "academic resource" component common among the functions of the library, writing center, and peer tutoring programs made this particular union a natural beginning for a broader range of partnerships across the divisions of academic and student affairs. Furthermore, as meetings continued and more ideas were shared, it became apparent that the learning commons would serve as a model in the entire university's efforts to foster crossdivisional cooperation in support of student academic success.

With this shared purpose, the learning commons would necessarily need to blend with the rest of the library physically and managerially. After examining the proposed physical space with the dean of the library, coordinator of library services, interim dean of student affairs, the writing center director, and the peer tutoring coordinator in fall 2009, the campus architect held several design and planning meetings over the following year. These meetings examined the need for flexibility, fluidity, and accommodation for technology in the space. Eventually, participants came to consensus, with all parties compromising in order plan the space collaboratively.

By early summer of 2010, renovation plans were finalized along with funding sources from both the library and student affairs, space modification paperwork was completed and approved, and a local architectural firm was commissioned to produce blueprints based on the design meetings. Everything was in readiness for work to begin in the learning commons proper, but progress was halted abruptly in July 2010 due to the imposition of budget austerity measures by the Nebraska state legislature.

A new dean for student affairs, Dr. Joseph Oravecz, took office in August 2010. Dr. Oravecz immediately declared his support the project and joined other UNK administrators in the drive to fully fund its construction. One-time funding from the UNK administration and from the University of Nebraska system was awarded in December 2010 through the energetic efforts of the UNK Chancellor and the Senior Vice Chancellor for Academic and Student Affairs. New contracts were signed and construction crews began work in January 2011.

Leading up to the start of renovations, student affairs staff and library faculty and administration had done a good deal of planning behind the scenes. Library staff members cleared the future learning commons space of furnishings, shifted parts of the book collection, dismantled and stored shelving, and otherwise prepared the space for construction. The peer tutoring coordinator and her staff assistant, along with the library's coordinator of user services, interviewed and hired more than a dozen student workers to staff the learning commons welcome desk and to assist with scheduling of tutoring and writing consultation sessions. Student affairs personnel were also engaged in revising the management structure of the division, including changes for the writing center and peer tutoring. A search was conducted for an assistant director for the writing center, to replace the previous director-level position, which allowed the learning commons to open for business at the beginning of the fall 2010 semester. Another search for the position of Academic Success director, who will coordinate with the library for learning commons activities, is underway. The Academic Success director will oversee the writing center, peer tutoring, Learning Strategies, Disability Services, and student support services (TRIO federal grant), and will work with the library and other campus units to expand first-year student programs.

Although it is currently in operation in temporary quarters, a "soft opening" for the learning commons was planned in late April 2011 to honor Dr. Zeller on the occasion of her retirement. The learning commons will have an official grand opening celebration in its permanent location at the beginning of fall semester 2011. The new facility will include three glass-enclosed rooms for group study, two student computer "bars," a state-of-the-art welcome desk, a printing station, and ten technology carrels for laptop or other private study use, in addition to ample tutoring space.

In order to accommodate academic peer tutoring while the new space is under construction, learning commons operations were shifted to a popular thirty-six-hundred-square-foot quiet study area which provided workspace, public access computers and printers, and varied tables and seating adjacent to the library's main circulating collection. That the operations of the learning commons could be shifted to this location without seriously affecting student use of the library was due to the availability of new quiet study space elsewhere in the building, primarily on the main floor of the building. Like the permanent space designated for the learning commons, this area was opened up by an intensive months-long program of weeding to reduce outdated parts of the bound journal and print reference collections and replacing those materials with electronic resources. The library was also instrumental in hosting meetings and furnishing space, and it continues to furnish technology resources for meetings, webinars, and staff training for both the learning commons and the division of student affairs.

Library computer technicians provided significant support in the preparation and implementation of key technology pieces. Over the summer, nine desktops, five laptops, and four netbooks were configured for specific functions within the permanent learning commons space. For several months, the library's software coordinator worked diligently with a systems analyst in the information technology department to resolve issues between the learning commons tracking software and the required security set-up on these machines. Without the support of library technology personnel, accurate attendance figures for the learning commons would not have been reportable. At mid-semester, seven new desktop computers were installed in the temporary learning commons space in response to student feedback that requested more computer availability in that section of the building. Doing so not only benefitted the library as a whole, but also provided easy technology access during tutoring sessions, especially for students with electronic-only copies of papers or programming code.

MARKETING THE LEARNING COMMONS

In addition to coordinating space usage and technology support, the library, peer tutoring, and writing center programs have engaged in cooperative marketing activities. The first of these efforts was Game Night, cohosted by the learning commons and the library at the beginning of the fall 2010 semester. This event was intended to develop camaraderie among learning commons student peer tutors, writing consultants, and student clients by providing activities, board games, and refreshments. Held during UNK's opening week celebrations, Game Night was a great success, attracting over sixty students despite being scheduled opposite another event showcasing the university's popular intramurals program. Consideration is being given to the expansion of Game Night to include console or computer gaming, along with increased advertising and better scheduling. Game Night could become a popular addition in UNK's traditional repertoire of first-week student activities.

Other coordinated marketing efforts for the learning commons contributed to building a campus commitment which emphasizes the fundamental collaboration of the learning commons and its constituents. Prior to the fall 2010 semester, campus faculty and staff were informed about the development of the learning commons through various means. Student affairs personnel were updated on the project during regular meetings throughout the planning phases, while key academic departments most strongly connected to peer tutoring received e-mail messages about the changing space at the beginning and end of the summer of 2010. In July 2010, an article describing the development of the learning commons was published in a campus-wide electronic newsletter.

The UNK Learning Commons is currently under construction on the second floor of the Calvin T. Ryan Library! Opening in Fall 2010, this space will allow the Academic Success and Writing Center tutors to collaborate within the information resource context that libraries are transitioning to worldwide. Acting as another resource within the library, tutors will continue their tradition of helping students succeed by growing as lifelong learners and writers. Additionally, the Commons will feature two computer bars for student use, a networked student printing station, upgraded lighting and flooring, and ample study space. The varied configuration of the Commons will allow students to work either independently or in small or large groups, and future plans may include private study rooms in which students can collaborate for homework, tests, and presentations. A Learning Commons Council is being formed to ensure that the voices of faculty, staff, and students are included in the Commons' development. Certainly, ongoing partnership between Peer Tutoring, the Writing Center, and the Library will facilitate more efficient and effective services for the UNK community. Please join us for Game Night on Wednesday, August 25th to get a peek at the progress, meet our tutors, and see what the UNK Learning Commons is all about![13]

Finally, during the first week of classes, a campuswide e-mail invited all staff and faculty members to attend Game Night and briefly described the partnership existing among the library, peer tutoring program, and writing center. The result of these communication efforts was to create a perception of the learning commons as an exciting, shared opportunity for the benefit of the entire campus, one which promised to grow quickly for the benefit of UNK students.

The electronic presence of the learning commons is still developing. Current collaborations include the library website, which links the academic peer tutoring and writing center websites under its services menu. Library blogs and newsletters regularly include announcements for special events in the learning commons. The learning commons tutoring schedule is linked from the library website and available in printed form in the library and in other campus locations. The peer tutoring and writing center websites provide links to the library's main page, with plans to further emphasize the learning commons as a library entity when construction of the permanent space is completed in fall 2011. Social networking pages for the constituent units of the learning commons are separated at present, but can easily be connected under new or existing accounts that better emphasize their partnership. Additionally, integrating direct library/learning commons access into the university's online course management system may forge another path to establishing a virtual presence of the UNK Learning Commons for off-campus and distance students.

RESPONDING TO CHALLENGES TO A SUCCESSFUL START-UP

Aside from these managerial and administrative efforts, perhaps the greatest source of success for the learning commons rested in the collaborative efforts of its most essential participants: the peer tutors and writing consultants. The peer tutoring coordinator officially moved the tutoring program into office space shared with the writing center in May 2010. Over the next month, the writing center director prepared those involved with the program for her resignation, effective at the end of June. This significantly challenged the learning commons in its first semester of operation, in terms of both staffing shortage and the absence of the director's visionary leadership. However, tutors and consultants pulled together by rediscovering their common goal of support for the development of students' academic independence, just as the library and peer tutoring and writing center programs had realized their common goal of facilitating student success in the process through development of a shared space and a shared learning commons identity. As proof of the success facilitated by these tutors and consultants in fall 2010, the peer tutoring program experienced a 20 percent growth in number of visits compared to fall 2009, and the writing center maintained its record of over 1,500 consultations for the fifth straight semester.

While the absence of a writing center director and learning commons leader prevented a seamless beginning, the three-month process of hiring an individual to fill the position entailed further collaboration among the library, peer tutoring program, and writing center. Consisting of individuals from both academic and student affairs, the hiring committee crafted a position title and job description emphasizing strategic program development and then evaluated applicants based on their experience and abilities to collaborate, unite, and lead. Final candidates were interviewed by library personnel, student affairs staff, and several higher members of administration as well as by tutors and consultants. Finally, in December 2010, the Writing Center and Learning Commons Assistant Director position was filled, and spring semester commenced with a renewed vigor to set the pace for the future of the UNK Learning Commons.

LEARNING COMMONS SERVICES

In the current temporary space, the services include writing center consultations and peer tutoring in a wide range of subjects, including mathematics, biology, chemistry, Spanish, accounting, statistics, economics, finance, German, and a number of other subjects on demand. Furthermore, the peer tutoring coordinator and assistant director of the writing center and learning commons are both linked directly to the library's 24/7 ask-a-librarian service so that they can provide online assistance with citations and writing projects for both on-campus and distance students.

THE FUTURE OF THE LEARNING COMMONS

Future plans for the learning commons envision even broader campus involvement. The relocation of academic peer tutoring from the Memorial Student Affairs Building to the learning commons in the library has opened the way for development of a one-stop location for several other student-support functions. Long-term plans include the relocation of academic advising, career services, Learning Strategies, Disability Services, and student support services (TRIO federal grant) into the library wing currently occupied by the department of communications.

In particular, organizing and utilizing a learning commons focus group consisting of individuals from academic and student affairs, information technology, and the UNK student body will allow the learning commons to benefit from the support and expertise of other campus entities. Plans to mutually design and administer a learning commons survey to UNK students, faculty, and staff will help provide the library and peer tutoring and writing center programs with direct campus feedback on the effectiveness of learning commons' initial collaborative and marketing efforts. The results of that survey and the recommendations of the focus group will help develop marketing strategies for the learning commons that will enable it to better define and transmit its purpose. Campuswide input will also aid the development of learning commons student learning outcomes and other assessment pieces that can help staff and administration better identify and evaluate the academic impact of this collaboration. If correlations are strong enough to indicate direct effectiveness on student success, the UNK Learning Commons could set a precedent for program analysis, as literature about the direct academic assessment of these types of spaces is sparse at best. If academic success correlations are statistically weak, the learning commons will compare those results with surveys to determine what further improvements could potentially foster better effectiveness.

CONCLUSION

The flexibility, creativity, patience, and dedication of students, staff, faculty, and administration allowed the UNK Learning Commons to become a reality in a budget year that saw university systemwide fiscal restrictions, with the certainty of even more widespread budget cuts in the coming biennium. Administrators, managers, faculty, and staff all continued to work on the project even when it appeared that only partial funding might be available in the belief that even a minimal facility was much better than having the peer tutoring program continue to operate in space that was clearly inadequate.

The development of the learning commons was successful because everyone involved in the project exhibited a shared commitment to providing students with the best possible support and opportunities for their academic advancement. Careful attention was given to the establishment of good working relationships requiring integrity, objectivity, patience, willingness to compromise, and respect for other participants in the project. Development of and commitment to a shared vision enabled the program to succeed despite the challenges of uniting separate campus divisions with differing structures, separate funding, and traditions and programs that traditionally have been quite different in focus.

It is hoped that the example of the learning commons will serve as a positive example to other units on the campus and that more opportunities for collaboration among academic and student affairs will result in the development of a campus culture that is increasingly innovative, dynamic, progressive, and focused on the success of the students that we serve. Whether other universities pursue similar collaborations through more formalized planning or through a less structured, pragmatic process than outlined in this chapter, dedication to common goals rather than individual interests and preferences will be essential to success.

Notes

1. University of Nebraska at Kearney, *Phase I Strategic Plan: Mission, Vision and Planning Guidance,* Student Development Goal. Objective 1, January 2007, 9.

2. "UNK Factbook," 2010–2011, University of Nebraska at Kearney, Office of Institutional Research, accessed January 29, 2012, http://www.unk.edu/factbook/general/General_Information.

3. "UNK Factbook: Headcount Enrollment, Spring Semester," 2010–2011, University of Nebraska at Kearney, Office of Institutional Research, accessed January 29, 2012, http://www.unk.edu/uploadedFiles/factbook/enrollment/Course_Location.pdf.

4. APRs at the University of Nebraska Kearney consist of an in-depth self-study written by department personnel, followed by formal focused interviews by a review team external to the department. The chair of the external review team is a normally a faculty member or administrator from a peer university, while other review team members are faculty or administrative staff members from other UNK campus departments or divisions.

5. David L. Brandt and Keri A. Pearson, *Office Program Review Self-Study* (Kearney: University of Nebraska at Kearney, April 8–9, 2009) 24.

6. Ibid., Appendix C, 5.

7. University of Nebraska at Kearney, "Review Team Report, Academic Program Review of Office," April 8–9, 2009, 7.

8. Amanda Granrud, "UNK Writing Center: Administrative Program Review, Spring 2010 Self Study," April 8, 2010, 38.

9. Ibid., 45.

10. Nancy Schmidt and Janet Kaufman, "Learning Commons: Bridging the Academic and Student Affairs Divide to Enhance Learning Across Campus," Research Strategies 20 (2005): 243.

11. Mardi Mahaffy, "Exploring Common Ground: U.S. Writing Center/Library Collaboration," *New Library World* 109 (2008): 173, 181.

12. Emily Love and Margaret B. Edwards, "Forging Inroads between Libraries and Academic, Multicultural and Student Services," *Reference Services Review* 37 (2009): 21.

13. Keri Pearson, "New Learning Commons Opens in Library for Fall 2010," *News: A Newsletter form Academic and Student Affairs* 3, no. 16 (July 23, 2010), University of Nebraska a Kearney website, http://www.unk.edu/academicaffairs/enews.aspx?id=51359.

12

Effective Library Professional Development: A University Partnership for Improving Access and Inclusion for Patrons with Disabilities

Elizabeth M. Lockwood, Scott N. Friedman, and Linda Naru

Although most library and student affairs collaborations focus on developing programs and services for students, collaborative outreach efforts aimed at faculty and staff have the potential to broaden awareness and institutionalize change beyond a one-time program. In this chapter, Lockwood, Friedman, and Naru describe a collaborative training program developed for library staff. The result of the training was to improve services for students with disabilities by raising awareness and fostering systemwide commitment to personal responsibility and departmental improvement.

Libraries have been vital to the growth of academic knowledge since the beginning of the university structure. Most college students utilize the campus library as a place to study, complete research projects, and delve into worlds of literature. What happens though when a student is unable to access these resources? For many students with disabilities, collegiate libraries present barriers due to outdated physical infrastructure, lack of technological accessibility, and poor institutional policy.

The library at the University of Illinois at Chicago (UIC) realized that there were significant opportunities to make the library system more accessible. By working with staff from the Disability Resource Center (DRC), a strong partnership formed to develop a disability-related professional development program that would be directed to frontline library professionals. Due to the overwhelming success of this collaboration, library staff became advocates for significantly improving library access, revising policies and procedures, and appreciating the importance of serving every library patron with a disability. Since the partnership began, the library has shifted its philosophical and practical approaches, resulting in numerous improvements to advance accessibility for all patrons. Consequently, the purpose of this chapter is to highlight the effective outcomes of the collaboration between the UIC Library and the DRC as well as to provide replicable strategies for others.

The UIC Library has three sites in Chicago and a total collection of 2.6 million volumes. Its main library was originally constructed from 1961 to 1965 and houses collections in social sciences, humanities, and engineering. Approximately 1.1 million visitors a year utilize this site. The Library of the Health Sciences in Chicago opened in its own building in the 1970s to support the fields of medicine, dentistry, nursing, public health, pharmacy, and applied health sciences. Neither of these facilities was originally designed to accommodate patrons with disabilities.

The DRC at the Chicago campus is a centralized disability services office within the Division of Academic and Enrollment Services. With a primary goal of providing accommodations and services for students with disabilities, the DRC works to ensure access according to federal law. Though the DRC is rooted in these fundamental aspects, the office structure is also designed to provide opportunities for collaboration across the campus. Through a group of highly trained access consultants, DRC staff provide accommodations to students while also encouraging disability inclusiveness.

BRIEF HISTORY OF LIBRARY SERVICES FOR PATRONS WITH DISABILITIES

Individual libraries have made varying efforts for many years to accommodate individuals with disabilities. Early programs for large-scale service to patrons grew out of the Pratt-Smoot Act,[1] in which the Library of Congress and regional libraries made available embossed books to patrons who were blind.[2] As the disability rights movement and legal actions developed during the 1960s and 1970s, libraries across the country saw significant increases in the number of deaf and hard-of-hearing patrons and those with physical disabilities.[3] While most of the early accommodations were designed to remove structural barriers to access, growth of technology made access to information even more valuable. Technology has removed significant barriers by increasing access to collections, library websites, media, and academic library instruction.[4] Due to the proliferation of technological access and subsequent needs of patrons with disabilities, frontline library staff members have needed additional training to effectively assist these individuals and make the overall library environment more comprehensively accessible.

LITERATURE ON EFFECTIVE DISABILITY-RELATED LIBRARY PROFESSIONAL DEVELOPMENT

Although a scarcity of literature exists, there is support for disability-related library professional development. Miller-Gatenby and Chittenden stress the importance of regular disability-related professional development that addresses equitable access and service, confidentiality, appropriate service behavior, use of appropriate language, and library policies and procedures.[5] Similarly, the American Library Association (ALA) makes it quite clear in its policy manual that access must be improved because "many people with disabilities face economic inequity, illiteracy, cultural isolation, and discrimination in education, employment and the broad range of societal activities."[6] Within this policy, the ALA makes explicit the need for disability-related professional development on two levels. First, graduate programs should require that students learn about legal issues, accessibility, assistive technology, and the needs which both patrons and employees with disabilities may have in the library setting. Second, a strong statement aimed at current library professionals notes the importance of providing training opportunities to learn about best practices in serving the needs of people with disabilities within libraries. Not only has the ALA taken a clear stand on the significance of library access, it correctly utilizes language aligning with the commonly accepted philosophy of disability within the United States.

THE SOCIAL MODEL OF DISABILITY

Since the latter part of the twentieth century, people with disabilities have begun to mobilize as a social movement. The disability rights movement parallels other liberation movements, and, akin to new social movements, disability movements demand self-representation and control over resources necessary for quality living.[7] Through the disability rights movement's battle against oppression, ableism, and exclusion, the creation of the social model of disability emerged. Discussions about and focus on the body and impairment shifted to issues of participation and inclusion.[8] It is through this lens that disability is viewed not in the traditional medical perspective as an impairment, but rather emphasizing the interaction between the person with a disability and society.

In the medical model of disability, a disability is viewed as a deficiency or abnormality, being disabled is negative, disability is housed within the individual, the remedy for a disability-related issue is a cure, and the agent of remedy is the professional. Conversely, the newer social or minority/interaction model perceives disability as a difference from average, being disabled in itself is neutral, disability derives from the interaction between the individual and society, the remedy is changing the interaction between the individual and society, and the agent of remedy can be the individual, an advocate, or anyone who changes the interaction.[9]

The social model of disability is increasing in popularity and is being implemented in disability policies globally. Recent impetus for this action, the United Nations Convention on the Rights of Persons with Disabilities (UNCRPD), came into force on May 3, 2008. The UNCRPD is an international human rights treaty intended to protect the rights and dignity of persons with disabilities and importantly adopts the social model of disability by defining persons with disabilities as "those who have long-term physical, mental, intellectual or sensory impairments which in interaction with various barriers may hinder their full and effective participation in society on an equal basis with others."[10]

As expressed above, to create a more accessible society for persons with disabilities and for everyone, a shift in the interaction between the individual and society is needed. Thus, encouraging this type of interaction became the focus of the UIC library-based professional development trainings. The aim of the presentations was to provide relevant and practical information and strategies to the frontline library staff. The staff could then apply this knowledge to effectively provide access and accommodations for patrons with disabilities.

The strong collaboration between the library and the DRC was paramount in the success of our initiative, and thus it is important to briefly review models of collaboration. The social model of disability, along with the collaboration model, discussed below, created the foundations from which we worked.

MODELS OF COLLABORATION

There are three main types of connections: networking, coordination, and collaboration. Networking is the least formal, and collaboration the most structured. Networking usually entails only an exchange of information. Coordination builds upon networking and is more action-oriented, with two or more parties working toward a common goal or solution. Collaboration is the most complex, with a developed structure that enables the parties to meet the common goal.[11]

Specifically, collaboration is a more formal type of making connections between two or more groups or individuals who mutually benefit from achieving common goals. Most collaboration models include emphasis on having (1) common goals, (2) well-designed structures that are supported, and (3) a connection that is mutually beneficial.[12] Although the library-DRC partnership employed all three types of connections, the three key components of the collaboration model were carried out the most. The types of connections utilized by our initiative are highlighted throughout this chapter.

LAYING THE GROUNDWORK FOR THE PROFESSIONAL DEVELOPMENT SESSIONS

The UIC Library has long offered services to patrons with disabilities, including retrieving books and journals from stacks, assisting with making at-cost photocopies, and providing some limited assistive technology. In 2007 it became apparent that the library's facilities and services could be significantly improved in order to move toward universal access to buildings, collections, and services. The University Librarian appointed the Library Accessible for All Task Force (LAATF) to develop a philosophy statement for providing universal access to library resources and services and to audit physical facilities and equipment in the library buildings on the Chicago campus. Library staff and staff from the DRC served on the task force. The LAATF submitted a final report to the University Librarian and the director of the DRC in November 2007, which served as the basis for a successor task force, the Accessibility Implementation Task Force (AITF).

Of the many recommendations made by the AITF, the category of Employee Training and Awareness was easily implemented because of the strong relationships formed between the AITF and DRC staff members. This relationship was established when a representative from the DRC volunteered to work with the AITF, thus creating the network and coordination between the groups. The authors of this chapter coordinated monthly meetings in which the foundation for effective frontline library staff trainings was laid. These meetings were fundamental in establishing the structure of the mutual goal of providing a professional development seminar to frontline staff. Initial work began during March 2008 with a training targeted for midsummer. All tasks were developed based upon recommendations from the AITF and placed into a timeline with deadlines for completion. With a clear timeline, the team developing the training began to determine the needs of both library staff and patrons.

To effectively determine the needs for disability-related professional development, the team developed a simple needs assessment. It was designed to formally identify the gaps between current and desired outcomes, and then to prioritize an order to resolve these gaps.[13] The needs assessment started with the LAATF report and the goals identified by the AITF and administrators within the library. From these pieces, a simple needs-assessment survey was created to measure how much knowledge library staff had and what else they would need to know in order to more successfully serve patrons with disabilities. The questions answered not only by frontline library staff, but also by library administrators, behind-the-scenes staff, and—in a slightly different format—by students with disabilities who regularly used the library. A summary of the responses identified several accessibility features that had been implemented previously, but many staff requested additional information.

The needs-assessment results were beneficial in identifying the final target audience and sections of the training. Because of the contact that frontline staff have in serving patrons with disabilities, the presenters decided to focus on basic and effective best practices that the frontline library staff could implement. In addition, the responses indicated that a 90-minute session on the following topics would best benefit these staff members:

- how to treat patrons with disabilities
- services for patrons with disabilities available within the library system
- a hands-on activity about library accessibility
- technology and campus resources that library staff could utilize to support patrons with disabilities

Not only were the library task forces and administrators vital in outlining the training needs, but the addition of a needs assessment also provided guidance for directly relevant and practical professional development to serve the frontline library staff.

THE PROFESSIONAL DEVELOPMENT TRAINING SESSIONS

Through the alliances discussed above, the authors of this chapter collaborated to create a disability-related professional development training for the UIC Library in the summer of 2008. In addition to the authors, the DRC's assistive technology specialist, Kevin Price, also volunteered to present. The sessions were titled "Disability Training for Daley and Health Sciences Libraries." The presenters facilitated the same session four times over a weeklong period during July 2008. The session was presented twice at the Daley Library and twice at the Library of the Health Sciences–Chicago. In addition, a remote connection was established to share the presentations live with three regional health sciences libraries throughout the state. In total, nearly one hundred frontline library staff across the system participated in the sessions.

To use the time as effectively as possible, the presentation was divided into three sections. Section one discussed general background statistics about persons with disabilities nationally and globally, followed by tips on how to work effectively with students with disabilities in everyday and more specific library settings. Section two examined library services and policies that were currently in place to serve patrons with disabilities. Section three concluded with discussing general accessibility, assistive technology, and campus resources.

Between sections two and three, the training paused for a small-group activity to analyze a real-life situation that a library employee might encounter. Five scenarios were modified from actual student and staff complaints about inaccessibility at the library. Each group randomly selected a scenario, discussed and developed a plan to effectively work with the inaccessibility, and shared the issue and solution with the whole group. The detailed scenarios were these:

1. One student indicated that directional signs were not clearly posted, and consequently the student was lost in the library for over an hour. Considering that the library is on a tight budget

this year and could not afford to purchase permanent signage, what recommendations would you suggest for ensuring that future patrons do not get lost?

2. A staff member stated that the library tries and is compliant with the legal definition of access but does not provide the kind of access that would minimize intervention. What steps could be taken to increase access for a broad range of patrons with disabilities?

3. A student mentioned that parking for library patrons with disabilities was not located close enough to the building to be considered accessible. Imagine that the library staff would be responsible for a shift in policy. How would this impact the situation?

4. Both staff and students discussed the height of the circulation desk counters as a barrier to access. What changes would you make to remove this barrier? Also, what steps would you take if your budget did not allow for replacing or renovating the counters?

5. Staff members expressed their potential inability to assist students due to a lack of understanding on how to use some of the accessibility software on accessible workstations. What remedies would you provide to ensure that any staff member (even those who work behind the scenes but might run across a student while walking back to the office) could assist a student?

Although the scenarios provided a foundation for exploring accessibility issues, the presenters encountered unexpected obstacles, which were used to promote disability awareness. On the fourth and last day of presentations, a sign language interpreter for two participants did not appear and did not inform anyone of the cancellation. This was a difficult situation because the presentation was aimed at providing accommodations to all patrons with disabilities, yet the interpreter was not present. Fortunately, one of the presenters was fluent in American Sign Language (ASL) and could interpret and present simultaneously during the presentation. These conditions were not ideal, but the presenter was able to highlight access and accommodate the deaf and hard-of-hearing participants while still successfully presenting. An unexpected benefit from this experience was that hearing participants became more interested in the presentation because of the unplanned use of sign language. Many postpresentation questions and survey responses for this session revolved around interest in sign language and communication access for deaf and hard-of-hearing patrons. The presenters used this unexpected pitfall as a teaching tool to demonstrate to the library staff the importance of communication and information access for everyone. In the end, this situation not only showed the practical value of providing access, it also provided an unexpected opportunity for increased awareness and a very positive impact.

In wrapping up each session, the presenters asked participants for session feedback. The overall response rate for the total presentations was fifty-six evaluations returned from the ninety-one distributed (or a 62 percent response rate). The smaller sessions at the Library of Health Sciences–Chicago yielded a 100 percent return rate. The larger Daley Library sessions had much lower return rates, possibly due to the very tight space that was available for the sessions. The evaluation questions and common responses were as follows:

1. Are you interested in learning more about Accessibility/ Disability topics?
   Sixty-six percent of the respondents stated they were interested in learning more about disability topics.
   ○ If yes, in what aspects are you interested?
      The most frequently requested topics for future presentations included assistive technology, policy-related aspects, and sign language. The ASL Club was discussed only in the last two presentations, and the use of ASL during the last session sparked a great deal of interest.

2. What suggestions do you have to improve the presentation?
   Some respondents would have preferred a shorter presentation with fewer presenters. There was interest in learning directly from students with disabilities through a presentation and role-playing format about their experiences at the larger university and within the library.

3. What did you like about the presentation?
Many participants stated that the presenters covered a very broad topic but were able to explain it in a concise and relevant manner while also providing suggestions that were relevant to the university and library. Many respondents indicated that they enjoyed the group scenarios.

4. Additional comments
We received many kind comments and thank-you statements; plus a highlight of "This was not boring."

SUCCESS THROUGH CONTINUOUSLY GROWING OUTCOMES

Though the professional development sessions were vital to preparing front-line library staff to engage in work that would serve patrons with disabilities, this was only the beginning of a major effort by the library system. The LAATF developed an initial philosophy of service that endorses a shift from the individual with a disability to an emphasis on increasing the level of inclusiveness and the flexibility of the library environment for all users. The task force report included the following guiding principles:

1. The Library should strive to provide seamless accessibility to information in all formats as well as safe and comfortable learning and collaborative spaces.

2. The Library environment should be accessible to the degree that it is not incumbent upon individuals to come forward and self-identify in order to access resources and services efficiently and independently.

3. The goal of the University Library should be the support of optimal independence and self-sufficiency of all users.

4. The Library should move beyond ADA legal compliance to creating a universally accessible environment both physically and virtually.

The AITF took this charge and systematically began addressing the recommendations in the LAATF report. The professional development sessions were only a part of the foundational work that AITF members completed to make the library more accessible. By August 2008, the task force members had completed or assigned continuous responsibility to the following units:

Facilities

- Providing adjustable-height tables for computer workstations and study tables.
- Adjusting the height of public printers and purchasing accessible photocopiers.
- Assigning study carrels for patrons with disabilities who need to use JAWS (text-to-speech software) or to work with an assistant in a nonpublic space.
- Continuous review of the library's emergency plan to accommodate persons with disabilities.
- Constant monitoring of buildings to insure accessibility; for example, maintaining automatic doors and checking that the campus grounds crew removes snow promptly.

Electronic Access and Collections

- Organizing with other university libraries to pressure vendors to provide accessible electronic databases and indexes.
- Ensuring that the library's website is accessible.
- Updating the accessibility information on the library's website.
- Routinely purchasing captioned DVDs.

Assistive Technology and User Services

- Keeping up-to-date versions of assistive technology such as JAWS and ZoomText (software designed for blind and visually impaired individuals) available on library computers.
- Expanding the number of staff members assigned as liaisons to patrons with disabilities.
- Extending proxy borrowing privileges for patrons with disabilities.

Employee Training and Awareness

- Providing an initial librarywide awareness training session.
- Establishing a program of annual training or awareness sessions on working with patrons with disabilities.

The LAATF final report also included an administration section with a recommendation to hire a staff person to oversee the provision of accessible services and facilities. The AITF made a conscious decision to work to incorporate the philosophy and responsibility of universal access among all staff rather than to assign responsibility to just one employee. This decision has been effective, and two fortunate financial developments have enabled the library to put into practice its commitment to universal accessibility.

In fall 2008, the library began to receive funds from a campus library/IT fee to support facilities upgrades and additional services that would support student achievement. As a result of these new funds, the library has been able to purchase new study tables, computer tables, computers, and chairs and to undertake small facilities-improvement projects such as restroom renovations. The library chose adjustable furniture, acquired more copies of assistive technology software, and will be able to remove barriers in its restrooms. All of these things directly influence the library's ongoing efforts to pursue the goal of universal accessibility. As a continuation of this achievement, the library recently finished design of a 15,000-square-foot learning commons area that will be constructed on the first floor of the Daley Library beginning in late 2010. In addition to adjustable furniture and equipment, this new space will have accessible signage, service counters, and 24-hour access services.

The library benefited significantly from its close collaboration with the DRC, especially in the collaborative task forces during 2007–2008 and the training sessions led with the DRC in July 2008. DRC staff provided expertise on mitigating physical barriers, helped prioritize recommended improvements, and were the source of much insight into the needs of patrons with disabilities. The training sessions were particularly effective because the broad participation of library staff as the presenters encouraged them to see the library environment from the perspective of patrons with disabilities.

LESSONS LEARNED

The library and patrons with disabilities greatly benefited from the collaborations with DRC staff. Since networks and coordination were already established with the task forces, a successful collaboration was easily formed. The library and the DRC established and achieved common goals and developed well-designed structures that are still in use. Everyone who was involved benefited from the initiative.[14] The library staff more effectively serves individuals with disabilities, and the DRC successfully disseminated disability awareness throughout the campus.

Crossunit campus collaborations are not always easy or simple. Research supports the need for collaborators to respect each other's strengths and weaknesses and to be prepared to work through cultural differences in campus units.[15] The success of the UIC Library–DRC partnership is due to several factors, which may be able to inspire and educate others.

UIC supports and advocates for a strong commitment to diversity and inclusion, which both the library and the DRC share. It is helpful to have a university system which encourages diversity in its mission and policies since this creates a foundation from which campuswide collaborations can emerge. Specifically, UIC's *2010 Strategic Thinking* report seeks to create "a fully integrated institution" and to "contribute to the making of a more egalitarian society."[16] Providing the highest quality of services for students with disabilities and creating bridges parallel UIC's mission of promoting "a resource and destination accessible to all who share our ambitions and have the desire to excel."[17]

Leadership is another key factor in our collaboration. Leadership can be one of the most critical factors accounting for the success of a group, yet effective leaders must create a sharing and inclusive atmosphere and develop tactics that fit with the cultural framework of the community.[18] Since both the DRC and the library already exhibit strong leadership within their departments and across campus, it was relatively easy to collaboratively lead and successfully carry out this initiative. Because of effective leadership in both units, staff members were willing to undertake the work of task forces to develop and participate in successful professional development sessions. Moreover, cooperative leadership empowers individuals to work together toward common goals that will create change, transform institutions, and consequently improve their quality of life.[19] This was the long-term goal, and the process to implement this change at UIC has begun.

Both the library and the DRC are units that serve students across campus. A positive impact was that there was cooperation between the groups rather than competition because of the overarching goal to improve student achievement. Some of the literature about campus unit collaborations describes conflicts in working styles or the need for one unit to adapt to its partner's decision-making methods or formality of structure.[20] Despite the somewhat different management styles of the heads of the library and the DRC, those involved in planning and implementing the training had common objectives, compatible temperaments, and willingness to do whatever work was necessary to meet the shared goals.

Although UIC may differ from many other comprehensive universities, effective strategies emerged from this collaboration which can be replicated at other schools. First, it is important to assess the situation and agree on what needs to be done. This action should be a collaborative effort with all units involved. Second, get the agreement and support of unit heads regarding goals and the methods for achieving them. Third, meet in person frequently to discuss progress, review documents, and carry out steps in the process. In other words, work together as closely as possible and think of the two units as one agency trying to achieve specific goals. Finally, make sure to respect each other's cultures and learn from one another. An example encountered at UIC was that at times the library staff seemed a bit narrow in interpreting and following disability-related procedures. Consequently, the DRC worked with library staff to provide awareness of these processes to provide better service to patrons with disabilities. In viewing this collaboration as a long-term goal to effect real institutional and cultural change, the shared vision in this partnership led to positive outcomes that could be replicated at college and university libraries throughout higher education.

Final Thoughts

Without the hard work of many individuals, it is unlikely that the UIC Library would have made such amazing strides in such little time. Currently, library staff exhibit knowledge and appreciation of how they can best serve, not only patrons with disabilities, but every person with a range of human abilities. Although the partnership to develop disability-related professional development sessions led to highly successful outcomes, it never would have without the foundational work completed by the library task forces. The task forces' findings and recommended policies directed library administrators and staff to take advantage of a partnership that would bridge the knowledge of two vastly different student service areas in collaboration toward the common goal of creating more universal accessibility throughout the campus. The success of these sessions was never intended to merely provide general awareness of simple best practices. The real success is in the ongoing advocacy and knowledge that grows within all library staff as a common cause for truly making the library a place for everyone.

Notes

1. Pratt-Smoot Act, Pub. L. No. 71-787, 46 Stat 1487 (1931).

2. Ruth Velleman, *Meeting the Needs of People with Disabilities: A Guide for Librarians, Educators, and Other Service Professionals* (Phoenix, AZ: The Oryx Press, 1990).

3. Phyllis Dalton, *Library Service to the Deaf and Hearing Impaired* (Phoenix, AZ: The Oryx Press, 1985); Velleman, *Meeting the Needs of People with Disabilities.*

4. Katherine J. Miller-Gatenby and Michele Chittenden, "Reference Services for All: How to Support Reference Services to Clients with Disabilities," in *Reference Services for the Adult Learner: Challenging Issues for the Traditional and Technological Era,* edited by Kwasi Sarkodie-Mensah (Binghamton, NY: The Haworth Press, 2000), 313–26.

5. Ibid.

6. American Library Association, "54.3.2 Library Services for People with Disabilities" in *ALA Policy Manual Section 2,* last updated October 2011, 33, http://www.ala.org/ala/aboutala/governance/policymanual/index.cfm.

7. James I. Charlton, *Nothing about Us without Us: Disability Oppression and Empowerment* (Berkeley: University of California Press, 1998); Kevin Paterson and Bill Hughes, "Disability Studies and Phenomenology: The Carnal Politics of Everyday Life," *Disability & Society* 14 (1999): 597–610.

8. Bill Hughes and Kevin Paterson, "The Social Model of Disability and the Disappearing Body: Towards a Sociology of Impairment," *Disability & Society,* 12 (1997): 325–40.

9. Michael Oliver, "Social Policy and Disability: Some Theoretical Issues," *Disability, Handicap & Society* 1 (1986): 5–17; Carol Gill, "A New Social Perspective on Disability and Its Implication for Rehabilitation," in *Sociocultural Implications in Treatment Planning in Occupational Therapy,* edited by Florence S. Cromwell (New York: Haworth Press, 1987), 49–55.

10. UN General Assembly, "Convention on the Rights of Persons with Disabilities," Dec. 13, 2006, 4, http://www.un.org/disabilities/default.asp?navid=14&pid=150.

11. Arthur Turovh Himmelman, "On the Theory and Practice of Transformational Collaboration," in *Creating Collaborative Advantage,* edited by Chris Huxham (London: Sage, 1996), 19–43.

12. Doug Cook, "Creating Connections: A Review of the Literature," in *The Collaborative Imperative: Librarians and Faculty Working Together in the Information Universe*, edited by Dick Raspa and Dane Ward (Chicago: American Library Association, 2000), 19–38.

13. Roger A. Kaufman and Fenwick W. English, *Needs Assessment: Concept and Application* (Englewood Cliffs, NJ: Educational Technology Publications, 1979).

14. Cook, "Creating Connections."

15. Pauline S. Swartz, Brian A. Carlisle, and E. Chisato Uyeki, "Libraries and Student Affairs: Partners for Student Success," *Reference Services Review* 35 (2006): 109–22.

16. 2010 Strategic Thinking Committee, *2010 Strategic Thinking*, University Report (Chicago: University of Illinois at Chicago, 2010), 12.

17. Ibid.

18. B. Ann Bettencourt, George Dillmann, and Neil Wollman, "The Intragroup Dynamics of Maintaining a Successful Grassroots Organization: A Case Study," *Journal of Social Issues* 52 (1996): 169–86; Aldon Morris, "Reflections on Social Movement Theory: Criticisms and Proposals," *Contemporary Sociology* 29 (2000): 445–54.

19. Dolores Bernal, "Grassroots Leadership Reconceptualized: Chicana Oral Histories and the 1968 East Los Angeles School Blowouts," *Frontiers: A Journal of Women Studies* 19 (1998): 113–42.

20. Swartz, Carlisle, and Uyeki, "Libraries and Student Affairs."

13

The Library and Student Life: Activist Partnerships in First-Year Experience Programs

Michelle Maloney, Joanna Royce-Davis, and Elizabeth Griego

Maloney, Royce-Davis, and Griego illustrate the wide variety of collaborative efforts that are possible between libraries and student affairs. Although their collaboration started with only a few programs, it grew to include more partners and support multiple programs. In addition to demonstrating how collaborations can develop and expand over time, this chapter shows the value of moving outside the walls of the library to reach students in other "contact zones."

Given that the world's current information landscape is marked by ever-increasing volume and fragmentation, the best academic libraries must have an expansive sense of the patron "contact zone."[1] The new information paradigm necessitates that forward-thinking libraries invest not only in visibility, but also in fresh ways of cultivating relationships—both within and outside of the physical space of the library itself. This refers not only to new relationships with patrons but the possibilities of collaboration between the multiple campus sectors that serve them. Swartz, Carlisle, and Uyeki have extolled the virtues of intrainstitutional collaboration where units "successfully pool resources in order to promote and enhance student learning," noting that both libraries and student affairs professionals operate outside of the curricular structure and are thus particularly well-suited to create flexible, dynamic partnerships that can advance student learning outside of the classroom.[2]

This chapter describes such a collaboration between two of the co-authors who work in student affairs—Elizabeth Griego, Vice President for Student Life, and Joanna Royce-Davis, Dean of Students—and the third who works in the library, Michelle Maloney, Outreach Librarian. The chapter discusses particular programs identified as ideal partnership vehicles and provides samples of student feedback that suggest these new initiatives were well received. The chapter ends with a set of lessons or transferable insights that may be of use to others attempting new initiatives.

INSTITUTIONAL BACKGROUND

University of the Pacific, an independent, comprehensive university, currently enrolls four thousand undergraduate students, five hundred graduate students, and six hundred first-time professional degree students at its Stockton, California, location. In 2007, the University of the Pacific Library, under a new leadership team and with a new librarian invested in building outreach capacity, began systematically identifying ways to integrate the library more fully into the fabric of campus.

As the librarian asked to lead this outreach effort, Michelle Maloney brought lessons from the Social Diversity and Social Justice Education curriculum at the University of Massachusetts Amherst, as well as her experience of the University of Illinois at Urbana–Champaign's Undergraduate Library, a library which has invested heavily in the formation of a strong and welcoming identity vis-à-vis students. Through a variety of outreach efforts, both face-to-face and virtual, Illinois's Undergraduate Library proactively conveys the overall message to its diverse student body—"We're here for you! Here's how the library can help!" Adapting Illinois's approach to best suit the needs of Pacific meant that a survey of the landscape was in order. Where could Pacific's university library, which had not previously had a dedicated outreach program, begin to best cultivate the "relationship development zone"[3] with students that would communicate how the Library can support their success?

The first step was to identify key campus constituencies and corresponding unexplored partnership opportunities through which to elevate the library's visibility and unearth the connections between its resources—intellectual, material, and spatial—and the vibrant world of the campus. Though it had an established librarian liaison system responsible for outreach to academic departments and faculty, there was a desire to reach as-yet-untapped audiences, particularly students, through nontraditional means so as to better facilitate patron access to a wide range of library services.

As the library began to look outward in this way, the Division of Student Life immediately emerged as a strong potential partner. Recent literature, particularly since 2005, has noted the many similarities shared by libraries and student services professionals in regards to promoting academic retention and persistence. As librarians Emily Love and Margaret Edwards note: "Both aim to equip students with tools and resources needed to succeed in their studies and with their evolving personal, social, emotional and academic endeavors."[4]

As the librarian liaison to Pacific's Benerd School of Education, which offers a graduate degree in educational administration and leadership with a student affairs emphasis, the Outreach Librarian was able to foster a strong connection with Pacific's Dean of Students, who also serves as the director of the university's graduate program in student affairs, as well as with other key student life campus leaders affiliated with this program. Though fortuitous, this connection by no means automatically guaranteed a successful partnership, nor should those without such a program be dissuaded from seeking partnerships with student life or other units outside the library on their respective campuses. With the right approach, one can foster strong and sustainable partnerships between the library and numerous campus units, including student affairs.

Pacific enjoys a strong and talented student life presence, with many of its members having been recognized by the student affairs professional association, NASPA: Student Affairs Administrators in Higher Education. The student life team is led by two of the three authors of this chapter. As the Vice President for Student Life, Elizabeth Griego provides leadership for campus engagement in whole person learning, the development of an inclusive and supportive community on campus, and targeted outreach for student success and retention. Dean of Students Joanna Royce-Davis is responsible for the first-year experience program, designed to ease the transition to college, engender student growth and development, facilitate early connection to the university, and promote retention. As the Division of Student Life seemed an ideal partner, this led to several options for the Outreach Librarian, Michelle Maloney, to pursue.

NEW PARTNERSHIPS AT WORK

Once the library had identified a principal partner, it then examined where a library presence could most naturally and robustly complement existing student life programming. Since the first-year experience program provides students with a critical lens through which to view and contextualize their time at Pacific, the Outreach Librarian decided to approach student life about expanding participation in first-year experience programming for Pacific's newest students—both freshman and transfer students.

Student life and allied units make a broad and deep investment in the first year because first-year activities have the potential to play a critical role in students' academic and social integration and overall college success.[5] At Pacific, the first-year experience is purposefully designed by a universitywide committee of faculty, staff, and students who together develop curricular and cocurricular experiences that have the expected outcome of facilitating connections that result in a sense of community and an awareness of available university resources. The Outreach Librarian now serves on this committee and in various work groups associated with first-year initiatives and projects.

In addition, as someone newer to the campus and thus struck by the diverse student population, the Outreach Librarian was committed to discovering how the library could help support a welcoming and inclusive campus climate that would benefit all students, not only those new to campus but any from underrepresented ethnic or religious backgrounds. Given these particular areas of focus, the two divisions within student life that the library initially reached out to were the Office of New Student and Family Programs, responsible for much of Pacific's first-year experience programming, and the Office of Multicultural Affairs, whose programs play a key role in educating all students about issues of diversity and equity.

Orientation: Springboard to Deeper Connections

In 2008, the library coordinated with the Office of New Student and Family Programs to begin participation in first-year experience activities, starting with a presence at all three new student orientation information fairs—tabling/networking events for incoming students held outside on the campus lawn every summer. Library involvement in these events was well received by students, staff, and faculty alike. Yet rather than view its successful participation in information fair events as the culmination of its outreach work, the library instead chose to view it as a springboard for making and fostering deeper connections on campus, particularly with student life colleagues.

Harnessing Student-to-Student Power

One of the most powerful results of this connection building has been the development of new library-based programming with the Office of New Student and Family Programs, which not only coordinates orientation events, but also recruits and mentors a one-hundred-member team of student ambassadors and student advisors. This peer team manages many components of new student orientation and promotes leadership and student involvement while also working to assist students with different facets of the college experience. The library now runs dedicated sessions for these student leaders, thus harnessing the power of peer-to-peer networking and knowledge dissemination and providing the campus with another powerful tool to promote academic persistence. The student ambassadors and student advisors also serve as an early-alert system for students in academic difficulty, who can be helped through the writing center (located in the library), archival and other research support for assignments, and referral to tutorial services.

Transfers: Support for a Fast-Track Journey

Another result of the deepening partnership between the library and student life involves dedicated library sessions for incoming transfer students. Transfer students are a population particularly in need of library resources, and there previously had not been dedicated library outreach programming in place for all transfer students. This was recognized as an area of particular need by the Outreach Librarian, who then approached the Dean of Students and Vice President for Student Life with ideas for integrating library content into the transfer orientation program and how such integration could benefit students. This overture was received positively by both student life leaders, and the library now offers orientation programming for all transfer students. Student ambassadors and student advisors attend these sessions with new transfer students and provide information about how they use the library and what library resources they most value. Transfer student feedback from these sessions consistently ranks the library as one of the top two campus resources most helpful to learn about as they begin their accelerated educational journey. As one student remarked to the Outreach Librarian, "I feel like I can make it through here because faculty members and staff have my back, including librarians like yourself."

Partnering to Promote Inclusiveness

Diversity is a central part of the Pacific experience, which has a higher-than-average population of minority-identified students. To help engender a welcoming environment for new students from underrepresented backgrounds, as well as promote a general campus climate where all are respected and valued, the Outreach Librarian established a partnership with student life's Office of Multicultural Affairs.

This connection has resulted in a program of regularly featured book displays placed prominently in the library's main lobby that are tailored to cultural heritage months as well as to events celebrating LGBT and women's history. The items in these displays, which aim to broaden multicultural learning on campus and help enhance student identity formation, have higher-than-average circulation rates of 20 to 53 percent and provide opportunities for all Pacific students to make their own discoveries and connections about the world, thus further equipping them with the knowledge needed to be informed and interculturally competent global citizens. The Director of Multicultural Affairs communicates each semester's multicultural affairs calendar of events to the Outreach Librarian, aids with the logistics of procuring posters for the library displays, and suggests book titles for various exhibits.

Library outreach to multicultural affairs has also opened up other avenues of contact. As students of color and other underrepresented populations have witnessed the Outreach Librarian working with the Director of Multicultural Affairs and other multicultural center staff members to prominently display the works of underrepresented populations at the library, as well as to assist with various events sponsored by multicultural affairs, this has engendered a deeper sense of community and of trust. The Outreach Librarian has in many ways been "adopted" as the primary multicultural affairs librarian—the person that students and staff know and consult with for their information needs, whether by appointment at the multicultural center or at the library.

Additionally, librarian participation in efforts to engender a more welcoming and inclusive campus climate has been recognized by the larger campus community, with two librarians, the Outreach Librarian as well as a reference librarian active with campus LGBT PRIDE and Safe Zone efforts, having been awarded Pacific's Martin Luther King Jr. Peace and Social Justice Award, which honors students, faculty, and staff who make outstanding contributions to social justice and equality on campus.

M.O.V.E.-ing Forward: Librarians in the Wilderness

Through the emerging library–student life partnership, opportunities for contact with students transitioned to something more: relationships of shared interest and purpose. Among other new student orientation events, library faculty and staff participate in Pacific's Mountains, Oceans, Valley Experience (M.O.V.E.), a signature first-year program that includes all entering first-year students. This program is facilitated by student life staff, student leaders, and faculty and takes students to one of twelve regional locations to experience each other, nature, and shared impact through service projects.

Library faculty have been visible and recognized leaders among the program facilitators since the first pilot of this experience four years ago. In one illustrative example, the pilot program, A Taste of Yosemite, brought one hundred students to Yosemite National Park. The highlight of the trip was when the head of special collections shared John Muir's sketches and writing outside of the library's basement archives, which is home to an extensive collection of Muir's journals and photographs, and in the context of their natural environment. Students read Muir's diaries written in his own hand and describing the giant Sequoia redwood trees in the exact area of the valley where students were also recording for posterity the historic growth of the trees. It is not surprising that in their evaluations of this experience, students noted the presence of this library faculty member as enriching their learning experience.

Building upon this initial collaboration, the Outreach Librarian, as well as a newly hired member of the student life team whose primary focus was the coordination of M.O.V.E., worked to increase the number of library faculty and staff taking part in M.O.V.E. Both spoke to library faculty and staff about the benefits of engaging with students in this way, noting that M.O.V.E. presents an opportunity to promote early awareness of library resources. Thus, as M.O.V.E. expanded from a pilot program to include all first-year students, so did the participation of library faculty and staff expand in number and in depth of commitment to the program.

In their roles as facilitators, library faculty and staff, along with their student affairs partners, modeled what it means to be open to new experiences and the associated possibility of new insight and learning. In place alongside new students, facilitators stretched beyond their own comfort zones while simultaneously creating a space where students felt safe to take shared risks and to develop shared connections as a result. The stretch was both literal and metaphorical as groups challenged their physical endurance via hikes, service projects removing invasive plant species, rebuilding picnic tables and recreation spaces, engaging in camping adventures, planting California native groundcover, and contributing many hundreds of hours of service to regional organizations. The act of being exposed in this way humanized library faculty and staff; these experiential identifications with them literally gave face and voice to the library as a hub for accessing personally relevant information and developing expanded perspective on the world. As one student ambassador later remarked to a group of prospective students and parents during a tour of the library, "We met on M.O.V.E and now I have a relationship with [the librarian] and know I can consult her for help with research!"

Through M.O.V.E. and in partnership, library faculty and student affairs staff have responded to the documented value of common experiences in the first year and have, together, intentionally designed experiences to be attentive to opportunities for whole student learning and the inclusion of faculty and staff as participants in the experience.[6] As a result, students have reported finding staff and faculty to be more approachable and viewing them as viable resources for supporting their college success. Because students have had the opportunity to see and experience collaboration in action, they are better able to visualize themselves as a part of that same collaborative context and to both contribute to and benefit from the related learning outcomes.

Supporting Graduate Students in Student Affairs

Library involvement in the first-year experience also extends to first-year graduate students in Pacific's graduate program in student affairs. The Pacific graduate program is unique in that, through the graduate assistantships that almost every individual in this program holds, these students function in multiple staff roles in the university setting, requiring them to be competent in the use of university resources both for their own needs and to meet the learning needs of undergraduates whom they serve across the cocurricular environment. Library faculty have served as consultants and partners in the continued refinement of the graduate program curriculum and in achieving the goal of integrated learning outcomes and experiences. These program improvements have included the addition of library orientation days for many courses in the program. These orientation days have allowed resource overviews to be customized to the research assignments associated with a given class, while simultaneously giving students the opportunity to become more aware of professional student affairs literature.

This collaboration has been particularly important as it has enabled these graduate students to become not only informed users of resources but also competent student affairs practitioners who understand the impact of information engagement and overload on student development and learning. Perhaps most telling is that the graduate students themselves come to view the library faculty as coinvestors in their learning and the outcomes of their graduate program experience. As one 2010 program alumnus remarked, "I know that [the librarian] is an ally for me in my success at Pacific. She is unquestionably invested in my development as a scholar and as a student affairs leader. She is always available to problem solve a search or to let me know about an article that may be of interest for one of my projects."

Assessing Impact

Pacific's assessment data are beginning to show evidence that the library and student affairs work together is yielding positive learning results for students. There is the anecdotal feedback received, such as this note, which was sent to Pacific's Sciences Librarian after she and the Outreach Librarian jointly led a tour and advising session for new students:

> It was nice meeting you and Michelle today at the library and thanks for the great tour. As a freshman, I will be spending a lot of time reading books and using your resources and appreciate your assistance and guidance in advance!

Additionally, Pacific participates in the senior survey of the Cooperative Institutional Research Program (CIRP), which queries students about their satisfaction with various aspects of their university experience and also asks for data on how frequently they engage in certain behaviors related to their life on campus. Pacific students evidence higher satisfaction with the library compared to their peers at other private universities. They also report a steadily increasing positive participation trend of using the library for research or homework (see tables 1 and 2).

Table 1. Percentage answering "Very Satisfied" or "Satisfied" to the question "Rate your satisfaction with your college library facilities."

	Pacific	Private Universities
2010	71.8	66.7
2009	70.3	—
2008	76.0	65.8
2007	72.7	75.6

Table 2. Percentage answering "Frequently" to the question "Since entering college, how often have you used the library for research or homework?"

	Pacific	Private Universities
2010	52.4	53.6
2009	51.4	54.2
2008	45.8	50.2
2007	45.3	55.7

Further, results from the most recently available National Survey for Student Engagement (NSSE) reveal that 80 percent of Pacific students, compared to 71 percent of seniors at other NSSE institutions, believe that their university is "providing the support you need to help you succeed academically." Forty-two percent of Pacific students, compared to 36 percent of seniors at other NSSE institutions, believe that their university is "providing the support you need to thrive socially." The student life/library activist partnership group will continue to track these and other measures carefully to assess how the efforts to support student learning are perceived by students. The team will also continue to track various measures of persistence and retention to see whether the synergy of the strong working relationships result in improved measures of student success.

LESSONS LEARNED: PRINCIPLES FOR COLLABORATION

Libraries have traditionally been stereotypically regarded as locations of quiet contemplation and reflection. The phrase "activist partnerships" in the chapter title was specifically chosen to characterize the purposeful, participative nature of the collaboration that has developed at Pacific as library faculty and student life staff have shared in the cocreation of opportunities that support student learning and development outside the contact zone of the library building itself. For other colleges and universities interested in developing this kind of activist teaching and learning partnership, the following principles are offered to help guide decision making.

Decide on a Common Vision

The Pacific student life/library partnership grew from collaborative discussions designed to envision, plan, facilitate, and assess selected common experiences for students that would engender library visibility outside the physical library building. Physical contact zones on campus were identified (such as the Multicultural Center, the Women's Resource Center, and the residence halls), as well as on- and off-campus programs where library faculty might be particularly useful participants and contributors.

By moving the library faculty out of the "contact zone" of the library building, the vision of an evolving "relationship development zone" was brought to fruition, creating opportunities where integrated learning could be initiated, shared, assisted, and eventually, realized.[7] Library faculty learned with student life staff that as students interacted with library faculty in novel contexts in open learning environments, they become connected to the faculty in ways that move beyond typical student-educator relationships. Students become more willing to share their personal challenges and opportunities when investment in their learning is demonstrated through interactive experiences that move beyond the expected across-the-desk role relationships of librarian and advisor to the environs of active, connected discovery and meaning making. When students perceive the relational interest and investment in them as persons, their trust is facilitated as well as their experience, and the resulting learning deepens.

Design a Systems Approach

Plans for an active partnership at Pacific centered on what designated interactions with students might be most important and sustainable. The intentional sequencing of interactions started with the participation of library faculty in new student orientation advising sessions, extended to participation in the M.O.V.E. service trips, incorporated selected campus programs such as Transfer Connect (for prospective transfer students) and Transfer Orientation (for enrolled students), and ultimately reached to include coaching the student ambassadors and student advisors, who could then extend information about resources and assistance to reach many more students. Most recently, the library has begun collaborating with residential assistants to pilot library programming in the residence halls, bringing the library "home" to on-campus students.

Target Innovation

All innovation begins with a creative idea; ultimately, the creative idea must be implemented for innovation to occur. In the case of Pacific, as planning proceeded into active participation and partnership, the resulting enthusiasm generated fresh interest for both library and student life team members as they explored new ways of working with students and with each other. Envisioning learning resources in their broadest sense helped expand the view of the possible and working with new colleagues in engaged experiential learning helped accentuate how leadership is experienced at Pacific, by staff, by faculty, and by students themselves.

Identify Viable Partners

Innovators in the library sought out other campus idea champions who were already engaged and interested in the idea of activist partnerships. Student life partners were ideal collaborators as they had the decision-making power, resources, technology, and access to student groups like the student advisors and student ambassadors. Including key student groups in the partnerships ensured that ideas could be expanded and resources and information distributed more broadly. An outcome of the evolving library/student life partnership has been a renewed appreciation of the contribution that both make to student learning and development and how powerful combined resources can become when participants work across boundaries for the shared enterprise.

Approach the Partnership Empirically

Every partnership opportunity undertaken has had multiple opportunities for evaluation, including systematic observation, embedded student surveys, and written student reflections, which can be deposited into their electronic portfolios. The student life/library partnership members were conscious that the collaborative work would change expectations, norms, and the vision that students had for the library. Assessment allows the staff to check on how, and in what ways, those changes have made a difference for students.

Activate Persistence and Engagement

As at Pacific, the results of an activist partnership may not be fully realized until relationships with students change and deepen. Survey trend data revealed how students perceived the resources available to them and demonstrated the attainment of this goal. Faculty and staff perceptions of their own work also changed as a result. The dominant philosophy of universities has been that students must come to the teachers and that students must adjust to the institution in order to succeed. The activist partnerships at Pacific are helping faculty and staff recognize that their conceptions of teaching and learning must change, that they must cultivate campus cultures where faculty and staff meet students in a common space, where faculty and staff become learners as well as teachers, and where faculty and staff can facilitate students being advisors and teachers to one another. This objective is best achieved when faculty and staff are in the learning space participating alongside students, both affirming and engaging them in the integration of their own learning.

Prioritize Diversity

Both student life and the library recognize that diversity must be foregrounded if staff and faculty are to fully reach and serve the student constituents. Emerging models of outreach in librarianship reveal that a commitment to diversity must be enacted not only in the familiar sense of welcoming and responding to demographic differences but also in terms of working with diverse campus sectors and those holding different roles within them. As Steven Bell states:

> Any community, and particularly an academic one, benefits from strength in numbers. Partnering with fellow academic administrators enables us to accomplish more through a united front than by seeking change individually. Your goals will sometimes differ and may even conflict, but it will almost always be advantageous to have allies in your community.[8]

Ultimately, partnerships around diverse campus functions strengthen the academic mission by integrating the multiple facets of a student's experience.

Recognize That Collaboration Is Sometimes Messy and Requires Work

Campus partners can assist in deepening perspectives about work, while also adding energy to faculty and staff efforts; however, even with the benefit of shared purpose, investment, and commitment described throughout this chapter and called out in each of the principles, collaboration of this kind does not come without challenges. While the library/student life partnership has been fortunate to find ways to efficiently communicate and come to understanding of goals and expected outcomes together, faculty and staff members have also been continually challenged to create and preserve the dedicated time required to share perspectives and come to agreement.

Additionally, while library faculty and student life staff have realized the necessity and value of expanding working relationships to purposefully include each other, as well as additional campus partners, they have also recognized the importance of clearly articulating the benefits of such collaboration within each respective unit. Such "early and often" communication can help to reassure the colleague more wedded to traditional ways of doing things and who may have a more difficult time envisioning the shared benefits such intrainstitutional partnerships can provide. Beyond conveying the potential advantages of collaboration, it is also necessary to cultivate a risk-friendly climate, one in which ideas can be tried and discarded if not of benefit to users.

CONCLUSION

The new information paradigm means that library faculty cannot assume that students come to the bricks-and-mortar library in the same ways; instead, library faculty must increasingly meet students where they are—whether that is in new virtual spaces, other spaces on campus, or even in the wilderness beyond the campus. What the Pacific example of activist partnerships demonstrates is that purposeful work on the shared design, facilitation, and assessment of first-year learning experiences can move librarians from what previously existed as the "contact zone" in the library to an evolving "relationship development zone," a place where integrated learning occurs and is realized through interactions among students and library staff. As students experience library staff in novel contexts and via unexpected interactions, students become connected to staff in ways that move beyond typical student-educator relationships. Oftentimes, both the library and student affairs are viewed simply as services that are available to support student learning. Instead, this partnership demonstrates the opportunity to develop authentic relationships with students and positions faculty and staff as co-investors in student learning and success. The recognition of a "relationship development zone" redefines student affairs and library collaborations as contexts for establishing the foundational elements of learning, relationships and academic and social integration that lead to student success.

Acknowledgement

Author Michelle Maloney gratefully acknowledges the contributions of Karen Cardozo-Kane, whose comments and suggestions were most helpful in the preparation of this manuscript.

Notes

1. James Elmborg, "Libraries in the Contact Zone: On the Creation of Educational Space," *Reference & User Services Quarterly* 46 (2006): 56–64.

2. Pauline S. Swartz, Brian A. Carlisle, and E. Chisato Uyeki, "Libraries and Student Affairs: Partners for Student Success," *Reference Services Review* 35 (2007): 109.

3. Sheila Kasperek, Amber Johnson, Katie Fotta, and Francis Craig, "Do a Little Dance: The Impact on Students when Librarians Get Involved in Extracurricular Activities," *The Journal of Academic Librarianship* 33 (2007): 118–26.

4. Emily Love and Margaret B. Edwards, "Forging Inroads between Libraries and Academic, Multicultural and Student Services," *Reference Services Review* 37 (2009): 21.

5. Betsy O. Barefoot, "The First-Year Experience," *About Campus* 4, no. 6 (January 2000): 12; Marybeth Hoffman et al., "Investigating 'Sense of Belonging' in First-Year College Students," *Journal of College Student Retention* 4 (January 2003): 227–56; George D. Kuh, Ty M. Cruce, Rick Shoup, and Jillian Kinzie, "Unmasking the Effects of Student Engagement on First-Year College Grades and Persistence," *Journal of Higher Education* 79 (Sept. 2008): 540–63.

6. George Mehaffy, "Preparing Undergraduates to Be Citizens: The Critical Role of the First Year of College," *First-Year Civic Engagement: Sound Foundations for College, Citizenship and Democracy,* edited by Martha J. LaBare (Columbia, SC: New York Times Knowledge Network and the National Resource Center for the First-Year Experience and Students in Transition,, 2008): 5–8.

7. Gary R. Pike and George D. Kuh, "First- and Second-Generation College Students: A Comparison of Their Engagement and Intellectual Development," *Journal of Higher Education* 76 (2005): 276–300.

8. Steven J. Bell, "A Passion for Academic Librarianship: Find It, Keep It, Sustain It—A Reflective Inquiry," *portal: Libraries and the Academy* 3 (2003): 638.

14

The Phoenix of Cooperation: How a Collaborative Team Can Rise from the Ashes of a Campus Political Disaster

Randall Schroeder, Matthew Chaney,
and Michael Wade

The course of collaboration is not always smooth, and many chapters in this book allude to problems that were encountered and addressed. However, this next chapter is uniquely inspirational in that the partners started with a seemingly insurmountable challenge—misunderstandings and resentment over the allocation of space on campus. The authors were able to form a partnership by eliminating territorial rhetoric and seeking common ground, in this case a desire to improve student retention, and being willing to look beyond past problems to forge something new.

This case study presents two problems not necessarily related to each other. Most closely related to the theme of this book is how a medium-sized state-funded university, Ferris State University of Big Rapids, Michigan, looked to creating a partnership of common goals between its library and multicultural student services. The other, and more serious, difficulty was creating that partnership in the middle of campus tension and strife regarding the move of the multicultural student services office into library space. Was it appropriate to have library space taken up by what was regarded at the time a service not related in any way to library operations? On the other hand, why were the librarians not welcoming this office to a building with large areas of underutilized space? Could such a partnership survive a very difficult start?

THE SITUATION IN 2008

In the summer of 2008, the administration of Ferris State University in Big Rapids, Michigan, decided to move its Office of Multicultural Student Services (OMSS) to the Ferris Library for Information Technology and Education (FLITE). There were sound campus-planning reasons for such a move. For years, OMSS had been housed in a back hallway of the university's aging and overcrowded student union. OMSS also desired a more visible location on campus closer to the main entrance and parking. FLITE had space that was available and suitable.

Conversations took place between university administrators and the dean of the library. Unfortunately, many librarians did not find out what was going on until carpenters and painters showed up to start working on the first-floor extended-study-hours lounge that had been allocated for the new OMSS. Some library faculty saw this as an uninvited space grab without their input and opposed the move. Though it was made clear by the university administration that in some indefinite future OMSS would move back to a renovated and expanded student center, given the economic challenges for the state of Michigan, let alone in higher education, when the new student center would be built was a complete unknown. Meanwhile the library was to house this office. To many librarians, this seemed like uninvited guests taking over the living room.

OMSS in the meantime had been struggling for decades to find a new space. Students who used OMSS services wondered if the resistance to the move to a more visible and usable space was consciously or unconsciously motivated by the racial demographics of the organization. The leaders of OMSS did not attribute such noxious ideas to the library faculty. Anyone viewing the situation, however, had to wonder why the Office of International Education, which had moved to some empty space on the fourth floor of FLITE the previous winter, received no resistance. The librarians argued that the fourth floor was not prime public space and had been vacated by a non-library operation, the Faculty Learning Center, so the situations were not analogous.

THE CHALLENGE

Regardless of the merits of the arguments, the ingredients were present to create a hot, simmering stew of a campus political disaster for the library. That summer, a team of librarians and members of OMSS led by Dr. David

Pilgrim, Chief Diversity Officer, met to see how this project could go forward. Thanks to the diplomacy skills of Rick Bearden, chair of the library faculty, and the goodwill of Matthew Chaney, director of OMSS, a compromise was worked out that benefited all sides. In return for the library giving up the space in the Extended Studies Lounge, the university would pay to create a handful of new study rooms in the main part of the library. These study rooms were desperately needed. That compromise, however, was not reached without some pain.

Pilgrim, Chaney, and Bearden held a series of "village forums" before construction started to explain the renovations and to hear from the librarians and the clientele of the OMSS. The forums were, to say the least, unfortunate. Intemperate statements led to emotions running high. Many left the forums in anger, no longer willing to listen to the other side. OMSS was moving into the library, but relations were strained to the breaking point.

CHANGES IN LIBRARY THINKING

The library administration at this point believed that there needed to be a different way to think about this move for all involved. The two academic department heads, Leah Monger, library systems and operations, and Randall Schroeder, public services, realized that the library was coming apart and burning bridges with the multicultural student population on campus. Monger was appointed interim dean of the library that summer after the previous dean abruptly resigned. At that point, the administration team adopted a new narrative for the library before the situation got completely out of hand. It was time to think of the building not as the library's space but a space where learning takes place and the library resides.

This new narrative reflects a larger trend. Academic libraries as a whole are in a state of transition. Few in the field seriously defend the idea of library as warehouse, and collections and space are evolving to reflect the change in purpose of the library and university. In its simplest form, the paradigm that has traditionally governed higher education is this—a college is an institution that exists to provide instruction. Subtly but profoundly, higher education is shifting to a new paradigm—a college is an institution that exists to produce learning.[1] This new paradigm creates a freedom for librarians to seek new layouts and new partners in the enterprise of producing learning.

Learning is fostered by many factors, not the least of which is feeling comfortable in the space provided. Beyond comfortable chairs and pleasing colors, comfort also comes from community. Scott Bennett wrote that "good study space is responsive to the academic and social dimensions of study in ways that allow students to control them both. Such space encourages study and fosters learning by fostering a sense of community among students, allowing them to be seen as members of that community while they take strength from seeing other community members."[2]

THE SOLUTION

For various reasons, many first-year students are ill-prepared to succeed academically. Among them are some who are the first in their families to go to college and who lack tacit knowledge about what college will be like. Other traditional-age students may not have the skills necessary for college-level academic work. As Kuh, Boruff-Jones, and Mark observe:

> For these and a host of other reasons—most of which they cannot control—students struggle academically and socially. Indeed, some sizeable fraction is figuratively lost at sea. They see few markers on their daily horizons that direct them toward familiar activities, allow them to build on their strengths, give them confidence to try new things, and motivate them to invest the necessary time and energy to meet academic challenges. These are among the behaviors associated with success in college. But for many reasons, large numbers of students do not engage in them often or well enough, though they are capable of doing so. The result? They leave college. Many never return to try again. It does not have to be this way. Along with their faculty and student affairs colleagues, academic librarians can play a key role in changing the culture of college campuses to enhance student and institutional performance.[3]

It seems like a radical thought in the midst of campus turmoil with emotions running hot, but in reality OMSS and the library had very similar missions that addressed one of higher education's biggest challenges—retention. Schroeder approached Chaney immediately after one of the village forums and asked if he would be interested in a learning partnership and joint programming since there was an opportunity with OMSS sharing library space. Chaney seemed relieved to find a friendly face and an offer of cooperation in the library.

Although this may seem like an abrupt change, it was clear to Schroeder and Chaney at the time that the poisonous atmosphere and the rhetoric of the village forums could not continue. These were conclusions that Schroeder and Chaney reached independently of each other much earlier in the summer. It was complicated, however, by the sudden resignation of the library dean. What emboldened Schroeder to reach out to Chaney was that the new interim dean, Monger, had also reached the same conclusion. Monger and Schroeder brainstormed ideas as to how to address the issue, and reaching out to Chaney seemed an easy first step. It was believed that by having OMSS and Office of International Education in the library as partners, all three units could foster learning by creating community even if they appeared to be strange bedfellows unwillingly cast together in the same building.

One of the functions of OMSS is to orient its clientele, many of whom are the first members of their families to attend college, to life in higher education. Michael Wade, the Special Programs Coordinator, leads a program entitled T.O.W.E.R.S. As described on the program's website,

> T.O.W.E.R.S. stands for Teaching Others What Establishes Real Success. The T.O.W.E.R.S. program was created to encourage, motivate and inspire youth of today to become the leaders of tomorrow. T.O.W.E.R.S. participants, *(LEADERS & PROTÉGÉS)*, will engage in both educational and social activities sponsored by the Office of Multicultural Student Services. Students will gain the fundamental resources needed to become successful in their careers.[4]

T.O.W.E.R.S. is a peer-based leadership program that trains successful student leaders from the clientele of OMSS to lead sessions for incoming students. The program was an opportunity for the library to reach a population that would greatly benefit from an introduction to the concepts of information literacy.

As time went on and passions cooled, Chaney, Wade, and the instruction librarians realized the benefits of the partnership. At a meeting with the library administration, university president David Eisler encouraged the librarians to make this partnership a priority.

WHAT DOES THIS MEAN FOR STUDENTS AND RETENTION?

Now that the discussion of a partnership with OMSS was taking place, the primary question to be considered was what initiatives would be in the best interests of the library and the clientele of OMSS? One area that would enhance the library's mission to create information-literate students and would also assist OMSS with the persistent problem of retention rates would be using the library instruction staff to make the library a less frightening learning space for the students.

One block to academic success for any first-year student is library anxiety. For many, this is their first encounter with research materials of the magnitude found at a university library. Compound this with a reluctance to ask for help or lack of knowledge about where to find help, and students struggle. That struggle can result in unsatisfactory grades, academic suspension, and, finally, dropping out, perhaps never to reenroll in higher education.[5] Universities have long realized that it is a more efficient use of resources to retain students rather than recruit new students. The student engagement premise is deceptively simple, even self-evident. The more students do something, the more proficient they become.[6]

Minimizing library anxiety and thus promoting academic success is achieved with student engagement with the library. At the most basic level of engagement, the librarians are just around the corner from the OMSS where students are able to get help. Sometimes students are more comfortable talking about their academic challenges with their peers. With librarian engagement with T.O.W.E.R.S., identified student leaders within OMSS have the opportunity to share information literacy skills with their peers.

THE FLIGHT OF THE PHOENIX

So what is next? The program is in its first year, so there is no assessment evidence of where this will lead. On the other hand, it has accomplished one very important thing. The staff of OMSS and the public services department of the library are willing and enthusiastic partners in an endeavor to serve the students of Ferris State University better. Given where the relationship was in the summer of 2008, that is no small accomplishment.

The opening of the partnership with the T.O.W.E.R.S program has encouraged other initiatives between OMSS and the library. Monger invited OMSS staff to the library's administrative team meetings to enable each unit to share what is going on in the building with the others. This practice was widened to include the Office of International Education, since it is also located in the library building.

As the units learn to work together, other opportunities have opened up. Library staff actively participated in the Martin Luther King, Jr. Day teach-in sponsored by the university inclusion office and OMSS. Three librarians read at the teach-in, which was very well received by OMSS. The symbolism of assisting OMSS with its programming has helped to dissipate the tensions of the previous years. Further, a similar partnership is starting with the Office of International Education. That partnership includes a new speakers convocation series in the reading room, which was also an underutilized space in the library.

Another new partner for the library will be the Jim Crow Museum of Racist Memorabilia. Earlier in 2010, Ferris State University received a matching grant to expand and find a permanent structure for its nationally known Jim Crow Museum of Racist Memorabilia. The museum collects, exhibits, and preserves objects and collections related to racial segregation, civil rights, and anti-Black caricatures. The museum promotes the scholarly examination of historical and contemporary expressions of racism while promoting racial understanding and healing. The library will donate a space that was formally used for storage to be the permanent home of the Jim Crow Museum. The university will use the matching grant to upgrade the space to be a museum showplace.

CONCLUSION

So, what has been learned through these experiences at Ferris State? What can be learned by hearing the story of these painful events and their successful resolution? There are many lessons to be learned from this case study.

First, in the face of a campus political disaster for the library, the library administrators thought to repair the situation by focusing on students. Fortunately for the library, the offended party, OMSS, was led by a director who was willing to let the unfortunate rhetoric of both sides go and listen to a proposal. It was clear to both parties that cooperation was in their best interests to restore peace on campus, but more importantly, it could accomplish something incredibly important to the students they serve. It would help keep students in school by giving the students the tools to succeed.

Second, even if the librarians are not looking at the underutilized space, then, as at Ferris State, administrators across campus are looking at vacated library footprints on campuses strapped for space. It is in the best interests of the librarian to look for partners even if they are not the typical contacts.

If the partnership is an imposed one, it is the wise librarian who sits back, examines the situation, and ponders how a productive partnership can be made.

Finally, this case study demonstrates that partnerships do not always emerge from happy circumstances. It provides the lesson that shared goals can triumph over circumstances.

Notes

1. Robert B. Barr and John Tagg, "From Teaching to Learning: A New Paradigm for Undergraduate Education," *Change* 27, no. 6 (1995), 12–25.

2. Scott Bennett, *Library as Place: Rethinking Roles, Rethinking Space* (Washington, DC: Council on Library and Information Resources, 2005), 17.

3. George Kuh, Polly Boruff-Jones, and Amy Mark, "Engaging Students in the First College Year: Why Academic Librarians Matter," in *The Role of the Library in the First College Year*, edited by Larry Hardesty (Columbia, SC: Association of College & Research Libraries and the National Resource Center for the First-Year Experience & Students in Transition, University of South Carolina, 2007), 17.

4. "T.O.W.E.R.S.: Multicultural Leadership Development Program," Office of Multicultural Student Services, Ferris State University, accessed January 29, 2012, http://www.ferris.edu/htmls/studentlife/minority/towers.

5. Kuh, Boruff-Jones, and Mark, "Engaging Students in the First College Year."

6. George D. Kuh, "What We're Learning about Student Engagement from NSSE," *Change* 35, no. 2 (2003): 24–32.

15

Strategic Partnerships across Divisions: Aligning Student Affairs and the University Library to Increase Diversity in an Academic Institution

Annette Marines and Yolanda Venegas

In this chapter, Marines and Venegas describe the Faculty Mentor Program at the University of California, Santa Cruz, a program designed to attract and prepare underrepresented students for graduate study. The authors provide an example of collaborative outreach to a specific group of students and show how programs can develop over time, demonstrating that such development is not an indication of weakness but a recognition that "change is constant."

This chapter focuses on a partnership between the University Library and Educational Opportunity Programs (EOP), a student affairs unit, at the University of California, Santa Cruz (UCSC). The collaboration between the instruction librarian and pregraduate programs student affairs officer (FMP coordinator) centered on the Faculty Mentor Program (FMP), a pregraduate program aimed at preparing underrepresented juniors and seniors for graduate studies in the arts, humanities, and social sciences. The collaboration continues a long tradition at UCSC of supporting racial, ethnic, and cultural diversity through the campus curriculum and programs that support the academic needs of underrepresented students.

In this context, the librarian and FMP coordinator worked together to enhance the FMP and improve the students' experiences and preparedness for graduate study. The partners built on an existing program steeped in a rich history and poised for change. From the outset of their collaboration, their work together was marked by a communication style that promoted flexibility and openness. They took risks by experimenting with changes and adjusting approaches when needed. They had mutual experience with and interest in working with underrepresented students, which cultivated a sense of trust and cooperation. Their diverse perspectives, including their individual work styles as well as their disciplinary conventions and practices, generated a stronger understanding of the work involved on both sides of the partnership, which enriched their work as they revisited their goals in FMP and the ways in which they would accomplish them.

Over the course of three years, the two focused their collaboration on the redesign and implementation of the FMP's curriculum to improve the critical and information literacy skills of students participating in the program. More specifically, their work to redesign the FMP curriculum led to an assessment of the participants' information literacy skills, development of strategies for shaping these skills, and explicit instruction to teach critical literacy skills to participants. Their individual contributions and the synergy of their collaboration created a stronger program that vastly enriched vital student outcomes.

SUMMARY OF LESSONS LEARNED

The librarian and the FMP coordinator were successful in strengthening the goals, standards, and expectations in FMP. Their work created a stronger, student-centered focus in the FMP research seminar and in the supplemental support offered to participants. Ultimately the collaborators were better prepared to respond to organizational changes and improve on efficiencies because they had better information. The two entered the collaboration with enthusiasm for working with underrepresented students and were committed to doing a good job. By the end of the three years, both had been profoundly impacted by their work together and the lessons they had learned from the experience.

INSTITUTIONAL CONTEXT

UCSC is a large research and doctoral-granting university that has a core focus of bringing together research from multiple disciplines. Of the approximately 16,000 undergraduates on the campus, nearly 3,800 are underrepresented students. The University Library consists of two libraries: McHenry Library, which houses the arts, humanities, and social science collections, and the Science & Engineering Library. In fiscal year 2006–2007, UCSC had one librarian for approximately every 615 students and thirty-three faculty. One librarian oversees outreach to the campus's underrepresented students through her connections with the student affairs units. The student affairs units oversee all nonacademic student services. The EOP, which administers the FMP, is part of the student affairs unit charged with ensuring the retention, academic success, and postgraduate preparation of first-generation college students from low-income and educationally disadvantaged backgrounds. Through the FMP, EOP aims to help the cohort of students become stronger graduate and professional school applicants and acquire the skills to prepare for graduate and professional studies.

The program requires FMP Fellows to identify and complete a research project while working under the guidance of a UCSC faculty sponsor who acts as a mentor. Fellows and faculty mentors meet regularly throughout the two-quarter time frame of the fellowship. In addition, fellows participate in a two-quarter weekly seminar focused on academic research methods, writing, and oral presentation skills as well as peer input and critique. Each fellow presents his or her research findings in a paper and a presentation at the annual FMP Undergraduate Research Colloquium, which is held at the close of the spring quarter and is open to the entire university community.

INFORMATION AND CRITICAL LITERACY

Two major learning objectives guided the collaboration. The first was information literacy, which is centered on preparing students for the first year of graduate study. Regardless of the discipline or field a student chooses to pursue in his or her graduate studies, a student must have well-developed information literacy skills in order to succeed. One of the challenges of teaching the FMP Undergraduate Research Seminar was that students often arrived with a broad range of library skills and experience. In order to gauge the information literacy skills of students entering FMP, the librarian developed an information literacy skills questionnaire and asked admitted students to submit it before the program began. The results of the information literacy skills questionnaire gave the librarian a sense of where the new cohort of students was, as a whole, and enabled the adaptation of the series of information literacy skills workshops to best fit the needs of the particular cohort.

The library workshops are based on the *Information Literacy Competency Standards for Higher Education.*[1] The librarian works on developing higher order and advanced library research skills, while at the same bringing students up to speed on the basics. By the end of the program, participating students have developed advanced library research skills, including the use of research databases and bibliographic software.

The other major learning objective of the collaboration centered on developing the students' critical literacy skills. The curriculum of the FMP research seminar is designed to take students through the series of steps one takes in order to develop a research project beginning with an area of interest or research question. In the meetings with their faculty mentors, students received the disciplinary or field guidance they needed as they developed their individual research projects from research question to research proposal, annotated bibliography, and research essay. Such one-on-one meetings with their mentors might focus on how one writes a research proposal in psychology or what an annotated bibliography in world literature looks like. What the students may or may not learn from their one-on-one meetings with their faculty mentors is a critical literacy that enables student participants to understand scholarship as academic discourse. The critical literacy objective teaches students to understand the *"secret secrets"* of the university. As junior scholars learning to write within a discipline or field, they are learning to master a discourse, to reproduce the discipline's boundaries and authority. Critical literacy enables students to "call discourse into question, to undo it in some fundamental way."[2]

Since most of the students participating in the FMP plan to pursue a PhD, it is important that they have a clear understanding of how their chosen discipline or field constructs knowledge. What are valid questions? How does the discipline ask questions or define a problem? What can be learned about the discipline's way of seeing things from the way it forms a thesis? What counts as reliable (or unreliable) evidence? What does this discipline or field do with experience? These are the kinds of questions that teach students to understand scholarship as academic discourse by members of an academic community— by a group of people working together on an ongoing problem or issue.[3]

BACKGROUND OF THE PARTNERSHIP

FMP was established in the early 1980s at UCSC as a response to the growing number of underrepresented students on campus and the call to increase the number of underrepresented professors in academia. Initially the program was established at Oakes College, the residential college at UCSC that has historically emphasized racial, ethnic, and cultural diversity. According to Rosalee Cabrera, former EOP counselor and FMP program coordinator, who was interviewed for this chapter, after an initial restructuring, the university's graduate school division took over the FMP. The division withdrew its support after a few years. Shortly thereafter, with new funds to the campus and an emerging interest in affirmative action programs, EOP reestablished the FMP in 1989.

The collaboration between the University Library and FMP dates back to the late 1980s, when a concerted library effort was made to recruit a multicultural services librarian. The position would "provide leadership in library services for the campus multicultural community."[4] A librarian was hired in 1988 and charged with developing a library outreach program. Part of her outreach effort, Cabrera explained, included establishing a collaborative relationship with Cabrera, then the coordinator for FMP. The two soon forged a partnership to revise the curriculum of the FMP research seminar.

As part of this early collaboration, the librarian developed class sessions that focused on research methods and asked faculty in different disciplines to lead sessions introducing students to their disciplinary research methods. While the librarian focused on developing the undergraduate curriculum in a way that insured students in the research seminar had a thorough introduction to research methods in their discipline or field, the FMP coordinator focused on including class sessions about the graduate school application process and managing the administration of FMP. Eventually, the librarian left her position to return to school, and the curricular developments that she and the FMP coordinator had initiated were instituted into the FMP course.

By the time the current instruction librarian arrived in 2001, the program had been reshaped by the librarians who had served in the role in the interim, leaving the new librarian with a program steeped in multiple legacies. In contrast to the multicultural services librarian position of 1988, the current librarian was hired as an entry-level reference librarian. Within her duties in reference services and instruction, she was assigned the role of coordinating the library outreach efforts that had already been established. Related to FMP, she established the connection by meeting with the longtime FMP coordinator. The librarian's work in FMP at the time involved connecting with the FMP coordinator, matching each student in FMP with one of ten to twelve librarians for individual consultations, and overseeing the library workshops that were embedded in the FMP research seminar. In 2004, the librarian was invited to take part in the steering committee that selects the FMP student participants. She continues to be a member of the committee.

Since the late 1980s, the pregraduate program has been one of three ways EOP meets its charge to support underrepresented students. The FMP coordinator administers FMP, which has a competitive application process and accepts fifteen to twenty participants each year. She also administers the Graduate Information Program and advises students, thus providing outreach to the broader community of underrepresented students. In FMP, she oversees the steering committee and the curriculum, hires the graduate instructor, plans all the major FMP events during the two quarters, advises the students, and evaluates the program.

CURRENT PARTNERSHIP

The collaboration under consideration here began in 2006 with the arrival of the new FMP coordinator. The scope of the partnership between the FMP coordinator and the librarian currently encompasses the FMP student selection process, the content and timing of library workshops, librarian-student one-on-one consultations, and setting goals, standards, and expectations for working with the students. This work supports FMP's primary components: the two-quarter research seminar that is led by a graduate student, the research project, and the student-faculty mentor relationships.

The arrival of the new FMP coordinator presented opportunities on both sides of the collaboration. Up to that point, the FMP and its curriculum had remained unchanged for some time. The partnership was initiated with a meeting when the FMP coordinator was meeting those involved with the program and learning more about their contributions. The librarian was eager to meet the new FMP coordinator and ready to get started with the next round of the program. In addition to their dedication to the community of students, the thing that was most clear during their first meeting was that each had a different understanding of the student cohort, based on their own vantage point, and thus how the library should support them. For example, the FMP coordinator had assumed that the students, because of their status as juniors and seniors with respectable grade point averages in their major, would be ready for advanced library research skills, while, with her five years' experience, the librarian understood that the level of information literacy varied among the students. It was clear that the two needed to come to a consensus over the goals of the program and the standards and expectations to which students would be held.

To start, they agreed that students should have some level of experience with the databases in their field as well as peer-reviewed sources. If they did not have that, they would have to receive their basic training prior to the start of the research seminar. The two collaborated on a questionnaire that would assist them in developing a profile of each student. The students who demonstrated a lack of information literacy skills would be asked to meet on an individual basis with the librarian so that they could be brought up to speed and learn what they needed to work on. The questionnaire was administered before the quarter started, so the information was available to the students prior to the start of the research seminar.

The FMP coordinator and librarian then worked to come to an agreement on mutual standards and expectations for students' performance in the research seminar. The two discussed the previous syllabus and other elements of the program, including the library workshops, as well as the problems students typically encountered. With the librarian's institutional knowledge of the program, the two were able to identify areas that needed improvement. To address the issue of students falling behind in their assignments, the FMP coordinator, in consultation with the librarian, created a sequenced research project with benchmarks ensuring that students were completing their project in a timely manner and could receive feedback when it could still be used for revision and improvement. Failure to meet the benchmarks would send an alert to the coordinator allowing her to address the issue. Another area of concern was the students who were falling behind in their meetings with their faculty mentors, who provide guidance and direction on the projects, or librarians, who provide guidance on literature reviews. With this information the FMP coordinator set the number of meetings students were required to make with faculty mentors and librarians and a recommended timeline for scheduling the meetings.

The next step was for the FMP coordinator to develop a better understanding of the role of library resources in the FMP research seminar curriculum. She turned to the librarian for a discussion and personal training on the very resources that the librarian used in the workshops. The two were then able to discuss how to better integrate the assignments with the content of the library workshops. Because one of the goals of the FMP research seminar centers on helping students define the conventions of their academic discipline, the library's subject encyclopedias became the most valuable tool for the FMP coordinator.

The final point that emerged from the initial meetings was that the two needed to look to each other as a network of support to improve their assistance to the students. With renewed goals as well as standards and expectations for the FMP students' performance, the librarian and FMP coordinator also needed to make sure that these changes were working for students. At the time, the best way to do this was through tracking the work of the students and alerting one another when a student was falling behind or not performing well. The two also exchanged any information they learned—from their conversations with the students in question or through evaluating their work—with one another in order to provide consistent support.

After the first year of the collaboration, the librarian and the FMP coordinator concluded that the individual librarian-student matches could no longer be sustained because of the dwindling numbers of librarian participants and because the expectations of the librarians had evolved. Though the librarians who participated had enjoyed the work, the statistics indicated that students were underutilizing the service and, increasingly, there were not enough librarians to support all the students. As a result, the instruction librarian became the sole contact for the fifteen to twenty FMP students. This new approach has improved the network of support because the librarian is interacting directly with all the students and is able to track their work as a cohort.

An added benefit of the librarian as the single point of contact in the library is the ability to identify patterns in some of the problems that students were reporting. As a result, the librarian was able to alert the FMP coordinator and the research seminar instructor that multiple students were reporting the same problems during their consultations with the librarian. The three discussed the situation and determined that the librarian would visit the class to discuss the issues because the instructor would be available to elaborate further on his expectations. The librarian then invited any student who was experiencing similar problems to make an appointment for a consultation with her.

TYPICAL TIMELINE

The FMP timeline is kicked off in spring in preparation for the two-quarter research seminar the following winter and spring. In May, the first round of applications is due, and the steering committee meets soon after to select the FMP participants. A graduate student with significant teaching experience is hired before the fall quarter to teach the research seminar. In the fall the second round of applications is due. This latter round is in place to ensure that new transfer students are eligible to apply. The steering committee meets in November to admit the second group of students. After the cohort has been selected, the information literacy skills questionnaire is administered.

In winter quarter the FMP research seminar officially begins. By the start of the quarter, students should have begun meeting with their faculty mentors, who will guide the students' research projects throughout the two-quarter program. The first library workshop is held during the first weeks of the seminar. In this session, the librarian establishes a rapport with the students and sets a context for the library in the research project. The workshop is paired with the annotated bibliography and "Conventions of Your Discipline" assignments. The focus of the session is on narrowing one's research question and using discipline-specific databases and resources. The second library workshop takes place one to two weeks later. The focus of that session is on organizing references using bibliographic software; it also serves as a follow-up on problems students are encountering with library research at that point.

The individual consultations between the students and librarian take place throughout the two-quarter research seminar; students begin contacting the librarian after the first library workshop. The consultations generally take place in the winter when students are composing annotated bibliographies and literature reviews. The librarian makes an additional visit to the research seminar classroom in the winter to follow up on the students' library research, discuss problems, and invite students to make appointments for consultations if they had not already done so.

The second quarter of the research seminar begins in the spring. Students are generally completing their research projects during this quarter, including administering their own surveys, conducting interviews, or analyzing archival material. Midway through the spring quarter, the final library workshop takes place. The focus of this workshop is on specialized collections, including government documents, statistics, archives, and special collections. The seminar culminates in the FMP colloquium during which students present their research findings to an audience. They submit their research papers during their final class meeting.

LESSONS LEARNED

During the three-year partnership, the librarian and FMP coordinator worked together to bridge the elements of the program to better integrate the students' research projects and the library. Reflecting on the three-year partnership, the authors learned valuable lessons as they worked across their departmental divides. Though the lessons are specific to the FMP, the overall themes—flexibility, mutual goals, working efficiently and effectively, and clarity of roles in sustaining a partnership or program—are applicable to other library–student affairs collaborations and partnerships.

Change Is a Constant, Be Flexible

Changes—organizational, personnel, budgetary, technological, and so on—are a constant in education today. At the outset of the collaboration between the librarian and FMP coordinator, the meetings were characterized by openness to different viewpoints, flexibility with the existing structure, and an interest in working with underrepresented students and enabling their success in FMP. This mutual understanding allowed the two to weather the changes that were going on, including administrative and organizational changes, budget shortfalls, and hiring freezes, and to be able to produce a successful program during the three-year partnership.

Establish Goals at the Outset

In the initial meetings, it was clear that the two collaborators had different ideas about the standards that students should be held to. For example, the librarian approached the workshops in a way that was reactive to the general problems she had observed in the previous FMP students cohorts, while the FMP coordinator had a much more proactive approach and higher expectations for the students. Once they agreed on a general goal for the first workshop—advanced-level, subject-specific research skills and strategies that would allow students to start their research right away—they determined a way to provide supplemental assistance to the students who were not fully prepared so as to not interfere with the momentum of the research seminar. This was the first step toward developing a more integrated connection between the library and FMP. In addition, the librarian has adopted the proactive approach in her work in public services and library instruction generally.

Strategic Support

Influenced by the initial planning, the librarian re-evaluated the FMP student-librarian matches to determine a strategic way to carry out that work. The librarian utilized the information available to her—accounts of students not meeting with their librarians, confusion as to the role of the librarian in the research project, new library strategic goals to focus on the user, and a better understanding of the FMP's goals as a result of the new partnership—to reorganize that portion of the program. Librarians would no longer serve as guides for the FMP students; however, they would still be called upon for their areas of expertise by referral. The change was welcomed by the librarians, who had new responsibilities in collection development and outreach to the academic departments. The librarian's work of supporting students is now focused on assisting them in a consistent manner rather than managing and facilitating the multiple librarian-student matches. Having one point of contact in the library proved to be an advantage for identifying specific problems students were encountering, not only for library-related problems but in other areas of the program. The librarian has been able to address library-related problems and refer other problems to the FMP coordinator and the research seminar instructor.

Roles in Sustaining Partnerships

Though FMP is more than just the librarian–FMP coordinator partnership, the program has had few opportunities to convene all the contributing parties for a meeting. Perhaps this is the reason the librarian–FMP coordinator partnership has been so successful. The most recent FMP cycle started without the FMP coordinator, who left to return to school. As a continuing participant, the librarian has already established connections with the interim coordinator and has been able to support her as she learns the job. As they have worked to do this, it is clear that FMP would benefit by formalizing the roles in FMP and that the partnership needs to be extended beyond the librarian and FMP coordinator to include other contributing parties.

CONCLUSION

Those looking to establish new, or refine existing, partnerships between the library and student affairs should undertake projects that have the potential to produce mutual benefits while advancing goals toward students' academic achievement and inclusiveness. In working with FMP, the librarian has come to understand the importance of working within a community and of embedding the library within the context of the program rather than attempting standalone efforts in information literacy and library instruction. In working with the librarian, the FMP coordinator had a collaborator who was accessible and who added an important perspective to FMP.

Librarians and student affairs officers should look internally at their existing programs to determine if they can benefit from an outside perspective. Traditional cultural climates that reinforce structural divisions and static practices are not sustainable in the current climate of reduced budgets and hiring freezes, nor do they aid in personal and professional growth.

With their distinct areas of expertise, librarians and student affairs officers can benefit tremendously from gaining insight into how they put their respective expertise into practice. The partnership between the librarian and FMP coordinator extended beyond FMP and into the way they performed their other professional duties. The two would refer students to one another when they encountered students in need of library help or pregraduate counseling. Overall, understanding one another's work opens up the potential for partnerships or collaborations in ways that one may not have imagined.

Notes

1. Association of College and Research Libraries, *Information Literacy Competency Standards for Higher Education* (Chicago: ACRL, 2000), http://www.ala.org/ala/mgrps/divs/acrl/standards/standards.pdf.
2. David Bartholomae, "What Is Composition and (If You Know What That Is) Why Do We Teach It?" in *Composition in the Twenty-First Century: Crisis and Change*, edited by Lynn Bloom, Donald Daiker, and Edward White (Carbondale: Southern Illinois University, 1996), 14.
3. Patricia Bizzell, *Academic Discourse and Critical Consciousness* (Pittsburgh, PA: University of Pittsburgh Press, 1992), 129–52.
4. Allan J. Dyson, "Reaching Out for Outreach: A University Library Develops a New Position to Serve the School's Multicultural Students," *American Libraries* 20 (1989): 952.

16

Conclusion: Lessons on Collaboration

Melissa Autumn Wong and Lisa Janicke Hinchliffe

The chapters in this book have much to share on two levels. First, they provide excellent examples of the services and programs that can be developed when librarians and student affairs professionals work together. The authors provide inspiration and advice for a wide variety of activities and around a wide variety of topics, including career preparation, academic success, leadership development, integrity, and civic engagement. Certainly readers of this volume can take away numerous ideas for partnering and programming at their own institutions. Of larger significance, however, are the lessons that can be learned about collaboration. The editors encouraged authors to reflect not only on the *what* of their collaborations, but also on the *how*. In this conclusion, the editors summarize the authors' thoughts on successful collaboration and direct readers to essays of interest for particular topics.

THE ROLE OF ENVIRONMENT IN COLLABORATION

Many authors state that their institutions explicitly encourage teamwork and collaboration, including interdepartmental partnerships. These authors believe that collaboration between the library and student affairs was a natural evolution of the work they were doing, that supervisors and colleagues were supportive of and encouraged such work, and that structures existed to facilitate the collaboration.

These authors often mention campus or department leadership as being key in creating an atmosphere conducive to collaboration. Elizabeth M. Lockwood, Scott N. Friedman, and Linda Naru note that "effective leaders must create a sharing and inclusive atmosphere" that will enable transformative work and collaboration. Nancy E. Adams and Jennifer K. Olivetti describe their institution as one "which encourages cooperation, boundary-spanning, and the wearing of multiple hats," and Chad Kahl and Janet Paterson portray their campus as one where librarians and student affairs professionals see one another as "partners in the educational process."

Chapters in this book also illustrate that collaborations can flourish in seemingly unfavorable environments. Randall Schroeder, Matthew Chaney, and Michael Wade demonstrate how, in an atmosphere of friction and distrust, overtures on the part of one person were a significant factor in creating a positive, cooperative relationship. Other authors note the presence of conditions that might seem to hinder collaboration—budget woes, technological changes, and colleagues leaving for new positions—and demonstrate that these challenges are surmountable with creativity and persistence. Thus, the lesson is that, while some institutions are already receptive to interdepartmental collaboration, librarians and student affairs professionals also have the power to shape the environment in which they work and create a positive climate for collaboration.

BEST PRACTICES FOR COLLABORATION

Regardless of the campus environment, the authors in this volume note several practices essential to productive, sustainable collaborations.

Mutual Goals

In reflecting on their work, all of the authors mention that a library and student affairs collaboration must be centered on a shared vision and goals that are clear and attainable. Based on years of research on collaboration in nonprofit settings, Paul W. Mattesich, Marta Murray-Close, and Barbara R. Monsey suggest that any successful collaboration will have a unique purpose, one that is different from the goals and approaches of the partners acting independently, and will provide benefits that neither partner can realize on their own.[1]

Lockwood, Friedman, and Naru partnered to create staff training and improve library services to students with disabilities, a goal they describe as "mutually beneficial" to the library and the Disability Resource Center. Maria T. Accardi, Ruth Garvey-Nix, and Leigh Ann Meyer brought three departments together to establish a plagiarism education and prevention program, a project in which everyone had a natural interest in the outcome, while

Nicole Eva and Jeremy Girard's collaboration grew out of a mutual desire to support students' academic success.

Authors also suggest that keeping their focus on the shared goal enabled them to continue a collaboration even as the specific logistics or personnel changed over time. Annette Marines and Yolanda Venegas describe a program to support minority students' preparation for graduate school that has undergone many changes but continues to be successful because it has evolved, while Ronald L. Wirtz and Keri A. Pearson share their multiyear work developing an information commons. As Schroeder, Chaney, and Wade so eloquently state, "shared goals can triumph over circumstances."

Process and Structure

Many authors wrote that while collaborations may emerge almost serendipitously, partners should be mindful of the need to develop processes and structures to sustain projects over the long term. Michelle Maloney, Joanna Royce-Davis, and Elizabeth Griego describe this as taking a systems approach and advocate developing sustainable practices for practical considerations like funding and staffing.

Kathryn M. Crowe, Mary L. Hummel, Jenny Dale, and Rosann Bazirjian cite the need to designate financial resources to sustain a project, as do Connie Scott and Cindy Price Verduce. Scott and Verduce also advise would-be collaborators to candidly discuss and define their roles and expectations and to identify "complementary leadership skills" that each can contribute.

Understanding and Respect

The authors in this volume uniformly cite the need to develop mutual respect and trust, as well as an understanding of the social norms and expectations of one another. They argue that partners should take time to learn about one another and that genuine collaboration cannot be rushed or conducted ad hoc.

Adams and Olivetti write that "each partner must have a clear understanding of the other's professional culture, values, and strategic goals" and suggest that through sharing expertise in the course of the collaboration mutual understanding and respect can develop. They advise that partners must "offer to share professional expertise with each other and to be open to receiving expert assistance from the other." Crowe, Hummel, Dale, and Bazirjian contend that this mutual understanding involves respecting not only differences in work styles and delivery methods, but also differences in daily logistics such as work hours.

Flexibility

Developing shared goals and mutual understanding lead to another factor that many authors cite as critical to their success—flexibility. Julie Mitchell and Margot Bell write that there are challenges with departments operating in different ways; however, collaborators must find common ground and be "flexible about the approach" they take to programs and services. Wirtz and Pearson also cite flexibility as essential, while Marines and Venegas demonstrate that long-term collaborations can be sustained if the collaborators are open to change.

Communication

Nearly all of the authors cite the importance of open, ongoing communication as essential to collaboration. Kahl and Paterson contend that collaborators should communicate not only with one another, but with other colleagues in their departments and institutions; they demonstrate that such widespread communication allowed them to draw on the expertise of other colleagues in printing, mounting, and displaying artwork and in publicizing events.

Physical proximity can encourage frequent communication. Adams and Olivetti state that having offices next door to one another naturally led to frequent interaction and information transfer. Mitchell and Bell describe the presence of a "library-based student affairs staff member" whose position is jointly funded by the library and student affairs and who is housed in the library, but "remains part of a strong community of [student affairs] practice on campus."

Co-located offices are not, however, essential to communication and success. Many of the authors in this text worked in different buildings on large campuses. These authors cite frequent communication through face-to-face meetings, e-mail, and phone calls. In these cases, the partners made a commitment to communicate openly and frequently, and each took personal responsibility to ensure communication was ongoing.

Persistence

Numerous authors relate the challenges they faced in bringing their ideas to fruition, and it is clear that a final, crucial factor in success for all of the authors was persistence. In writing that collaborators must persevere beyond the inevitable problems, Natalie Maio and Kathryn Shaughnessy advise readers to adopt the attitude that they will "leave no partner behind" and to recast challenges as "surmountable obstacles."

THE FUTURE OF LIBRARY AND STUDENT AFFAIRS COLLABORATIONS

As the essays in this book have shown, potential collaborations between librarians and student affairs professionals are numerous. Large or small, short-term or ongoing, they can be realized on all types of campuses. Such collaborations support integrative learning and foster holistic student development, providing new avenues for libraries and student affairs to realize their missions.

Note

1. Paul W. Mattesich, Marta Murray-Close, and Barbara R. Monsey, *Collaboration: What Makes It Work,* 2nd ed. (Saint Paul, MN: Amherst W. Wilder Foundation, 2001).

Resources for Further Reading

Melissa Autumn Wong and Lisa Janicke Hinchliffe

The following is a selected bibliography of publications on student affairs, strategies for collaboration, and library and student affairs collaborations.

STUDENT AFFAIRS

American College Personnel Association. "The Student Learning Imperative: Implications for Student Affairs." American College Personnel Association. 1996. http://www.myacpa.org/sli_delete/sli.htm.

A core reading for understanding the field of student affairs, this brief document outlines the key role cocurricular learning plays in college student development.

Barr, Margaret J., Mary K. Desler, and Associates. *The Handbook of Student Affairs Administration*, 2nd ed. San Francisco: Jossey-Bass, 2000.

The majority of this book is devoted to practical advice on leading student affairs departments; however, Part I has excellent chapters on the philosophy and organization of student affairs as well as key factors influencing current student affairs work and would be useful for readers seeking an introduction to the profession.

Doyle, Jeff A. "Where Have We Come From and Where Are We Going? A Review of Past Student Affairs Philosophies and an Analysis of the Current Student Learning Philosophy." *College Student Affairs Journal* 24 (2004): 66–83.

Doyle examines three philosophies that have guided student affairs work: student services, student development, and student learning. In addition to providing an historical overview of the philosophies and their impact on the profession, Doyle explores the implications of the student learning model for current student affairs work.

Hamrick, Florence A., Nancy J. Evans, and John H. Schuh. *Foundations of Student Affairs Practice: How Philosophy, Theory and Research Strengthen Educational*

Outcomes. San Francisco: Jossey-Bass, 2002.

The authors examine theories of student development and strategies for fostering student learning in key areas of personal, social, and intellectual development.

Keeling, Richard P., ed. *Learning Reconsidered: A Campus-Wide Focus on the Student Experience.* Washington, DC: National Association of Student Personnel Administrators and American College Personnel Association, January 2004. http://www.myacpa.org/pub/documents/learningreconsidered.pdfA core document in student affairs, *Learning Reconsidered* argues for the importance of a campuswide holistic approach to student learning. It was followed by *Learning Reconsidered 2,* which provides advice on implementing the ideas in *Learning Reconsidered.*

Keeling, Richard P., ed. *Learning Reconsidered 2: A Practical Guide to Implementing a Campus-Wide Focus on the Student Experience.* Washington, DC: American College Personnel Association, 2006.

A follow-up to *Learning Reconsidered,* this volume discusses the nature of learning and how student affairs units can promote holistic student development. This is a core document for student affairs professionals, and librarians will benefit from familiarity with it.

Komives, Susan R., Dudley B. Woodard, Jr., and Associates. *Student Services: A Handbook for the Profession,* 4th ed. San Francisco: Jossey-Bass, 2003.

Intended as a handbook for student affairs professionals, this is an excellent volume for readers seeking a broad introduction to the profession. The authors explore the theoretical foundations of student development and student affairs work, discuss how student affairs professionals can support student development, and outline the skills needed for this work.

Kuh, George D., Jillian Kinzie, John H. Schuh, Elizabeth J. Whitt, and Associates. *Student Success in College: Creating Conditions That Matter.* San Francisco: Jossey-Bass, 2005.

Kuh and his coauthors provide an excellent overview of holistic student development and suggest ways colleges can create environments, inside and outside of the classroom, that engage students and lead to holistic development.

Pascarella, Ernest T., and Patrick T. Terenzini, *How College Affects Students.* Vol. 2, *A Third Decade of Research.* San Francisco: Jossey-Bass, 2005.

Pascarella and Terenzini explain how students develop across range of dimensions, including the intellectual, psychosocial, ethical, and attitudinal, and explore the long term effects of college on quality of life.

COLLABORATION

Elmborg, James K., and Sheril Hook, eds. *Centers for Learning: Writing Centers and Libraries in Collaboration.* Chicago: American Library Association, 2005.

Focused on collaboration with writing centers, the chapters collected in this volume provide useful models of how librarians can seek to understand and find common ground with colleagues on campus.

Hansen, Morton T. *Collaboration: How Leaders Avoid the Traps, Create Unity, and Reap Big Results.* Cambridge, MA: Harvard Business School Press, 2009.

Although the examples in this book are primarily taken from the business world, readers can extrapolate to academic settings and find essential ways of thinking about collaboration and excellent practical advice.

Iannuzzi, Patricia. "Faculty Development and Information Literacy: Establishing Campus Partnerships." *Reference Services Review* (1998): 97–102, 116.

Although Iannuzzi writes about outreach to faculty, throughout the article she offers excellent advice on creating partnerships that is applicable to any collaborative effort that librarians would like to initiate.

Mattessich, Paul W., Marta Murray-Close, Barbara R. Monsey, and Wilder Research Center. *Collaboration: What Makes It Work.* 2nd ed. St. Paul, MN: Amherst H. Wilder Foundation, 2001.

The authors review the research on collaboration in nonprofit settings and identify key factors for success. The book includes practical examples and advice as well as inventory for self-reflection.

Raspa, Dick, and Dane Ward, eds. *The Collaborative Imperative: Librarians and Faculty Working Together in the Information Universe.* Chicago: American Library Association, 2000.

Although focused on working with faculty, Raspa and Ward's model of the "5 P's" (passion, playfulness, project, persistence, and promotion) is applicable to any situation. Chapters by Raspa, Ward, and others provide excellent advice on collaboration.

Shane, Jordana M. Y. "Formal and Informal Structures for Collaboration on a Campus-Wide Information Literacy Program." *Resource Sharing and Information Networks* 17 (2004): 85–110.

Shane argues for the importance of collaboration to achieve the library's goals, including promoting student learning and meeting accreditation standards, and draws on the literature of collaboration to outline best practices for working successfully with others on campus.

LIBRARIES AND STUDENT AFFAIRS IN COLLABORATION

Crowe, Kathryn. "Student Affairs Connection: Promoting the Library through Co-Curricular Activities." *Collaborative Librarianship* 2 (2010): 154–58.

As part of an article on outreach to students in cocurricular settings, Crowe describes the library's cooperation with student affairs to participate in campus activity fairs and establish librarian liaisons to student affairs offices and student organizations. The author also profiles other outreach activities, including social events and a student advisory council for the library.

Cummings, Lara Ursin. "Bursting Out of the Box: Outreach to the Millennial Generation through Student Services Programs." *Reference Services Review* 35 (2007): 285–95.

Cummings describes a variety of outreach efforts to market the library's resources and services to students through collaboration with student affairs units, including residential life, TRIO, athletics, and new student programs. The article includes practical advice on successful collaboration and creation of marketing materials.

Dahl, Candice. "Library Liaison with Non-Academic Units: A New Approach for a Traditional Model." *Partnership: The Canadian Journal of Library and Information Practice and Research* 2, no. 1 (2007): 1–12.

Dahl notes that many libraries have liaison programs with academic departments; these programs are formalized through structured job responsibilities and administrative and financial support. In contrast, relationships with nonacademic departments are characterized as "outreach" or "collaboration" and are informal in nature. Dahl argues that libraries would benefit from extending formal liaison programs to include student affairs and other nonacademic departments.

Dugan, Mary, George Bergstrom, and Tomalee Doan. "Campus Career Collaboration: 'Do the Research. Land the Job.'" *College & Undergraduate Libraries* 16 (2009): 122–37.

The authors outline a library-led collaboration with campus career centers to create a wiki of job hunting and career information that took advantage of the expertise of each department and highlighted resources and opportunities available to students across campus. In addition to articulating the many possibilities inherent in library and career center collaborations, this article is an excellent example of collaboration to create a virtual resource.

Engle, Lea Susan. "Hitching Your Wagon to the Right Star: A Case Study in Collaboration." *College & Undergraduate Libraries* 18 (2011): 249–60.

Engle describes her collaboration with a first-year experience program to reach students during orientation. In addition to providing numerous concrete ideas for orientation-related outreach, the author has developed an excellent ten-step guide to creating partnerships.

Forrest, Laura Urbanski. "Academic Librarians and Student Affairs Professionals: An Ethical Collaboration for Higher Education." *Education Libraries* 28 (2005): 11–15.
Forrest notes the lack of literature on library and student affairs collaborations and argues that librarians should pursue such partnerships because they benefit librarians, student affairs professionals, and students. She also notes that guiding documents in both professions promote such partnerships.

Hinchliffe, Lisa Janicke, and Melissa Autumn Wong. "From Services-Centered to Student-Centered: A 'Wellness Wheel' Approach to Developing the Library as an Integrative Learning Commons." *College & Undergraduate Libraries* 17 (2010): 213–24.
Hinchliffe and Wong introduce the "Wellness Wheel," a framework for developing programming frequently used by student affairs professionals, and show how it can be used as the basis for programming in libraries and for collaborations with student affairs colleagues.

Hollister, Christopher. "Bringing Information Literacy to Career Services." *Reference Services Review* 33 (2005): 104–11.
Hollister describes a successful collaboration between a library and a career center and shows how such collaborations can support and expand information literacy efforts on campus.

Karle, Elizabeth M. "Invigorating the Academic Library Experience: Creative Programming Ideas." *College & Research Libraries News* 69 (208): 141–44.
Karle argues for the importance of creative programming to attract students and shape the image of the library on campus. She provides five programming ideas, including suggestions for campus offices that could serve as partners.

Kelleher, Mary, and Sara Laidlaw. "A Natural Fit: The Academic Librarian Advising in the First Year Experience." *College & Undergraduate Libraries* 16 (2009): 153–63.
Kelleher and Laidlaw show how librarians can serve as academic advisors to the benefit of students, librarians, and the advising program. There are a number of publications about librarians participating in or collaborating with advising programs, and the authors provide a thorough review of the literature.

Kraemer, Elizabeth W., Dana J. Keyse, and Shawn V. Lombardo. "Beyond These Walls: Building a Library Outreach Program at Oakland University." *The Reference Librarian* 39, no. 82 (2003): 5–17.

The authors profile a variety of outreach efforts conducted through collaboration with student affairs colleagues; programs and services were aimed at first-year and transfer students, multicultural groups, on-campus residents, and students in the Honors College.

Love, Emily, and Margaret B. Edwards. "Forging Inroads between Libraries and Academic, Multicultural and Student Services." *Reference Services Review* 37 (2009): 20–29.

Love and Edwards profile a variety of collaborative efforts with campus departments, including the career center, health center, academic advising, and multicultural student services, that simultaneously brought those departments into the library and extended the reach of the library beyond its own walls. The authors include tips for establishing and sustaining partnerships.

"Meeting the Student Learning Imperative: Supporting and Sustaining Collaboration between Academic Libraries and Student Services Programs." Special Issue of *Research Strategies* 20, no. 4 (2007).

Following an introduction to the volume by special issue editors Scott Walter and Michele Eodice, seven articles profile collaborative efforts.

O'English, Lorena, and Sarah McCord. "Getting in on the Game: Partnering with a University Athletics Department." *portal: Libraries and the Academy* 6 (2006): 143–53.

The authors describe a multifaceted collaboration with the athletics department. One aspect of the collaboration was outreach to student athletes to support academic success; the other aspect was a marketing and development partnership that benefitted both parties.

Strothmann, Molly, and Karen Antell. "The Live-In Librarian: Developing Library Outreach to University Residence Halls." *Reference & User Services Quarterly* 50 (Fall 2010): 58–58.

Strothmann and Antell outline the benefits of reaching out to students through the residence halls and offer many ideas for programming. One of the authors served as a faculty-in-residence and admits her work was eased by that role; however, the authors specifically address how any librarian can establish a positive, collaborative relationship with residential life.

Swartz, Pauline S., Brian A. Carlisle, and E. Chisato Uyeki. "Libraries and Student Affairs: Partners for Student Success." *Reference Services Review* 35 (2007): 109–22.

The authors describe collaborative efforts to create workshops and educational resources on academic integrity. Although the article provides some information on the resources that were created, the focus is on advice for initiating and sustaining collaborative relationships.

Walter, Scott. "Building a 'Seamless Environment' for Assessment of Information Literacy: Libraries, Student Affairs, and Learning Outside the Classroom." *Communications in Information Literacy* 3 (2009): 91–98.

Reminding readers that learning takes place not only in the classroom, but outside the classroom through cocurricular programs as well, Walter highlights the work student affairs professionals have done to assess cocurricular learning and encourages librarians interested in assessment to look at this work for lessons applicable to the library.

Walter, Scott. "Moving Beyond Collections: Academic Library Outreach to Multicultural Student Centers." *Reference Services Review* 33 (2005): 438–58.

Walter provides a case study of working with multicultural student offices to conduct an information needs assessment in order to improve library services to students of color. The article includes a thorough literature review on service to diverse communities in academic libraries and a copy of the survey instrument that was used.

Young, Courtney L. "Incorporating Undergraduate Advising in Teaching Information Literacy: Case Study for Academic Librarians as Advisors." *Journal of Academic Librarianship* 34 (2008): 139–44.

Based on her experience as an academic advisor, Young shares the parallels between academic librarianship and advising. She argues that serving as an advisor is a natural fit for librarians' skills and provides unique insights into students and the curriculum.

Zitron, Lizz. "These Are the People in Your Neighborhood, A–L." April 7, 2011. *The Outreach Librarian* (blog). http://theoutreachlibrarian.com/2011/04/07/these-are-the-people-in-your-neighborhood-a-l/.

Zitron provides an excellent list of departments on campus, accompanied by ideas for interesting and innovative collaborations. For the second half of the list, see "The People in Your 'Hood, M-Z" at http://theoutreachlibrarian.com/2011/04/12/the-people-in-your-hood-m-z/.

Contributing Authors

Maria T. Accardi is Assistant Librarian and Coordinator of Instruction at Indiana University Southeast in New Albany, Indiana. She holds a master's degree in English from the University of Louisville and a master's degree in library and information science from the University of Pittsburgh.

Nancy E. Adams is Associate Director and Coordinator of Education and Instruction at the Penn State Hershey George T. Harrell Health Sciences Library and was formerly the University Librarian and Director of Student Services at Harrisburg University of Science and Technology. She earned her master's degree in library and information science at Wayne State University.

Rosann Bazirjian is the Dean of University Libraries at the University of North Carolina at Greensboro. She received her master's degree in library and information science in library service from Columbia University and a master's in social science from Syracuse University.

Margot Bell is Associate Director of Student Development at the University of British Columbia. She has a master's degree in educational counseling from the University of Ottawa.

Matthew Chaney is the Director for the Office of Multicultural Student Services at Ferris State University. He received his master's degree in education, focused on career and technical education, from Ferris State University.

Kathryn M. Crowe is Associate Dean for Public Services at the University Libraries at the University of North Carolina at Greensboro. She has a master's degree in library science from Indiana University and a master's degree in history from the University of Georgia.

Jenny Dale is the First-Year Instruction Coordinator at the University of North Carolina at Greensboro Libraries. She holds a master's degree in library and information science from the University of North Carolina at Chapel Hill.

Nicole Eva is a professional librarian at the University of Lethbridge. She received her master's degree in library and information science from the University of Western Ontario and has a bachelor of commerce degree with a major in marketing from the University of Saskatchewan.

Scott N. Friedman is Director of Access and Disability Services and 504/ADA Coordinator at William Rainey Harper College in Palatine, Illinois. He holds a master's degree in adult and higher education from Northern Illinois University and is currently completing his doctoral research in the field of disability studies, along with a second master's in special education, at the University of Illinois at Chicago.

Ruth Garvey-Nix is the Vice Chancellor for Student Affairs at Indiana University Southeast. She earned her doctorate in higher education administration from the University of Southern Mississippi.

Jeremy Girard was president of the University of Lethbridge Students' Union in 2009–2010. Jeremy completed his bachelor of science degree, majoring in neuroscience, at the University of Lethbridge in December 2011.

Elizabeth Griego is Vice President for Student Life as well as professor of education at the University of the Pacific in Stockton, California. She has a bachelor's degree in speech and hearing pathology and audiology from the University of Nebraska, Lincoln, a master's in student personnel work from the Ohio State University, and a doctorate in higher education administration from the University of California, Berkeley.

Lisa Janicke Hinchliffe is the Coordinator for Information Literacy Services and Instruction and an associate professor for library administration at the University of Illinois at Urbana–Champaign. She has master's degrees in educational psychology and library and information science from the University of Illinois at Urbana–Champaign as well as a bachelor of arts degree in philosophy from the University of St. Thomas in Minnesota.

Mary L. Hummel is Assistant Vice President for Student Affairs at the University of Maryland. She was formerly Director of Housing and Residence Life at the University of North Carolina at Greensboro. She received her doctorate from the Center for the Study of Higher and Postsecondary Education at the University of Michigan. Her master's degree and undergraduate degree are both from the Pennsylvania State University.

Chad Kahl is the subject librarian for criminal justice, law, military science, and politics and government at Illinois State University's Milner Library. He received a master's in library and information science, a master's in political science, and a bachelor's degree with majors in political science and history from the University of Illinois at Urbana–Champaign.

Elizabeth M. Lockwood is an adjunct professor at the University of Arizona South and vice president of Deaf We Can, a nonprofit organization that provides advocacy, training, and legal representation to deaf communities globally. Elizabeth holds a doctorate in disability studies and a master's degree in public policy focusing on immigration and disability policies.

Dallas Long is Head of Access Services and assistant professor at Illinois State University. He holds master's degrees in higher education administration and library and information science from the University of Illinois at Urbana–Champaign and a bachelor's degree in psychology from Webster University. He is currently pursuing a doctoral degree in higher education administration at Illinois State University.

Natalie Maio is the Associate Director of Leadership Development at the Queens Campus of St. John's University. She holds a bachelor's in English and secondary education from Hofstra University, a master's in education, specializing in college student development, from Long Island University— CW Post, and a doctorate in education, specializing in student development in higher education, from St. John's University.

Michelle Maloney is a reference librarian at the University of the Pacific in Stockton, California. She has a bachelor of arts in communication from the University of Massachusetts and a master's degree in library and information science from the University of Illinois at Urbana–Champaign.

Annette Marines is the subject librarian for sociology and writing and is the instruction and outreach coordinator at the University of California, Santa Cruz. She received her bachelor's in sociology from the University of California, Santa Barbara, and a master's in library and information science from San Jose State University.

Leigh Ann Meyer is Director of the Writing Center at Indiana University Southeast and also teaches writing and literature. She has an associate's degree in journalism, a bachelor of science in secondary education—English, and a master's degree in secondary education—English.

Julie Mitchell is the Interim Coordinator for the Chapman Learning Commons in the Irving K. Barber Learning Centre at the University of British Columbia. She has a master's degree in library and information studies from the University of British Columbia.

Linda Naru is Assistant University Librarian for Administrative Services at the University of Illinois at Chicago. She has a master's degree in library sciences from the University of Michigan and a master's in public administration from the University of Illinois at Chicago.

Jennifer K. Olivetti was previously a student services professional at Harrisburg University of Science and Technology, most recently serving as Assistant Director of Academic Success Programs and Services. She earned a bachelor's degree in psychology from Shippensburg University and a master's degree in higher education from Geneva College. Olivetti is currently a doctoral student in clinical psychology at Philadelphia College of Osteopathic Medicine.

Janet Paterson is the Dean of Students as well as an adjunct professor in the College of Education at Illinois State University. She received her doctorate from Texas A&M University, a master's in education from Indiana University, and a bachelor's with majors in psychology and sociology from Millikin University.

Keri A. Pearson is the Tutoring and Assessment Coordinator for Academic Success at the University of Nebraska at Kearney. She holds bachelor's degrees in mathematics and physics from the University of Nebraska at Kearney and began her work with peer education as an undergraduate tutor for Student Support Services during her studies.

Joanna Royce-Davis is the Dean of Students at University of the Pacific in Stockton, California, as well as an associate professor and Director of the Specialization in Student Affairs in the University's Benerd School of Education. She has a bachelor's degree from Indiana University, a master's from San Jose State University, and a doctorate from Syracuse University.

Randall Schroeder is the department head for Public Services at the Ferris State University Library. He received his master's degree in library and information science at the University of Iowa.

Connie Scott is the Director of the McMillen Library at Indiana Tech. She has a master's of library science from the University of Wisconsin–Milwaukee and a bachelor's degree in English from Indiana State University.

Kathryn Shaughnessy is Assistant Professor of Instructional Services in the St. John's University Libraries and a Senior Fellow in the university's Center for Teaching and Learning. She holds a bachelor's in philosophy from Loyola College in Maryland, a master's degree in philosophy from Fordham University, and a master's degree in academic and digital librarianship from St. John's University.

Yolanda Venegas is a writer and teacher currently teaching first-year composition at Santa Clara University. She received her doctoral training in ethnic studies at the University of California, Berkeley, and is currently enrolled in the master's degree program in English composition at San Francisco State University.

Cindy Price Verduce is the Director of Learning Support Services and Career Planning and Development at Indiana Tech. She received her master of education degree in student personnel services with a cognate in employee relations and personnel from the University of South Carolina, where she also obtained her bachelor of arts degree in history and political science.

Michael Wade is the Assistant Director for the Office of Multicultural Student Services at Ferris State University. He received his bachelor's degree in business administration with a minor in human resource management from Ferris State University. He is currently pursuing his master's degree in career and technical education postsecondary administration, also at Ferris State University.

Ronald L. Wirtz is the Coordinator of User Services at the Calvin T. Ryan Library of the University of Nebraska at Kearney. He has a doctorate in education as well as master's degrees in library science and French.

Melissa Autumn Wong is an adjunct faculty member in the library and information science schools at San Jose State University and the University of Illinois at Urbana–Champaign. Melissa formerly served as Library Director at Marymount College, California, and as a librarian at the University of Southern California. Melissa received her master's degree in library and information science from the University of Illinois at Urbana–Champaign and her bachelor of arts degree from Augustana College in Illinois.

Index